CSUK 7177 £15-99

LABOUR'S RENEWAL?

Labour's Renewal?

The Policy Review and Beyond

Gerald R. Taylor

Senior Lecturer in Politics
LSU College of Higher Education
Southampton

First published 1997 by
MACMILLAN PRESS LTD
Houndmills, Basingstoke, Hampshire RG21 6XS
and London
Companies and representatives
throughout the world

ISBN 0–333–65247–9 hardcover
ISBN 0–333–65248–7 paperback

A catalogue record for this book is available from the British Library.

10 9 8 7 6 5 4 3 2 1
06 05 04 03 02 01 00 99 98 97

Printed in Great Britain by
The Ipswich Book Co. Ltd, Ipswich, Suffolk

To my parents,
Robert and Lilian

Contents

List of Tables

List of Figures

Preface

This book had its origins on 15 March 1981 at a dark and uninviting Oddfellows Hall in Teignmouth, Devon. It was there that I was persuaded to first join the Labour Party. From a practical involvement in politics came a desire to understand political debate and activity better. This led me back into full-time education, to my PhD, and to the writing of this work. Much has happened in the years in between, but my desire to understand politics, and my membership of the Labour Party have remained constant. It is these two factors which are reflected here – in particular a desire to understand why Labour have not been more successful as an electoral and political force than they have.

Whilst this is clearly a partisan intention, I hope that this is also a work of academic value. This work is intended to contribute, constructively, to the debate on Labour's future and to help us all understand the problems Labour faces. It does not suggest solutions to these problems, though it does criticise the attempts of 'renewal' and 'modernisation' which have been designed to provide Labour with new direction. Indeed it is these attempts at reconstruction of the Party which are used to illustrate and examine the Party's problems.

As with any work which has taken many years to come to fruition the final form owes a great deal to the criticism and commentary of others. The whole has been deeply informed by a series of interviews conducted from 1988 to 1995 with Shadow Cabinet members, MPs and MEPs, Party officials, individuals in Neil Kinnock's Leader's Office, pressure groups, various individuals involved in the Policy Review, the Commission on Social Justice, and the reform of Clause IV. Many asked to remain anonymous, but I would like to record my gratitude for their assistance. The final work has also been shaped by innumerable conversations, discussions and arguments with Party activists and local officials at Teignbridge, Colchester North, and more recently Southampton.

In addition various parts of this book were read and criticised by various people over the same period. I would particularly like to thank David Sanders who must have been very tired of some of my arguments, and my phone calls, by the end. David's comments were particularly valuable, especially with chapter 5. I have not managed to incorporate all the changes he recommended and I am sure that the final product suffers as a result. Thanks are also due to Jim McCormick at IPPR who was a great help with chapter 6 and sharply critical of its contents. I would also like to thank various other friends and colleagues for support and criticism at various stages. These include David Marsh, Ken Newton and Hugh Ward when I was at Essex, Martin Smith, and Adrian Smith, Frank Cogliano and Paula Coonerty at LSU College. Others who must be mentioned include: Chris Fegan, Dave Fallows, Jane Fensome, Jane Franklin, Chris Sparks, Bob Kennedy and Mark Gardner. I would also like to thank students I have taught at Essex, Westminster, and now at LSU College for occasionally making me think. Eric Shaw kindly gave me permission to use an unpublished research paper.

Finally my deepest gratitude must go to my partner, Sylvia Chin, and our daughter Sarah.

Gerald R. Taylor
LSU College, Southampton

List of Abbreviations

1 Introduction

The Labour Party has been a focus for academic debate for many years. Some of this work has concentrated on specific aspects of the Party. These have included: the development of Labour's internal Party discipline (Shaw, 1988); the link between Labour and the trade unions (Minkin, 1991); and the role and importance of Party members and activists (Seyd and Whiteley, 1992b). Another area of interest has been the nature and importance of change within the Party (Shaw, 1994; Smith and Spear). The future of the Labour Party, its prospects of obtaining government office, the principles it is likely to advance and the policies it will pursue, all of these will be significant deciding factors in the style and content of British politics for the foreseeable future. Beyond this the dramatic demise of Labour in the 1980s, the problems the Party now faces, and its reaction to these problems may tell us something about the behaviour and environment of political parties, particularly social democratic political parties, in liberal democracies.

This work represents an attempt to combine these approaches. It looks at specific attempts to renew and modernise the Party in the context of the Party's wider history and development. It asks whether changes since the commencement of the Policy Review under Neil Kinnock in 1987, through John Smith's instigation of the Commission on Social Justice, to the reform of Clause IV undertaken in 1995 under the leadership of Tony Blair, have addressed Labour's fundamental problems.

The Policy Review represented not merely a development of Party policy, but a fundamental attempt at restructuring the Party, which many modernisers regard themselves as continuing (Blair, 1993). In 1982 Labour had published a comprehensive policy statement (Labour Party, 1982). This represented a codification and restatement of Party policy based on Party Conference decisions, and provided the basis of Labour's manifesto for the 1983 General Election (Labour Party, 1983). This respect for Conference decisions and attempt to promote an awareness of Party policy well in advance of the General Election was probably itself a reaction to the way in which the wider Party had been excluded from the drafting of the 1979 manifesto (Seyd, 1987, 121–4). The scale of the disastrous result of the 1983 General Election led to the belief that all that was done in 1983 was a contributory factor to the disaster (Heffernan and Marqusee, 28). Neil Kinnock, elected Party Leader at the 1983 Party Conference, was determined that the perceived mistakes of 1983 would not be repeated.

1

Writing in this period Paul Whiteley sought to define Labour's problems. Whiteley suggested that there were three aspects to Labour's overall crisis. These were: an ideological crisis, marked by an ideological split between the Party's members and activists and its elected representatives in Parliament and on local councils; a membership crisis as membership figures continued to decline; and, perhaps most importantly, an electoral crisis, made dramatically clear by Labour's stunningly poor performance in the General Election of 1983. All these added up to a cumulative crisis of potentially catastrophic proportions (Whiteley, 1).

These three crises were all addressed by different aspects of the Policy Review. The Review contained specifically ideological aspects, notably the publication of *Democratic Socialist Aims and Values* (Labour Party, 1988). The review process itself attempted to involve Party members and supporters in policy-making directly for the first time. Fundamentally, though, the Review was an electoral strategy: a sophisticated attempt to alter Labour's image and policies to improve their electoral position. This electoral approach consciously linked policy with both image and the Party's electoral appeal, and strikingly with the personal leadership of Neil Kinnock (Hughes and Wintour, 4–5).

In effect, the Review was an ambitious attempt to overcome Labour's fundamental problems and provide a comprehensive settlement which would satisfy the most important elements of the Party organisation, and the majority of the Party's supporters. In doing so, it was hoped that the Review would provide a basis for an electorally resurgent Party capable of challenging for power and perhaps again becoming 'the natural party of government'.

The developing crises of the 1980s were themselves the product of traditional divisions and debates within the Party. The strength of these divisions was demonstrated by an increasingly divisive Conference (Minkin, 1991, 311). This presented severe problems to the Kinnock leadership in the aftermath of the 1983 General Election disaster and the perceived weaknesses of the leadership of Michael Foot. Kinnock addressed them in typical Labour leadership fashion by demonstrating 'a willingness to stand up, without flinching, to "the left"' (Shaw, 1988, 259).

In this, and other respects, the first Kinnock period of opposition (1983–7) did much to establish the priorities Kinnock and his supporters wished to promote (Minkin, 1991, 460). Indeed the 1983 to 1987 period was a very important run-up to the Policy Review itself, in particular introducing policy-making procedure changes that brought together the Party's National Executive Committee (NEC) and Shadow Cabinet in joint policy committees (Minkin, 1991, 400–1). A process later to be built on by the Review (Hughes and Wintour,

12). Nonetheless, in the Policy Review Kinnock and his supporters turned the groundwork of this earlier period to more ambitious ends.

The electoral strategy was the central theme and structuring force of the Review. Phase one of the Review was intended to provide the foundations for the review process. There were two elements to this foundation: the ideological statement, mentioned above, and an assessment of Britain's political situation in 1991, the earliest likely date for a General Election, including an extensive survey of public attitudes. This work resulted in the initial statements of the policy review groups published in the document: *Social Justice and Economic Efficiency.* The 'final reports' of the policy review groups were collected together a year later in the phase two document: *Meet the Challenge, Make the Change.* The electoral objective of the review process was underlined by the fact that this document was published during the 1989 European election campaign and became an element in Labour's campaigning for European seats. Phase three of the Review produced *Looking to the Future*, which was intended to refine and simplify the groups' final reports for wider consumption and campaigning purposes. This was intended as an interim step between the Review process and the preparation of an election manifesto for a General Election initially expected by the Party in 1991. The failure of an election to materialise in 1991 led to the publication of a fourth round of documents, most importantly *Opportunity Britain,* which did little more than reaffirm the major points of previous documents.

The important point to bear in mind is that the Review timetable was aimed at the eventual production of an election manifesto. At each stage of the Review the central documents were accompanied by policy statements in a variety of different areas based on the work of the Review. Here it is the central Review documents which are the subject of discussion, and not the parallel policy statements released during these years.

The Policy Review as a self-contained, coherent and sophisticated attempt to deal with Labour's core problems represents the main area of concern of this work, and is the subject of Part 1 below, but attempts to transform Labour have not ended there. Partly this is because the Review did not succeed in its attempt either to win the 1992 General Election, or to resolve Labour's problems. Instead Labour's latest Leader, Tony Blair, has sought to stamp his own identity on the Party by transforming a process of 'renewal' into 'modernisation'. One central aspect of this new attempt to address Labour's problems has been the reform of Clause IV of Labour's constitution, its statement of ideological belief, which will be considered in chapter 7.

The immediate response to defeat in the 1992 General Election fell to John Smith, elected Leader after Kinnock's post-election resignation. His most significant action to follow Kinnock's attempts at resolving Labour's problems was to initiate the Commission on Social Justice, whose work will be the subject of chapter 6. Both Smith, in his short time as Party Leader before his premature death, and Blair have pursued parallel approaches to those of the Policy Review. The question considered here will be to what extent any of these initiatives have really addressed Labour's core problems.

In order to consider this question Labour's core problems and their antecedents must be more clearly identified and consideration given to the way the development of Labour has been seen during this period. The Policy Review has been portrayed in at least five distinct ways: it has been seen as part of the creation of a 'new model party' (Hughes and Wintour); as an instrument of the resurgence of a right-wing hegemony against the democratic reforms pursued by the left in the late 1970s and early 1980s (Heffernan and Marqusee); as part of a continuing ideological and intellectual slide away from a nascent social democracy and towards 'social liberalism' (Elliott); as a means to affect policy changes and 'renew' the party (Smith and Spear); and as a means of affecting changes in the Party's policy-making system (Shaw, 1989). This debate has continued into the era of modernisation which has been seen as a 'catching-up' of the agenda set by Thatcherism (Hay), as a process of modernisation owing much to Labour's heritage (Smith, 1994), as a clean break from Labour's past (Mandelson and Liddle), or as an attempt to introduce the Fordist state structures of other countries (Wickham-Jones). What are the areas of agreement and departure between these views and the argument pursued here?

The Review has been portrayed in terms of breaks and continuities with the past. For example, both Smith and Elliott see the Review as marking a step in an ideological departure. For Smith the Review marked Labour as at last accepting its social democratic identity (Smith, 1992, 223), whilst Elliott saw it as an abandonment of social democracy in favour of a more liberal alternative (Elliott, 17).On the other hand supporters of modernisation tend to portray the Party as embodying a long-standing belief in ethical socialism (Mandelson and Liddle, 29–30); this compliments Blair's firm Christian beliefs.

These various claims must be considered in the light of Labour's ideological history. It will be argued below that this has been predominantly electorally pragmatic rather than either socialist or social democratic. From this perspective the Review and reform of Clause IV represent both a continuity with and a departure from Labour's past.

These changes lead to the first of three interrelated problems for Labour which form the basis of this study: a loss of ideological identity. This does not mean that Labour's problems originate from its move away from 'socialism' or even 'social democracy', but rather that Labour's lack of a stronger ideological foundation meant that it became identified with its

5 views of PR 1. 2. 3. 4. 5.

Smith–SD   Elliot–liberal social'sm

Lab ideologically pragmatic – not socialist or SD hence PR in continuity & change.

Labs weak id. foundation led to dependence on record.

pragmatic use of British state power. In particular this became an 'ideological association' with the practice of the 1945–51 Labour government. When the postwar consensus was challenged this prompted a policy reassessment for Labour, but given Labour's ideological association with the postwar state, this also resulted in an ideological crisis for the Party. Labour's support for the British state is noted by both Smith and Elliott (Smith, 1992, 224; Elliott, 190) This provides support for the second of Labour's three core problems: its lack of an effective critique of the British state.

prompted *policy reassess* *ident.* *crisis*

The concerns of renewal and modernisation are consistent with Labour's historical concerns, particularly with its electoral pragmatism. The problems on which the Review foundered are long-standing ones for the Party. However, the Review can be seen as a break from Labour's more recent past, in particular 'the Bennite rebellion of the late 1970s and early 1980s' (Heffernan and Marqusee, 9).

It was claimed by some that the Policy Review had succeeded in renewing the Party (Seyd and Whiteley, 1992a, 30). Renewal suggests that either the Party's electoral recovery was due to the efforts of the Labour Party itself, or that Labour had developed as a Party into a more efficient and credible force, or both. That belief is not shared here. On the contrary it will be argued that it is Labour's deeper problems which sidelined the Review, rather than the Review which fundamentally affected the Party. It might be added that if the Review had provided the 'renewal' it was intended to produce then it is unlikely that the Party would feel 'modernisation' to be necessary.

renewal *not stuff.* *modernisation* *also* *necessary*

The Review certainly did act as a focus for supporters of the Kinnock leadership. The development of a new grouping around the Party Leader had tentatively begun under the leadership of Michael Foot (Shaw, 1988, 224). This development was cemented by the struggle against *Militant* and the Review was both the product of and a contributing factor to the unity of this leadership group.

This unity of a leadership group able to push through its own agenda for reform has continued under Blair's leadership, and highlights the third major problem for Labour: Labour's poor contact with its members and its potential voters. The Review, the Commission on Social Justice, and the reform of Clause IV, all included attempts to involve Party members and supporters. Poor contact with its constituency has been a feature of Labour's postwar history. Patrick Seyd traces the move towards 'direct appeals' to the electorate from the 1950s onwards, with 'television, advertising and sample surveys, increasingly marginalising Party members and the trade unions as means of mobilising Labour support' (Seyd, 1987, 39). Party members, particularly activists, were increasingly seen as an embarrassment to, rather than a vital influence on, the Party (Seyd, 1987, 39–40). One thing which has been changed since 1987 is the attention given to Party membership and organisation, in particular to recruitment, and the by-passing of Party activists in decision-making processes. However, this has not reversed the trend towards the reliance on the media and public opinion surveys to deliver and assess Labour's message (Hughes and Wintour, 52).

Attempts to involve the wider Party membership in these years must be contrasted with the trend, noted above, of portraying the strength of the Party Leader by his ability to defeat opponents within his own Party (Heffernan and Marqusee, 82; Elliott, 137). The electoral wisdom of such a strategy might also be questioned (Elliott, 171). In addition Heffernan and Marqusee suggest that the review process represented a tightening of links with union leaders, again at the expense of ordinary Party and union members (Heffernan and Marqusee, 156).

The argument made here does not support the contention that Labour has undergone 'renewal', has become a 'new model party', or is in the process of 'modernisation'. Labour faces serious and specific problems which events since 1987 have illustrated, but not resolved. Labour's specific problems, of membership, ideology, and electoral decline (Whiteley), and consequent problems of finance, organisation and image, are themselves symptoms of a deeper malaise.

It is argued here that three interrelated factors are fundamental to Labour's problems. These are: an indistinct ideological identity; a lack of connection with its potential constituency; and a lack of a critique of the state form it seeks to administer. Whether or not Labour is capable of resolving these fundamental problems is not discussed here. However, it can be suggested that in order to do so Labour must provide a more substantial ideological *raison d'etre* than electoral pragmatism; an effective channel of two-way communication to its supporters, potential and actual; and, most importantly, a deeper understanding of the problems of utilising state power to aid those excluded from its exercise. In order to assess Labour's 'transformation' since 1987 we must consider its history in each of these areas in greater depth.

Labour's Ideological Development

It is usual to see the period from 1976 to 1983 as a period of ideological conflict in the Labour Party between the 'left' and the 'right' (Seyd, 1987). From this perspective the Kinnock leadership can be seen as a reaction to the 'lurch to the left' of the early 1980s and the electoral disaster of 1983 (Heffernan and Marqusee, 9). This is too simple to provide an adequate basis for analysis between 1987 and 1992. In fact, the historical events of the late 1970s and 1980s themselves have to be put into a broader historical context. In the 1980s the perceived threat of *Militant* did much to bring together the Kinnock leadership group and to foster the idea of the Policy Review (Heffernan and Marqusee, 63–4).

Such conflicts have been a recurring aspect of Labour's history. In the 1950s the perceived threat to the 'right' leadership were the Bevanites, in the interwar years there was the danger of Communist infiltration and the challenge of the Popular Front (Callaghan, 1990), and before that a changing relationship with the Independent Labour Party (Brown, 1988).

The ideological divisions of the 1980s must be seen as part of a continuing trend, a trend in which there has been 'little fundamental socialism' (Leach, 117). Despite the adoption in 1918 of a constitution with at least one specific socialist objective, (Callaghan, 1990: 74–5) Labour remains largely a 'trade union reformist party' (Leach, 135; Elliott, xiii). Nonetheless, battles over Clause IV proved protracted until its final abandonment. It is perhaps indicative of Labour's curious ideological history that a clause written by the Fabian Sidney Webb (Callaghan, 1990, 74) and a system of state ownership largely the creation of the equally 'moderate', Herbert Morrison (Morgan, 1987, 182–3), should have become the sacred cows defended by the Party's 'left' against incursions from the reforming 'right'.

Clause IV had come under attack more than once in the Party. In the 1950s the Gaitskellite leadership wished to see the clause revoked on the grounds that it was outdated. Whilst the existence of Clause IV was not called into question during the Review period, the 'producer centred' approach of the Labour Party was raised (Heffernan and Marqusee, 303; Beishon). During its existence the Party's original Clause IV was never a serious basis for policy-making and political action, apart from the one policy of nationalisation, and even here it had been interpreted in a particularly narrow and highly specific fashion.

The real importance of Clause IV was not what it said, but rather its role as a statement of faith. As Drucker pointed out:

> Clause IV, so fundamentally associated with the Labour Party, was more than a sentimental symbol. ... It puts a principle between Labour and the Tories. As long as it retains Clause IV, the Tories can never assimilate all of Labour's achievements or demands. (Drucker, 38)

The failure to regard Clause IV as an effective guide to policy action left the Party with the appearance of a lack of ideological commitment (Callaghan, 1989, 23). This 'doctrineless' approach was clearly in contrast with the other European social democratic parties (Padgett and Paterson, 15). The division between fundamentalism and revisionism in the Labour Party has been a largely redundant one. The dominant ideological strand in Labour's

Guiding principles derives from experience not theory

history has been one of pragmatism. This does not mean that the Labour Party is unprincipled, as it is quite possible that a pragmatic approach to British politics can be married to a clear set of guiding principles, but it does mean that these principles are themselves derived from practical experience rather than theory.

In fact Labour's ideological identity is fundamentally based on its practical politics, its actions. As Jones and Keating have put it, after the 1945–51 Labour Government: 'Socialism became what the Labour Government had done' (Jones and Keating, 61). The perceived successes of the Attlee administration proved the basis for the belief that some form of transformation, socialist or not, had been achieved (Callaghan, 1989, 29).

Though nationalisation may be identified as Labour's 'project' (Drucker, 28), the other elements of the postwar settlement, Keynesian economics and Beveridgean welfare, are far from unequivocally Labour concerns (Callaghan, 1990, 129). Neither Beveridge nor Keynes saw themselves as associates of the Labour Party (Foote, 140). Both were concerned with the efficient working of the existing social system, not with its replacement; and both had their ideas accepted, in principle at least, under Churchill's wartime coalition, and later applied by Labour under Attlee.

In addition, all three of these elements can be seen as state based. Beveridge called for the extension of state welfare, Keynes for state control of aggregate demand, and nationalisation was undertaken by the state. This reflected a shift away from municipal, cooperative politics, toward state and central government (Beilharz, 55; Taylor, 1980, 16).

In effect Labour's ideological identity with the principles embodied in the Attlee Government were an acknowledgment of Labour's pragmatic soul. It was an identification with a series of practical responses to the experiences of the interwar years. As such Labour became the defenders of the 'historic gains' of an administration from which: 'the predominant feature which emerges is not so much socialism as *statism*' (Jones and Keating, 61, emphasis in original).

Drucker has argued that Labour's lack of doctrine is compensated by a distinctive Party ethos (Drucker, vii). Whilst Drucker may be right, how does this help us? How can we know what this ethos consists of and how it interacts with other aspects of Party activity? How does it change over time and what are the determinants of such change?

In fact the central debate over Party ideology has focused on the relationship between power and principle. The challenges to Clause IV which have occurred have been on the basis of the need to change the Party's ideological position for electoral gain (Foote, 231). Others have seen the defence of the class interests Labour was created to represent as fundamentally more

party id

power & principle · change id to gain power.

important than the search for 'Parliamentary honours' (Taylor, 1980, 7). This conflict between the desire to represent the Party's class-based interests and the desire for wider support to win General Elections has been a continuing factor in Labour's ideological struggles.

Whilst Aneurin Bevan could argue that principles were no use without the power to implement them (Foot, 1975a, 146), he also believed that this did not require a compromise between Labour's principles and power, but rather that Labour could not hope to gain the support it desired without holding to its principles (Bevan, 126). This suggests that the Party's ideological differences are crucially related to electoral strategy. Ideology also has implications for membership and this has also long been understood (Foote, 196). Both of these factors emerge in the Policy Review and subsequently in the reform of Clause IV.

The question that needs to be asked is how does this division between principle and power set the context for Labour's renewal? The ideological schism Whiteley suggested within the Labour Party was not so much a division between the leaders and the led, but more a division amongst the party's elite. On the one side stand those with little or no experience in elective office. These are young, radical activists generally to the left of their more 'moderate', elder, right-wing comrades who have already spent some time as Members of Parliament or local councillors (Whiteley, 24–50). This schism could be attributed on the one hand to elected activists being absorbed into the tradition of British political life, and on the other to the radical nature of activists untempered by the experience and wisdom engendered by office.

Whiteley remains ambivalent about the orientation of individual members and potential Labour voters, not because they lack political orientation (Seyd and Whiteley, 1992b), but rather because their views are not as structured, or certainly not structured in the same way, as Party activists or elected politicians. Wainwright argues that activists represent the views of ordinary members more accurately than elected politicians because of their more recent and intimate links with the grass roots (Wainwright). Whatever the accuracy of this claim, the point here is that their views are articulated differently in internal Party debates.

This observation is intensified by the different perspectives of the two groups involved. The need to transfer the opinions, attitudes and priorities of Labour's grass roots into the language of a leadership concerned with elected office presents real problems of understanding, comprehension and compatibility. The same can, of course, also be said for the reverse process, that it is sometimes difficult for grass-roots Labour supporters and members to comprehend the concerns and priorities of the Party's elite. Elite views are structured not just by the exigencies of the political opinions of voters, but are also informed by, and couched in terms derived from, the historical debates within the Party itself, and the various theoretical models which have arisen and continue to arise within elite discussion.

The debate over power and principle stretches back to the formation of the Labour Representation Committee in 1900. Its formation, and subsequently that of the Labour Party, was designed to secure the election to Parliament of socialists and members of the working class (Callaghan, 1990, 63–4). Whether or not that aim has been achieved is not important here, the point is that once Labour had achieved first parliamentary and later governmental office it became transformed from a party struggling for power to one defending its power bases. A key problem for all parties once elected is: what changes will secure the existing electoral base, and which will destroy it? There is a tendency for those already elected to view the power structure which has rewarded them with election as positively beneficial, or at worst neutral.

The desirability of defending the elected position of certain individuals may not be as self-evident to non-elected Labour Party members, particularly for those most active in the Party. For those elected, and for their supporters, the desire to defend these power bases may come to be seen as the need to preserve existing institutional structures, or at least elements of them. Such a view in turn fosters a conservative attitude to the operation of the existing political system. This goes some way to explaining the schism Whiteley perceived between Labour's elected elite and its non-elected activists.

A conflict, for reformist or revolutionary parties, between short-term electoral considerations and long-term programmatic priorities almost inevitably arises. To the extent that Party support is genuinely based upon its reformist, or revolutionary, pretensions, short-term priorities may lead to a long-term deterioration in electoral performance (Przeworski).

In Britain, Whiteley has claimed, the failure to deliver promised benefits to its supporters once in office has contributed to Labour's long-term electoral decline (Whiteley, 12–18). Whilst similar problems are experienced by social democratic parties throughout Europe (Przeworski, 23–9), the structured views of Labour's elite appears as one of its particular manifestations in the British context. Labour's history has been marked, in practice, by the primacy of electorally pragmatic considerations above the desire to implement the Party's agreed policies (Callaghan, 1990, 240), themselves the outcome of the Party's elite debate.

The lack of a deeper ideological base is itself the consequence of Labour's uncritical acceptance of the British state as a neutral political instrument, and the resulting belief that all that is needed is the achievement of power to enact 'socialist', or at least 'labourist', policies. The consequence has been that Labour had no deep roots to protect it against the breakdown of postwar consensus, which has been the British manifestation of the global crisis of social democracy and failure of the left (Smith, 1992, 14).

The pragmatic basis of Labour's ideology, and its identification with Labour in government, and therefore with Labour's parliamentary leadership, has itself contributed to an ideological gulf between Labour's elected elite and Party activists (Whiteley). It is the relationship between Labour's elite, its supporters and members, which provides the second of the three fundamental problems Labour faces.

Labour and Its Supporters

An increasing distance between Labour and its potential, or actual, constituency has been marked in a number of ways: declining membership, poor electoral performance, and an increasingly exclusive policy-making system. Electoral appeals and reform of Labour's policy-making systems were an integral part of the periods of renewal and now of modernisation, whilst membership recruitment was seen as an important, if ancillary, element of both.

As mentioned above, an ideological split between Labour's activists and its elected elite has often been observed. Commentators have seen Labour's activists as essentially more 'extreme' or 'militant' than the leadership (McLean, 39) and this perception seems to be shared by that leadership (Seyd and Whiteley, 1992b, 5). Indeed suspicion of activists amongst Party leaders is nothing new (Seyd and Whiteley, 1992a, 40; Elliott, 32). Occasionally this conflict has emerged amongst the Party elite when the 'activists' have found champions within the elite group, perhaps most notably with Aneurin Bevan in the 1940s and 1950s (Howell; Foot 1975a and 1975b) and Tony Benn in the late 1970s and early 1980s (Seyd, 1987; Kogan and Kogan). It can also be traced through the development and exercise of Labour's disciplinary procedures (Shaw, 1988).

Party activists are seen, by Party leaders, commentators, and academics, as an electoral liability rather than a resource through which potential supporters can be reached largely because they are perceived as 'unrepresentative' of either Labour's membership as a whole, or of the Party's wider support (Seyd and Whiteley, 1992b, 100).

This perception has been compounded by the decline in Labour's working-class electoral base (Denver, 143–4; Crewe, 1991). The point here is not to debate the accuracy, or otherwise, of these perceptions, but merely to observe that they have blocked off one of the main avenues by which Labour might have contacted its potential constituency, both to exercise Party influence and to determine the reactions of that constituency to the Party's programme.

As a substitute for such contact Labour has used media presentations to reach its constituency, and public opinion surveys to gauge its reaction. Media presentation and surveying techniques were both developed in the Review through the creation of the Shadow Communications Agency, under the control of Peter Mandelson (Hughes and Wintour, 61). It is important to bear in mind two aspects of the nature of this strategy.

Firstly, by attempting to reach potential supporters through non-Party means Labour has separated out opinion forming and opinion receiving. Labour seeks to determine public opinion through sample surveys, and to influence it through the media. This means that the determination of public opinion is essentially passive. There is no opportunity for debate with the mass of Labour voters and supporters, or the public as a whole. The experience is one of discovery and response. Secondly, in bypassing Party channels crucial aspects of Labour's attempt to reach potential support are outside of its control. The media and polling organisations are crucial filters between Labour and its audience. Of course it could be argued by the Party's leadership that these are more acceptable filters than would be presented by the Party itself, but this might tell us as much about the Party leadership as it does about the wider Party.

Real attempts to establish new contact within the Party and revitalise the Party as a political tool for the leadership have been a feature both of Labour's renewal and of its modernisation. There appeared a genuine feeling amongst many involved in these changes that the Party must be rejuvenated and that renewal provided an opportunity for that. The results of these attempts have been mixed. Membership recruitment rose both during the Policy Review and the early period of Blair's leadership, but the first rise was subsequently reversed, and the implications of the second have yet to become apparent. Attempts were made to consult the membership directly, but these also provided mixed responses. These experiences suggest that Labour does not have a channel to its real or potential support which is reliable enough for the Party to adequately represent its concerns or express its message convincingly.

The fact that Labour has seen its function as the achievement of state power has meant that broader ideological or activist concerns have been seen as troublesome and irrelevant to the main interest of the Party, and something to be curtailed. It is the relationship to the state which now needs to be addressed.

Labour and the State

Labour's attachment to the view of the state as a neutral administrative instrument has frequently been observed (Leach, 42). According to Jones and Keating, Labour's problem is not that it embraces state power as such, but that it uncritically embraces the British state as the form of state power (Jones and Keating, 2). In this sense the Labour Party is a highly conservative body (Marquand, 1992, 46).

Even those on the left of the Party have tended to see Parliament as 'the ultimate guardian of democracy, and hence the bulwark against tyranny' (Benn, 1991b, 38). This sanguine view of the British state is not shared by all on the left. Many socialists, democratic or otherwise, have had deep misgivings about attempting to administer a liberal democratic state, particularly one as profoundly conservative in nature as the British state, for broadly socialist ends (Miliband, 1982). Despite this, socialism has been far from certain in producing an alternative.

Marx may have had a theory of the state (Draper, 20), but his proscriptions for the socialist state were not such as to prevent Lenin advancing his own state theory as that of Marx (Beilharz, 12–13). Current debate about the nature of the state amongst socialists contrasts a view of 'the state as the instrument of the transition to socialism' (Clarke, 1991a, 31) with a belief that the state must be seen as 'one aspect of the social relations of capital' (Holloway and Picciotto, 109). The latter seems to imply that the state must be regarded as an equal, perhaps a greater, problem than the social conditions it administers. This approach certainly could not be married to Labour's perspective. The former also seems to be alien to Labour's traditional views. Whilst Labour has seen its role as achieving state power, it is difficult to argue that this has been the first step in the 'transition to socialism'. Lacking a critique of the British state, Labour has consequently lacked any idea of how the state might be used to achieve a socialist society, even if that were an unequivocal objective of the Party. Nor does one need to be a socialist, or a revolutionary, to regard a critique of the state as important. From an economic point of view, for example, it has been argued that a major problem of the British state is the institutional power of the finance sector and the policies this dictates (Pollard; Hutton, 1993b; Elliott, 190). State reform is also implied from decentralising environmental perspectives (Bromley, 117).

This lack of a critique of the British state has become particularly troublesome for Labour as the British state has been challenged from two sources. The first have been the Conservative Governments of Margaret Thatcher, which adapted a critique of the state based on New Right public choice theorists (Dunleavy, 154–61). A second challenge is presented by the developing European Union (Ellis, xii). For renewal and modernisation the more important of the two has undoubtedly been that of Thatcherism (Hay), both because it presented a sharper and more obvious break with Britain's postwar history, and because it was focused at the national level at which Labour's leadership operates.

Labour's attempt to respond to this challenge is complicated by its equivocal nature. Whilst critical of 'state intervention' Thatcherism was forced to use the state for its own ends (Elliott, 96; Marquand, 1988, 101; Gamble, 1988, 28). The exercise of state authority to guarantee the 'free market' and protect the economic power of the 'individual' was one thing, state interference to regulate the market or to bring about preconceived 'political' ends quite another. For Labour this was bad news as this is precisely the form of state power with which they have been associated (Elliott, 34–5).

This lack of a critique of the British state also affects the nature of the Party and of its activities. Labour's relationship to the state bears implications for Labour's internal democracy and policy-making system. After all, Labour is one part of the machinery of political power in Britain, and its willingness to participate in the British political system lends credibility and legitimacy to that system. Meanwhile, the British political system itself contributes to the structure of the Labour Party and its mode of operation. McKenzie has argued that this means that the 'final authority' in British political parties rests with the Parliamentary leadership (Drucker, 2).

This view of political parties as run by the 'final authority' of the Parliamentary leadership does not fit well with some outlines of the Labour Party which see it as dominated by the trade unions (Minkin, 1991) or Party 'extremists' (Seyd and Whiteley, 1992b). Nonetheless, to say that Labour's Conference never had the central policy-making role the Party's constitution accorded it is not to say that it lacked importance. Conference may have provided an important mechanism for frustrated Party activists to 'let off steam', and the changing nature of its role in Labour's policy-making system may leave the Party without a safety valve for such frustrations.

Another consequence of Labour's lack of critical appreciation of the British state is the Party's approach to policy, and in particular the effectiveness, or appropriateness, of state activity with regard to policy options. The Policy Review sought to address this through the concept of 'market socialism' (Le Grand, 12). This was seen entirely in opposition to command economies in much the same way that the modernisers were later to portray the need to reform Clause IV (Thompson, 1995a, 2). Nonetheless, in a collection of articles discussing the concept, Le Grand and Estrin had argued that 'market socialism' demanded 'a change in our understanding of the appropriate role of the state' (Estrin and Le Grand, 1). Despite this bold statement, the remaining essays provided no extensive discussion of what the 'appropriate role' of the state might be.

In the Review itself it is difficult to see how 'market socialism' differs from the earlier concept of the 'mixed economy' except in the fact that the mix will involve less state ownership of industry and more state regulation. In fact another published collection of contributions to the Review (Cowling and Sugden) called for extensive state intervention to promote training and other economic ends. In comparing British industrial development with that of countries like Japan and Germany the authors came to the conclusion that a more integrated and extensive state and industry relationship was vitally important.

This confusion about the role of the state was in clear contrast to the approach of Labour's political opponents (Harris, 1989, 4). Not only did Thatcherism question the legitimate role of the British state, it also questioned the role of all organisations intervening between the state and the individual. This is an approach which Labour would find it very hard to adopt. Hence, in seeing the British state as a neutral instrument for the wielding of political power Labour has found itself with little to offer in response to the Thatcherite challenge.

Interestingly, the constitutional challenges the British state faces were considered in the review process (Dearlove and Saunders, chapter 5; Marquand, 1992). In fact Labour has been prepared to countenance far-reaching changes to the form of the British state (Elliott, 74). Debate on electoral reform had been one 'spin-off' of the Review with the commissioning of The Plant Report (Plant Commission), whilst reform of the House of Lords has been a long-standing Labour policy (Crossman, 339–40). The point is not that Labour is incapable of constitutional or state reform, but rather that these policies are piecemeal and ad hoc, not strategic or systematic. They are prompted by experience and practice, not critique or theory. In particular Labour's interest in the state's economic efficiency is generated by Britain's relative economic decline (Gamble, 1985), whilst the political reform of the state arises from declining electoral performance and the experience of government with small working majorities (Denver). In this, as in the other areas considered above, Labour is responding to circumstances, not determining them.

Conclusion

The analysis contained in the following chapters argues that renewal and modernisation are consecutive attempts to address a series of deep-rooted problems within the Labour Party. These problems have been perceived in a variety of ways by the Party leadership, fundamentally in electoral, pragmatic terms. This is entirely consistent with Labour's traditional approaches and perspectives. It is argued here that such strategies will not succeed unless they address three core problems: a lack of ideological identity; problems contacting and conversing with the Party's constituency and support; and a lack of an effective critique of the British state.

All of these problems emerged in some form or other throughout the period of renewal and modernisation. The Policy Review contained a specific statement of ideological belief as part of its initial phase, the Commission on Social Justice spent its initial phase discussing the philosophical meaning of social justice, and the modernisers targeted Clause IV for reform as the Party's ideological statement. Under the leadership of both Kinnock and Blair, membership recruitment was seen as a priority, not least to increase the power of 'moderate' members against 'extreme' activists. At the same time they both concentrated on developing media presentation, under the guidance of Peter Mandelson, and the Policy Review developed the use of opinion polls and sample surveys. Finally, whilst a commitment to market systems has been developing through this period, this has been married to a belief in state regulation to alleviate the 'excesses' of the market.

It is argued below that these attempts have essentially failed to resolve Labour's problems, and as a result have not helped Labour become more effective either as a party of government or as an electoral force. This does not mean that Labour will not win the next General Election. As is argued in chapter 5, the result of this will depend as much on the performance of the Conservative Government as on that of the Labour Opposition. What it does suggest is that once elected Labour will either have a programme which is not able to deliver radical change, or will not be able to deliver effectively its programme. As this may be one reason why Labour has been in electoral decline in the postwar period, a Blair Government may be incapable of halting or reversing this long-term decline. However, one thing that is not accepted here is that this is the result of 'betrayal' or bad faith on the part of Labour's leadership (Heffernan and Marqusee; Elliott). Such approaches fail to answer the question of why, given the repeated nature of such 'betrayal', Labour consistently elects this type of leader. If a proper assessment of the failures of renewal and modernisation are to be made a deeper analysis is necessary.

The attempts at modernisation under Tony Blair are frequently portrayed as a continuation of the renewal of the Party under Neil Kinnock (Blair, 1993, 9; Mandelson and Liddle, 2). Because of this, and the sophisticated nature of the Policy Review strategy, Part 1 consists of a detailed consideration of the Party's Policy Review undertaken between 1987 and 1992. In chapter 2 the ideological elements of the Review are considered. Chapter 3 considers the Policy Review's policy-making structures which, for a time, supplanted those of the Party itself and provided the impetus for wider change in Labour's policy-making structures. The policy output of the Review is examined in chapter 4, which focuses on economic policy to provide a clear analysis of Labour's use of the state as a tool for policy implementation. Finally, the Review as an electoral strategy is the focus of chapter 5.

The period since the Review is considered in Part 2, and in particular the Commission on Social Justice, initiated by John Smith; and the reform of Clause IV, brought about by Tony Blair. These chapters assess the move from Party renewal to modernisation. Chapter 6 considers the work of the Commission on Social Justice, and chapter 7 looks at the reform of Clause IV.

One important aspect to remember is that the renewal of the Party has focused on the need to break from Labour's past. This is partly dependent on Labour finding a convincing alternative which it can present, but it is also open to question whether Labour can divorce itself from its historical associations (Dunleavy, 30). Its ability to do so may depend on its ability to sustain a new image over a period of time. This in turn is dependent on the fundamental problems facing the Party and the resolution of these problems within the Party. The argument here suggests that renewal and modernisation do not provide a resolution to these problems, fundamentally because Labour has still not come to terms with the way in which its own structures and approaches are dictated by the elitist nature of the British state.

Part 1:
The Policy Review

2 The Ideological Foundation

Introduction

The ideological element of the Review was designed and intended to provide a base for the work of the review groups and for the policy output. The vehicle for providing this foundation was to be the phase one document *Democratic Socialist Aims and Values* (Labour Party, 1988, also referred to as *Aims and Values*). This chapter will look at the extent of the influence *Aims and Values* had on the Review's output through a detailed reading of its text.

Aims and Values attempted to clarify the Party's philosophy, an attempt subsequently taken up by the Blair leadership with the reform of Clause IV, considered in chapter 7 below. It was intended to provide the philosophical basis on which the Policy Review proper would be built. The possibility that the Review was based on principles other than those set out by *Aims and Values* must also be considered and explored through an assessment of the ideological content of other Review documents.

In examination of the underlying principles, the ideology, of the Review, the way in which the Review fitted with Labour's ideological history must also be considered. I have argued that one of Labour's problems has been a loss of ideological identity. This could occur either because the Party has moved away from its former principles and beliefs, or because these principles are increasingly difficult to marry to the perceived realities of the Party's situation. In this chapter it will be argued that Labour has been essentially pragmatic in its ideological approach, and that the Review continued this practice. The reason why this pragmatism did not provide a stronger philosophical identification in the nineties was the result of Labour's association with the nature of postwar state power, an association Labour has proved reluctant or unable to shake off.

In essence Labour's 'loss of ideological identity' was, therefore, not the result of a change in its ideological principles, but rather a reflection of its inability to come to terms with a new reality in practical and pragmatic terms. First the intended ideological statement *Aims and Values* must be examined to determine why this failed to provide an ideological basis for the Party in the 1990s.

Democratic Socialist Aims and Values

The Parliamentary leadership of the Labour Party first became convinced of the value of a modern restatement of socialist beliefs and values as a direct

21

result of the ideological conflict within the Party (Shaw, 1988, 233–4). Such a restatement would help to separate the mainstream Party from the perceived threat of trotskyite entryism in the shape of the *Militant Tendency*. However, this strategy opened the danger of splitting the Party in two, particularly given the strength in the Party of the wider left in the early 1980s (Seyd, 1987). As a result the leadership procrastinated until the regrouping of elements of the left, around the leadership of Neil Kinnock, ensured victory over the *Militant* threat, and removed any potential for disastrous internal division (Shaw, 1988, 259–63). This provided the opportunity for the long-awaited statement to see the light of day.

By the time it was published in March 1988, after its endorsement by Labour's National Executive Committee now dominated by the new elite group, *Democratic Socialist Aims and Values* was seen as the ideological foundation of the Policy Review which by this time had been agreed by Conference. This was the Labour leadership's chance not only to take another step in rebuilding the Party in its preferred image, but also to consolidate the groups broadly loyal to the Kinnock regime.

Aims and Values demonstrated no intention to compromise with dissenting voices within the Party, irrespective of the possibility of exacerbating existing conflicts. The document's authors were the Party Leader, Neil Kinnock, and Deputy Leader, Roy Hattersley, and its content relied heavily on Hattersley's own book, *Choose Freedom* (Hattersley), published the previous year.

Whilst amendments were invited before its ratification by the NEC, respondents were given barely a month to reply, and the structure and nature of the document made amendment virtually impossible (Heffernan and Marqusee). Under the circumstances it was perhaps hardly surprising that *Aims and Values* failed to galvanise the Party into constructive internal debate or to unite the disparate ideological positions within the Party. The best that can be said was that it did not rock Labour's, occasionally unstable, ideological boat, but, as one interviewee observed, this seems more because the statement was ignored than because of the force of its arguments.

Perhaps more surprising was the fact that the statement, intended and designed as it was to provide the ideological clout for the Policy Review itself, had little effect on the overall shape or product of the Review. Whilst the Review structure did include a committee, chaired by Tom Sawyer, which was responsible for ensuring the coherence of the final reports of the seven Review committees, little attention was paid to the ideological framework set out in *Aims and Values*.

This does not mean that themes stated in *Aims and Values* were not reflected in *Meet the Challenge, Make the Change*; they were, notably on the productive economy and market socialism. However, this was a reflection of the fact that the mainstream group which had formed around the Kinnock leadership already shared a common view of the political position, and it was this view which dominated both the Shadow Cabinet and the NEC.

Despite the lack of influence, and restricted authorship, of *Aims and Values,* an examination of this statement remains worthwhile as an indication of the ideological perspectives of Labour's highest echelon, and as a prelude to later changes.

I have argued that Labour's historical ideological base contains three major strands which can be defined in relation to Clause IV, part 4 of the Party's constitution: fundamentalism, revisionism and pragmatism. *Aims and Values* appeared to contain elements of all three. Revisionism can be seen in the attempt to establish freedom and equality, as defined by the Party leadership, in replacement of common ownership as the rallying cry for democratic socialists. Pragmatism was expressed by subsuming all objectives to what might prove practicable in the context of contemporary society, without creating social change of any great order. Yet the authors still felt it necessary to include Clause IV part 4 on the internal front cover of the document (Labour Party, 1988).

Freedom was undoubtedly the central ideological theme of *Aims and Values,* but contradictions concerning what is meant by freedom in a socialist context are already clear in the Neil Kinnock quote which prefaced the document:

> We are democratic socialists.
>
> We want a state where the collective contribution of the community is used for the advance of individual freedom. Not just freedom in name, but freedom that can be exercised in practice – because the school is good, because the work is available, because the health service is strong, because the law is fair, because the streets are safe.
>
> Real freedom with real choices and real chances. That is what freedom means to us as democratic socialists. That is why we want to put the state where it belongs – under the feet of the people, not over their heads...
> We must be the friends of freedom, for we know that for us as free people, freedom can have no boundaries. (Labour Party, 1988, 2)

The problem for Labour's concept of freedom, as expressed in the words of the Party Leader, was that the connection between freedom, in particular individual freedom, and social organisation was simply ignored or glossed over. According to these words of Neil Kinnock, it would seem that whilst Britons must be regarded as 'free people', this was 'just freedom in name' and not 'freedom that can be exercised in practice'. Leaving aside the problem of what 'freedom in name' can mean and whether freedom is a quantitative or indivisible attribute, the 'freedom ... in practice' was to be measured, it would appear, entirely in respect of the efficiency of government and state activity. It was to be assessed by the quality of the education service, the availability of work, the strength of the NHS, the 'fairness' of the law, and the ability to walk the streets.

The real problem with this attempted definition, which reflects a deeper problem with the Review and the Party as a whole, was the role of the state with regard to freedom. If freedom is defined by the efficiency of the state, does this mean that those areas in which the state is not involved are free by definition? Or rather that the state must involve itself in every area of society for freedom to occur? Wouldn't the cause of freedom then be best served by either advancing or curtailing the activities of the state rather than bothering with state 'efficiency' as such?

It is perhaps natural that a political party seeking to achieve state power should define its objectives firstly in the context of what it sees as the legitimate exercise of that state power. The point could justly be made that to attempt this kind of analysis on a brief introduction to one Party document by one Party individual is stretching a point. This is perfectly true and the point would not be worth making so emphatically if it were not for the role *Aims and Values* was intended to play as an ideological foundation to the Policy Review, and for the problems it demonstrated with Labour's undeveloped attitude to the state and state activity (Jones and Keating).

This has salience for two reasons. Firstly, though it would be asking far too much to expect to attempt to resolve the general problems of socialist political thought since the collapse of the 'actually existing socialist states' of Eastern Europe (Shaw, 1994, 154), as I have argued above, Labour's main focus of concern has always been the achievement of elected office, and thus the exercise of state power. Under these circumstances it is not unreasonable to suggest that the Party should have some consistent attitude to the legitimate exercise of the power its leadership seeks to wield. This point is reinforced by the second, which is that the Thatcherite style and ideology of the Conservative Party, the Party of government in Britain since 1979, has stressed precisely this point, the role of the state, and the relationship between the state and individual freedom.

Gamble has characterised Thatcherism as calling for a 'free economy and a strong state', but rightly points out that this is 'capable of several different interpretations' (Gamble, 1988, 31). He has also questioned whether these challenges to the role of the state are leading to a new consensus (Gamble, 1988, 208). Confusion over the rise of a new consensus may be at least partly due to Labour's equivocal response to the Thatcherite challenge to the legitimate role of the state.

If the Party Leader's introduction did not resolve these issues, what of the substantive content of *Democratic Socialist Aims and Values* itself? The opening paragraph put substantial flesh on the vague visions presented by Neil Kinnock (Labour Party, 1988, 3). It firstly identified the Labour Party as concerned with 'the fundamental objective of government'. The Party was, therefore, essentially interested in practical policy. It limited the Party in both its political and institutional intentions to the context of government as it exits within our current society.

It next stated that this fundamental objective 'is the protection and extension of individual liberty'. It then sought to describe the necessary requirements for such liberty which should, as such, be the basis of government action.

These were linked to absence of restraint, but beyond this to the positive possession of economic and political strength. They extend beyond the bounds of government activity to include 'state, corporate or private power of every sort'. Crucially they were linked to the second major philosophical theme of *Aims and Values*: equality. The economic power to make choices was stressed, but: 'economic change will not in itself and alone build the society which socialists wish to create. We need a more equal distribution of power as well as of wealth' (Labour Party, 1988, 3).

The commitment to greater economic and political equality, enabling the choices which are the mark of individual freedom to be made, was clear. What was also clear was that this must be achieved through government action and predominantly through the management of changes already occurring within society rather than by the development and promotion of radical alternatives. The objectives of economic and political equality leading to freedom were to be achieved through reformist, parliamentary activity.

This leads us back to Whiteley's assertion that Labour's problems, at least in part, stem from their poor performance as a party of government in achieving benefits which are available to everyone, by its failure to improve conditions for the working people upon which the Labour vote is based (Whiteley). If Whiteley is right, what evidence did *Aims and Values* provide that future Labour administrations will be any more successful than their predecessors?

Its introduction suggested that class, though still regarded as one form of power division within society, was by no means alone, nor can it in any way be regarded as more important or fundamental than any of the others. This was made explicit in the following section:

> If we are to achieve real equality between the sexes and the races and break down the barriers of prejudice which limit the life chances of so many women, condemn the ethnic minorities to second-class citizenship, divide

classes, leave young people powerless, and often place disabled people outside the community and restrict their quality of life, we must challenge the balance of power in Britain. (Labour Party 1988, 4)

Whilst 'institutional prejudice and social discrimination cannot be separated from the economic condition of those groups and individuals who are still denied the full rights of a free society' (Labour Party, 1988, 4), there was little here which would seem out of place in a statement of radical liberalism. Indeed, the emphasis on individual liberty divorced from social context accentuated the liberal tenor, though the stress on government objectives might have been seen as authoritarian by some liberals.

The fact that conflicts between individual liberty and social organisation had not been addressed was brought home in the next section. Here it was claimed that:

> real freedom can only be extended by cooperative action, by participation in democratic institutions at work, in the community and in public life, and by collective provision to gain and sustain individual liberty.

This was followed by the statement that:

> there is a clear responsibility on government to protect and defend its citizens by the maintenance of effective armed forces, by civilian policing and by the rule of law. (Labour Party, 1988, 5)

This obviously demonstrated the tendency of those in elected, state-authorised positions to see the organisation of the state as neutral, or, even, naturally beneficial (Jones and Keating, 65). It was not, therefore, the nature of the democratic or legal institutions which exist which create the problems, but rather the fact that they are not extensive enough, or that they are unfortunately, perhaps uncharacteristically, populated by the wrong sort of people.

In many ways the whole of *Aims and Values* was a classic demonstration of how this perspective not only denies the importance of existing power structures, but serves actively to discourage any analysis of the existing social order as a potential problem. This illustrates the consequences of Labour's lack of state critique. The discounting of existing power relationships as a contributing factor inevitably leads to a concentration on the individual, both in terms of the 'abuse' of power and the need for 'emancipation'. To this extent *Aims and Values* could be seen as a document representing reformist liberal, rather than socialist, philosophy. The only indication of a distinctively socialist view was the emphasis given to the distribution of economic, as well as political, power.

Immediately following the document's assertion of the importance of defence, policing and the rule of law came the statement that 'indeed, these commitments are among the fundamentals of freedom for our country and in our country' (Labour Party, 1988, 4). Once again Labour's philosophical statement suggested on the one hand that we had 'fundamentals of freedom', we were a 'free people', but that somehow this freedom was incomplete. It would seem, from the analysis given so far, that the primary reason for this incompleteness was the individual recalcitrance and contrariness of the British people in avoiding the extension of 'democracy' and in allowing the continuation of uneven power relationships.

The flavour of classical liberal philosophy which appeared to pervade much of *Aims and Values* was reinforced by the statement that:

> We do not believe in the intrusive state. We consider that the boundaries of liberty are drawn at the point where the exercise of freedom by one individual or group invades the freedom of others. (Labour Party, 1988, 4)

This compares interestingly with John Stuart Mill's advocation of self and other regarding actions as the basis for the assessment of individual liberty (Mill). Beyond this *Aims and Values* provided no criteria to assess who determines when one person's actions 'invades the freedom of others', or whose freedom should prevail in such circumstances.

In fact all that could be offered was the machinery of 'democratic' government to act as the final 'neutral' arbiter. This formula demonstrates a failure to analyse existing power relationships, and a consequent failure to prescribe a convincing and sustainable alternative. Instead Labour was thrown back, as in the past, on the need for a paternalistic and benevolent state administering the power structure whose decisions would be dependent on which individuals occupied elected positions.

The commitment to extended democracy, a more equitable distribution of economic and political power and enhanced individual liberty was necessarily subsumed within this requirement. In replacement the enforcement of law and order became, in a real sense, the 'fundamentals of freedom'.

As *Aims and Values* itself stated:

> That is the main reason why socialists contend for political power. To us, the state is an instrument for sustaining and enhancing the liberties of the whole community, no more, no less. (Labour Party, 1988, 4)

One could hardly ask for a clearer statement of reformist paternalism. As the following paragraphs made clear, 'liberties' were a matter of 'policing' and 'democratic government should be the main guarantor of fundamental

freedoms of citizenship'. This, apparently, was the individual freedom
Labour envisaged.

The assertion that:

> experience has shown how partial and how fragile [these fundamental
> freedoms] are, how inadequately they are protected and how easily eroded
> when government becomes the agent of centralisation, censorship and the
> constriction of freedom (Labour Party, 1988, 4),

merely demonstrated how inadequate and how unsuitable the proposed
formula had already proved itself to be. The remainder of *Aims and Values*
was given over to reasserting or reformulating these premises to cover a number
of situations.

This is not to deny that *Aims and Values* pointed to some interesting areas
of practical reform, and asserted important principles: for example the need
for democratic, independent trade unions; diverse ownership of and equality
of access to the media; and greater access to information. All these were
important and progressive points, but they merely confirmed the document's
reformist, paternalistic and essentially liberal nature in the face of its failure
convincingly to challenge the organisation of social power.

When *Aims and Values* turned to redistribution of wealth it justified this
objective, as might be expected, by reference to the need to enable individuals
to make effective choice. Commitment to redistribution must exist alongside:

> [a celebration of] excellence and initiative in scholarship, industry, the arts,
> in science, in sport, in craft, or in caring for others. We want to see merit
> recognised and rewarded. Socialists rejoice in human diversity. (Labour
> Party, 1988, 7)

Rejoicing in human diversity is a pretty sentiment, but it did not explain
how merit would be measured and rewarded or how such rewards would be
prevented from creating cumulative disparities in power and wealth without
resort to restrictive and interventionist state action (Nozick, 161–3). Whilst
this concentration on redistribution reflected Hattersley's own work, where
arguments in its favour were powerfully declared (Hattersley, 135–9), it seemed
to fit uneasily with the practical nature of the document as a whole.

This apparent discrepancy was explained by the view that:

> The divisions in our society are not only wrong in principle, they are
> damaging in practice. ... A divided society cannot prosper in the long term.
> (Labour Party, 1988, 7)

This introduces the fundamental outlook which in fact underlays the Policy
Review as a whole. It was expressly spelt out in the title of the initial Review

document *Social Justice and Economic Efficiency* (Labour Party, n.d.a, also referred to as *Social Justice*). This title was not just a cute phrase, it reflected the view within Labour's leadership that social justice and economic efficiency are not merely complementary concepts, they are in fact intimately and inextricably linked together. This was to be later reflected in the creation of the Commission on Social Justice (see chapter 6). With such an outlook it was not surprising to find in a philosophical statement a section on Socialism and the Productive Economy.

In fact this section, later transformed into the Productive and Competitive Economy for *Meet the Challenge, Make the Change* (Labour Party, n.d.b, also referred to as *Meet the Challenge*), formed the largest section of *Aims and Values*, stretching over four of its eleven pages. Starting with the assertion that 'demands [of an advanced industrial society] can and must be balanced by a collective approach to common economic problems' (Labour Party 1988, 8), the section then concentrated on the policy options best suited to this approach.

Whilst many of the options discussed were reflected and elaborated on in *Meet the Challenge, Make the Change*, the justifications for the particular options presented were also indicative. For example the statement's comments on science and technology seemed almost touchingly naive and quaintly antiquated (Labour Party, 1988, 8). Unfortunately, it did nothing to recognise the problems of 'technical fix' solutions, or environmental concerns about the relationship between technology and nature (Woolgar; Street).

The concentration on investment in science and technology was also strikingly reminiscent of Wilson's appeal to the 'white heat of technology' (Elliott, 3). This historical echo will be studied in more detail when we look at the structure of policy which emanated from the review groups themselves.

The need for 'a positive lead from government' was stressed, at least as far as 'investment in research, design and development, in schooling and further and higher education, and in training' was concerned. A commitment to environmental protection was also given, but this suggested environmental concern was subject to the need for agreed international coordination, with no clear idea of how this was to be pursued (Labour Party, 1988, 9). It also relegated environmental concerns below the need to create 'an economy which uses and develops resources in the widest national interests' (Labour Party, 1988, 9). Again no definition of contentious terms such as 'national interests' were provided.

Aims and Values then turned to social ownership:

We are not, and never have been, committed to any one form of public ownership, but the objectives we seek clearly require a greater sector of the economy to be socially owned. The primary case for social ownership does not rest on the precise forms which it can take in any particular part of the economy. It rests instead on each individual's right to control his or her own life, to have a say in the decisions by which he or she is affected, and to share fairly in the benefits to which each individual, by virtue of his or her participation in the whole social enterprise, contributes and is entitled. The organization of economic activity in order to achieve these aims, through both common ownership and extension of democracy at work to influence industrial policy, is likely to encourage greater efficiency and a better economic performance. But its fundamental justification is greater social justice and individual fulfilment and satisfaction. Social ownership, by enhancing the rights and power of each individual, is a basic protection against the concentration of social and economic power in the hands of a few individuals and institutions at the expense of everyone else. (Labour Party, 1988, 9)

This paragraph is worth quoting in full, not just because of its important central arguments, but because it provided an interesting gloss on Clause IV part 4 and the changes which were to come.

It provides a classic demonstration of how the majority of pragmatists, and occasionally revisionists, within the Party have happily coexisted with the commitment to common ownership. Whilst, quite rightly, claiming that Clause IV part 4 of Labour's constitution does not commit Labour to any particular form of common ownership, *Aims and Values* unequivocally equated common ownership to 'greater efficiency and a better economic performance'. Whilst it is true this is not 'its fundamental justification', it was nonetheless the expressed expectation.

This expectation has rarely been more clearly stated but, whether it has been achieved or not, it has constantly formed the basis of much Labour activity in government. It has provided the key to proclaiming common ownership in theory, whilst claiming the time was not right in practice. The expectation of improved economic performance and the actual economic performance of nationalised industries when compared, on usually less than favourable grounds, with private industry has been used as a reason for pushing the fulfilment of this objective, at least with regard to the 'commanding heights' of the economy, into the distant future.

Labour in practice were prepared tacitly to accept the justification of this prevarication on the grounds that either the relative poor performance demonstrated that the form of common ownership was wrong and a better system should be formulated once short-term problems were overcome, or this poor performance was what was to be expected from common ownership and Britain's short-term economic problems were such that the luxury of extended common ownership was simply not viable. This effectively postponed any large-scale common ownership programme to the long-term and, as Keynes once pointed out, in the long-term we are all dead.

In the light of these comments, the next paragraph struck a fascinating note:

> The public utilities are by their nature monopolies. They are also monopolies on which the rest of the economy depends. It is essential that they remain in public ownership – nationalised, in the original sense of the word, as single units owned by the nation through elected government, and capable of management in a way that meets national and community needs for efficiency, responsiveness to customers, satisfactory working conditions and coherent planning. In other areas it is necessary for the development of new forms of social ownership, including municipal enterprise and workers' and consumers' cooperatives. (Labour Party, 1988, 9)

Here we see the confirmation of the pragmatist sleight of hand. Whilst 'the development of new forms of social ownership' must occur 'in other areas', the public utilities, the only industries which for reasons of strategy and cost were likely to be brought into common ownership in the foreseeable future, must be 'nationalised in the original sense of the word, as single units owned by the nation through elected government'. Once again any extension of common ownership on grounds which might possibly prove more economically effective than what has gone before, or even more popular, was relegated to the long-term. Most interestingly, this passage ignored the criticisms made of the standard form nationalisation has taken till now, and which encouraged the document itself to suggest the need for the development of new forms of common ownership.

This was followed by the statement that:

> A party committed to the mixed economy must also encourage the development of forms of organization and ownership in which private and public enterprise and capital can be combined. (Labour Party, 1988, 9–10)

poverty

Arguments supporting a mixed economy were few and far between before this assertion, and no criteria were given for the nature of the 'mix'. Given that wider social ownership was seen as a means of protecting individuals against the social and economic concentration of power, it might have been expected that some justification for the necessity of a mixed economy, or some description of the legitimate role of government in restricting the possible negative consequences of private ownership, should have been given. However, none was forthcoming.

Although the possibility of using public resources as a means of opening up enterprises to industrial democracy was emphasised, this was still restricted by the term 'wherever practicable' (Labour Party, 1988, 10). Given Labour's record on industrial democracy in government this appeared another long-term commitment.

The distribution of output was discussed initially with some indication that markets and competition would face real restrictions, but this seemed little more than a cover to legitimise pragmatic intervention by government when deemed necessary. In fact:

> It is immoral as well as irrational to distribute some goods and services according to the market principle. Health care, education and social services must be allocated throughout the country irrespective of the purchasing power of those who receive such services. Good standards and adequate housing and transport must be available to those who cannot afford or do not choose to make private provision. Market forces have not and will not ensure provision or the real opportunities for choice in the basic necessities to which every citizen is entitled. (Labour Party, 1988, 10)

However this was dressed up it amounted to little more than saying that those services which were already provided publicly should continue to be so. Were these really the statements of a political party which believed in the extended application of their economic philosophy?

In essence this was a pragmatic defence of existing public provision on the grounds that it appeared to have worked well, and perhaps more significantly appeared electorally popular. No criteria for central intervention into markets was suggested, perhaps in the belief that if this were attempted it might serve to undermine existing public services. In short, this was not the statement of a party confident in its beliefs and determined to carry them through in contemporary circumstances. Instead it represented one seeking to defend its historical position on pragmatic grounds.

Indeed:

> To attempt the distribution of consumer goods by central direction and bureaucratic allocation is to risk the waste and inefficiencies of the command economies. ... We cannot afford the scarcities, the misallocation and the failure of supply and distribution which would follow if we ended all market allocation – any more than we can afford the exploitation, irresponsibility and waste of precious resources that comes from unregulated domination by the market system. (Labour Party, 1988, 10)

This repeated the links between ideas of social justice, misallocation, failure of supply and distribution, exploitation, irresponsibility and waste, economic efficiency and what we can 'afford'. It opened again the door to defining 'social justice', and presumably 'socialism', in terms of economic efficiency. The crucial question which remained unanswered was how economic efficiency should be measured. It seemed taken for granted in much of *Aims and Values* that current social measures of economic efficiency, profit, productivity, or output for example, should be our future criteria, except perhaps in the case of nationalised industries. Do these criteria really tell us any more about the 'social justice' of our system than that already taken into account in conventional social and economic organisation? Several answers to this question were possible, but the point is that in the context of *Aims and Values* the question was never asked.

The section ended with the kind of assertion that was prevalent throughout:

> The real choice is not between the unregulated market and the bureaucratic allocation of Soviet centralism. Democratic socialists believe in market allocation – but market allocation guided by agreement that the competitive system should pursue the objective of greater freedom, greater equality and greater choice. (Labour Party, 1988, 11)

This was another defensive statement. 'Market allocation' must be 'guided by agreement', but agreement between whom, over what and in what context? This was an inadequate attempt to maintain the necessity for some form of government intervention in markets in the face of the reassertion of market values by the political right in the eighties. As with so many other arguments in *Aims and Values*, there may be very good reasons in the actual economic history of Britain for government intervention, but the document failed to provide any general theoretical reasons behind this conclusion save the belief that it is more 'economically efficient'. Whilst this might be a valid argument given Britain's economic problems, and whilst it might be given a more general economic and philosophical basis, *Aims and Values* contained no argument of this kind.

In fact, the lack of any underlying principles of government action, and legitimate intervention, opened the way for arbitrary government involvement, restricting the personal liberty *Aims and Values* lauded, based on purely personal decision-making by government actors. *Aims and Values* sought to proclaim its difference from both Soviet centralism and unregulated markets, but its failure to define a convincing alternative leaves it firmly embedded in the uneven compromise between markets and regulation which has traditionally characterised postwar Britain. There was no real attempt to tackle the problems of power and liberty which this model has provided in Britain and therefore to recognise at least the existing difficulties.

The concluding statement of *Aims and Values* did indeed sum the document up:

> This description of the principles of democratic socialism is consistent with the great tradition of our movement. It is also attuned to the present and the future needs for justice and efficiency which must be advanced in times of great technological, economic, social and cultural change. The creation of the more equal, free and just society to which we aspire requires a persistent determination to bring that change about and to relate every policy to that object. Socialism and, therefore, the Labour Party, is, above all else, committed to the protection and extension of individual freedom. We are dedicated to that objective and to gaining and to using the democratic power to make it reality in practice. (Labour Party, 1988, 11)

This conclusion combined a measure of whistling in the dark with a bland assertion of Labour's position, ignoring its own history. It was absolutely true that *Aims and Values* appeared entirely consonant with 'the great tradition' of the Labour Party, if this was taken to mean the actions of Labour governments and the activity of Labour's leadership. In fact, most of *Aims and Values* appeared as a justification of the consignment of all ideology in the Party to a subsidiary role underpinning the practical concerns of managing a capitalist economy and being re-elected to run a capitalist society.

The bold statements which followed sounded as if the continued assertion of Labour's commitment to certain ideals would prove that actual commitment existed. Meanwhile the phrase 'socialism and, therefore, the Labour Party', evoked Morrison's statement that socialism is what Labour governments do.

In fact the overall impression left by *Democratic Socialist Aims and Values*, the ideological underpinning to Labour's Policy Review, was one of a Party leadership determined to assert a return to normal practice following the ideological challenges of the left in the late seventies and early eighties (Seyd, 1987; Kogan and Kogan). As mentioned above, the reason the leadership was enabled to again stamp its authority on the Labour Party in this way was because of the realignment of many elements of the left around the Kinnock leadership.

It was not, therefore, *Aims and Values* which resolved the ideological schism, which Whiteley outlined, in favour of Labour's leadership, rather it was the resolution of this schism which made the *Aims and Values* statement possible. *Aims and Values'* bottom line was stated in its concluding sentence where all principles are subsumed to conquering 'democratic power to make [them] a reality in practice'. The Labour Party after *Aims and Values* remained what it always was, primarily an electoral organisation within which ideologies are only as useful as, and should only be promoted to the extent of, the number of votes they win.

What we need to know here is not only how the ideological schism was resolved, but whether that resolution provided the basis of a sustainable solution to Labour's ideological problems in the face of the Party's condemnation to opposition by a fourth electoral defeat or of the rigours of a difficult term of government. The nature of the resolution achieved has been derived through internal Party politics, although, of course, the full implications of the left's marginalisation are not just internal. The origins of these philosophical differences have not been addressed, but have been submerged. This was the real significance of *Aims and Values;* reasserting the primacy of practical and pragmatic goals, the need to win and retain government power above all else. Whilst Labour's history shows this to have been a powerful force for order and calm within the Party approaching election times, particularly whilst in opposition, Labour governments in the sixties and seventies faced enormous internal opposition when they failed to deliver promised changes. Nothing in *Aims and Values* made the next Labour Government any more likely to be successful on this score than its predecessors. It represented an ideological compromise, forced by other events, which was likely to be sustained only until a Labour Government was in a position to act on its programme. Once government was achieved the maintenance of unity would depend on the performance of Labour's elite in the light of the expectations engendered.

Perhaps *Aims and Values'* obviously defensive nature and its advocation of the actual past practice of Labour's leadership led to its lack of influence on the content of the Policy Review itself. Perhaps this was because of its restricted authorship. Whatever the reason, the Policy Review developed independently of *Aims and Values* and with no reference to it as a provider of organising principles. Given this fact the Policy Review itself might present us with an ideological perspective which provided a more solid foundation for healing Labour's ideological rifts.

Social Justice and Economic Efficiency

Despite the statement of Labour's General Secretary, Larry Whitty, that: 'The Review is firmly rooted in Labour's aims and values, those of democratic socialism' (Labour Party, n.d.a, 1), it was the document in which this was maintained which was to provide the Policy Review's real focus, and not *Democratic Socialist Aims and Values*. Despite the existence of the Campaign Management Team, chaired by the Review's instigator, Tom Sawyer, and charged with overseeing the ideological and policy coherence of the Review

*practical not
id. consideration
directed review*

groups, *Aims and Values* was not influential in setting the framework for the groups themselves.

Instead it was the practical considerations outlined in the first phase of the Review by *Social Justice and Economic Efficiency* which really provided a solid base. To quote Whitty again:

> *Social Justice and Economic Efficiency* presents the first stage of Labour's Policy Review, and sets out the framework for the second stage of detailed policy development which is now to be undertaken by the Party. (Labour Party, n.d.a, 1)

So the review groups were effectively given two documents purporting to provide a structure for the body of the Review itself. One, *Aims and Values* was intended as a statement of the Party's ideology on which policy was to be based, the other, and in practice far more influential, *Social Justice and Economic Efficiency*, was practical in design.

Its precise nature as a document, and its detailed content, will be considered in the examination of policy formation and the policy output of the Review in subsequent chapters. The point to emphasise here is its essentially pragmatic form. *Social Justice and Economic Efficiency* was not intended as some grand statement of principle, it was a collection of statements effectively providing the preliminary reports of each of the policy review groups (Labour Party, n.d.a, 1).

In essence these provided the distillation of the consultation work undertaken by the review groups to date. They partly resulted from the ill-fated *Labour Listens* campaign, and partly from the beginnings of consultation within the Party and amongst interest groups. However, most importantly they were derived from private polling and specially commissioned assessments of the way Britain was likely to look in the 1990s.

This attempt at futurology formed the foundation stone of the Review process. It was an attempt to assess the practical problems a Labour Government would face, should one be elected at the next possible opportunity in 1991 or 1992. It also represented a conscious decision by the guiding lights of the Review, and the Party Leader, to transcend existing Party infighting on such issues as nuclear defence and the European Community. In doing so it was hoped that the narrow dogmatism of 'left–right' splits on such issues could be pushed aside and a new Party unity could be built around a common purpose for the nineties. This common purpose was itself to be based on the practical problems the Party would face in government, forming the bedrock of the Kinnockite alliance, from which the Review would emerge.

This concern with practical politics is, perhaps, not surprising from a party which had lost three elections in a row, nor the unity which this pragmatism helped to underpin. There were also other reasons why *Social Justice and Economic Efficiency* became the organisational touchstone of the Policy Review itself, rather than *Aims and Values*.

Firstly, *Social Justice* was a product of the review groups, it represented the views of those already involved in the review process and who would continue with that process through to its conclusion. It was not the product of a restricted authorship and it already had the authority of a consultation process, even if it was a somewhat imperfect one.

Secondly, as the product of the review groups, it was already organised into the areas of responsibility of the groups themselves. It did not demand interpretation in terms of its applicability to the differing areas of the review groups' remit.

Thirdly, *Social Justice* was a forward-looking document by its nature, seeking to come to terms with the practical environment in which a Labour Government would have to work. In contrast *Aims and Values*, I have suggested, was largely concerned, intentionally or otherwise, with justifying and restating the existing ideology of Labour's leadership, and the ideological practice of the Party since its inception. It presented nothing new or dynamic to galvanise interest. It must have seemed particularly unappealing to those, like Tom Sawyer himself, who had been involved alongside Tony Benn with various critiques of this ideological practice in the past.

Finally, *Social Justice* did represent a galvanising force. It provided those who had been excluded from power for eight years, considerably longer in the case of those many who, like Kinnock himself, were excluded from effective power under the leadership of Callaghan and Wilson, with the ability to play at government in advance. To determine a series of policy options and possibilities which could form the blueprint for a government within which they, at last, had some say (see chapter 1).

The accuracy and coherence of Labour's assessment of the future is not the point here; rather what should be noted is the essentially practical nature of this exercise, and the fact that this 'practical' document formed the real basis for the Review in place of the ideological statement *Aims and Values*, even though this too proved fundamentally pragmatic.

This does not mean to say that *Social Justice* is devoid of principle. Even the most empirical analysis has to assess the data available and resolve problems of statistical measurement; all of which requires value judgments. In an attempt at futurology these problems dominate and so to do the value judgments associated with them.

To the extent that there exists a single underlying principle, it is, as has already been claimed, the one embodied in the documents title. 'Social justice' is seen as inextricably linked to 'economic efficiency', to such an extent that economic performance, as a *de facto* measure of 'efficiency', might be seen as also indicating, in some sense, social justice. The policy implications of this we will examine later, though it is tempting to mention in passing the similarities between this view and the classical liberal view of industrial and social progress.

The importance of this perspective for the second phase of the Review, and also the general pragmatism of *Social Justice*, was demonstrated in the main report of the review groups, *Meet the Challenge, Make the Change*. In an introduction signed by Neil Kinnock the basic approach was set down clearly:

> This document is not an election manifesto. It is a statement of how our convictions apply to the challenges and changes confronting the United Kingdom in the final decade of this century and beyond. It offers an approach which, we believe, commands understanding and support throughout the country. All measurements of public opinion show that the Labour Party and the substantial majority of the British people continue to hold common values. It is those values which will guide Labour in government. (Labour Party, n.d.b, 5)

It is interesting to note that here Labour's 'common values' with 'the substantial majority of the British people' were stressed and that these 'continue'. Given the fact that the document represents the culmination of a comprehensive overhaul of Party policy, including a statement of values, this seems an extraordinarily complacent assertion to make. Perhaps the point was to place the Review firmly in the historical context of Labour's continuing, and maybe unchanging, values. Values which Whiteley has suggested have failed Labour in government in the past (Whiteley, 188). It might be that the statement's importance was more in drawing together Labour's views and those of the British people, as expressed in opinion polls, thereby justifying the Party's increasing reliance on private polling, a subject to which we will return when we examine policy-making.

This view needs to be tempered in the light of a later statement:

> The purpose has been and will be to secure the understanding and support of the people so that we can be elected to put our values – the values which we so clearly share with the great majority of the British people – into democratic power. (Labour Party, n.d.b. 8)

Here quite clearly the Party's values are those of which the public must be persuaded, though they still 'share' them and the precise relationship between Party values and public values, whether leading or led, is not entirely clear.

The most important aspect of the previous quote here, though, is the fact that *Meet the Challenge, Make the Change*, as its title implies, was seen as a statement relating 'convictions' to 'the challenges and changes confronting the United Kingdom in the final century of this decade and beyond'. This was precisely the point of *Social Justice and Economic Efficiency*.

All this was reinforced by the bulk of Neil Kinnock's introduction which concentrated on evaluating the nature of change under Thatcherism and giving potted descriptions of the policy options recommended by each of the review groups.

The introduction also confirmed Labour's position as a party of all the people. The position in the Party of the 'best off' in society was explicitly defended:

> Even amongst those who have done relatively well in the last decade, a growing number also sense that their personal gains have been accompanied by social loss. Divided communities and a divided country, eroded liberties, declining services, rising crime, congestion in the cities and pollution in the countryside, a general sense of falling standards: these, in the end, are not experienced simply as individual concerns, but as the community's loss too. (Labour Party, n.d.b, 5)

So, though Britain may not be a classless society, the Labour Party was intent on remaining a classless party.

Pragmatism and the primacy of the role of *Social Justice* were finally enshrined in the last few sentences of this introduction:

> It is time for a government that is dedicated to making our country a place of efficiency and justice, and a friend of freedom, fairness, security and peace across the world. (Labour Party, n.d.b, 8)

Conclusion

It might be said that to judge Labour's ideological position as flawed because it failed to address the problems which have caused a crisis in fundamental socialist philosophy in all its forms is harsh. After all, why should a practical electoral Party, whose socialist roots have never in any case been that clear, succeed where the rest of the socialist world has failed. Indeed, that form of judgment would be harsh, and is not the point of the criticisms made here.

Whilst it would be truly remarkable for the Labour Party to provide rigorous and convincing answers to the philosophical problems of international socialism, particularly as *Aims and Values* was essentially an abridged version of a book by the Party's Deputy Leader, some acknowledgment of the existence of these philosophical problems, and some sign of an understanding of their nature and importance, might have proved valuable. This view was reinforced by the fact that *Aims and Values* actively incorporated, and failed to resolve, one of the central problems of modern socialism, the connection between individual liberty and social action. This, in turn, reflected Labour's lack of a critique of the British state.

It is not even necessary to revert to this level to establish a serious critique of *Aims and Values*, it is possible to do so within the confines of the objectives the document had within the Labour Party. These were twofold, to provide: a clear ideological statement helping to unite the Party and marginalise elements perceived as extreme; and the ideological framework of the Policy Review. It failed on both counts. *Aims and Values* was, in its essence, no more than a reiteration and justification of historical Labour practice. It could safely be ignored in the policy review process because it said nothing new.

It was *Social Justice* that provided the basic framework for the Policy Review as a whole, and a solidly pragmatic framework it proved to be. It could be claimed that *Social Justice* sat easily with the principles of *Aims and Values* for the simple reason that pragmatism itself was nothing new to the Labour Party. The Policy Review's pragmatism was reinforced by the primacy of *Social Justice* over *Aims and Values*. This was essential if only for the fact that *Aims and Values* to some extent tried to hedge its bets through passing reference to the strands of fundamentalism and revisionism in Labour's history, and because it was, after all, intended as an ideological document. *Social Justice* had no such ideological association.

It would be wrong to claim that the Policy Review in some way subverted Clause IV part 4 as a result of its pragmatism. As was stated above, pragmatism survived quite happily alongside Clause IV part 4 for the same reason the Policy Review could; it was simply ignored. If the Policy Review represented an assault on Clause IV part 4 then it could rightly be called a revisionist work. It did not and it was not. Clause IV part 4 did not enter into the calculations of the Review which was primarily concerned with the creation of practical policy options for a future Labour Government.

However, a clear problem remained for Labour's leadership, dependent as it was on the realigned Party elite. The ideological elements of the Policy Review achieved nothing more than a restatement of historical Labour party positions, including the reaffirmation of the primacy of pragmatism. The ideological banner which flew over the Policy Review was very much a flag of convenience whose design had been transmitted from the past.

In an age where socialist thought is in crisis, and Labour's association with state power has been questioned by the political thought of the New Right, the Policy Review failed to halt the erosion of Labour's ideological identity. Whilst Labour's ideology could always be regarded as essentially pragmatic, and never particularly strong, until the 1980s Labour could be portrayed as in some sense a socialist party, and in some sense pursuing the principles embodied in Clause IV, part 4. The Review failed to recognise, or convincingly respond to, the ideological challenge of the New Right both to socialism as a whole, and to Labour's identification of 'social ownership' with the operation of the British state.

Having considered the ideological elements of the Review which were supposed to provide the basis for its future deliberations, those deliberations themselves must now be considered. The following chapter analyses the policy-making structures of the Review itself and the way these affected Labour's existing policy-making system, this is followed by a consideration of the policy output of the Review as exemplified by the Review's economic policies, and an examination of the electoral impact of the Review. With the failures of the attempt to provide an ideological underpinning in mind attention must now be given to how the Review was actually put together.

3 The Policy-Making System

Introduction

Having considered the ideological aspects of the Review, and argued for its essentially pragmatic nature, we must now consider the creation of the central Review documents, its policy statements, and the conduct of the Review itself. The conduct of the Review required its own policy-making system within the Party. In essence this usurped Labour's existing policy-making structures at least for the period of the Review, and these new systems were in turn considered as possible replacements for perceived weaknesses in Labour's policy system.

For some of the Review's initiators it represented an opportunity to institute a more inclusive policy-making system. This chapter will argue that this attempt failed for two reasons. Firstly, there remained a distinction of approach and attitude between the Party's leadership and its grass roots. This meant that the attempts of the Review to consult members and supporters provided material which was not in a form, or of a type, which could readily be assimilated and presented by the Party leadership. Secondly, the Party leadership consistently underestimated the importance and misunderstood the true function of key elements in the Party's policy-making process, notably Party Conference.

The Policy Review and Policy-Making

Each of the four phases of Labour's Policy Review completed between 1987 and 1991 had its own characteristics and concerns. Phase one, resulting in the publication of *Democratic Socialist Aims and Values* and *Social Justice and Economic Efficiency*, was primarily concerned with setting the ideological and practical context of the Review.

Phase two provided substantial policy output in the shape of *Meet the Challenge, Make the Change*, which was endorsed at the Party's 1989 Conference. This was refined and repackaged for electoral purposes in phases three and four of the Review, producing the statements *Looking to the Future* and *Opportunity Britain*. The substantive policy and the effectiveness of Labour's electoral strategy will be considered in subsequent chapters, but the impact of the Review was not confined to policy alone.

The conduct of a comprehensive review required the creation of a separate policy-making system. Existing Party policy-making structures were not designed to cope with the scale of the Review or to work with the speed needed if it was to be completed by the time of a probable election in 1991. Besides which, the perceived weaknesses of the existing policy-making structures were one of the reasons for conducting a review in the first place.

The initial suggestion for the Review came from the Executive of NUPE, and in particular from the union's Deputy General Secretary, Tom Sawyer (Sawyer, 11; Shaw, 1989, 1). Sawyer used his position on Labour's NEC to propose and advance the Review. The Review was to have two major functions: firstly, to close the perceived gap between the Party and the electorate on policy issues; secondly, to help overcome internal disunity which was also perceived as an obstacle to Labour's electoral aspirations. On both fronts Sawyer's intentions were far more wide-reaching and ambitious than the Review was able to achieve.

The need for a comprehensive examination of Party policy was suggested by the Party's recent electoral history. The electoral disaster of 1983 was blamed on the Party's 'extreme' policy programme and internal disunity. In 1987, whilst some of the policy alternatives had been moderated, many important radical elements remained (Callaghan, 1989, 45–6). Meanwhile the Party appeared more united and presentation had improved beyond recognition. Yet still the Party's electoral performance was poor. As Shaw has said, 'Only one conclusion could be drawn: promotion had been massively improved, so it was the product that was defective' (Shaw, 1989, 2).

The results of Labour's private polling were damning:

> Labour was seen as outdated, identified with an old agenda. Its policies no longer matched people's personal and family aspirations. Labour as a party was seen as having an alien internal structure: male-dominated, and intent on telling people how they should run their lives, rather than enabling them as individuals to make their own choices. (Hughes and Wintour, 61)

The Shadow Communications Agency presented these findings to the NEC, the intention was to shock the NEC into the conclusion that change was imperative. However, findings suggesting Neil Kinnock was poorly perceived as Party Leader were deliberately suppressed (Hughes and Wintour, 62). Clear implications were taken both for existing Labour policies and for the fitness of the policy-making structures which had brought them about. The idea of persuading the electorate towards Labour was largely abandoned.

This starting point could have provided some interesting and exciting outcomes if the initial work had been used as a context for wider debate. This was certainly the intention of Sawyer himself (Shaw, 1989, 1). As a NUPE official Sawyer wished to see Labour adopt membership participation practices of the kind his own union, amongst others, had been implementing. Disunity was not simply a question of splits amongst the parliamentary elite. The Review needed to provide a policy-making system which had such authority and respect within the Party that it was effectively incontrovertible. As MPs and trade unions could already be brought onside by the Party leadership, the crucial element was a greater participation of Party activists, members and supporters.

The ideal was a mass membership participatory party, and this ideal was to be pursued through the instigation of a membership drive towards the end of the Review period. The Review could not wait for the ideal, but even so: '[Sawyer] urged a Policy Review organised in such a way as to invite rather than exclude membership participation' (Shaw, 1989, 1). Policy documents were published early in the year to allow debate at local level and to facilitate a more informed debate at Conference, thus attempting to utilise existing policy-making structures. In addition the Party organised a series of meetings under the banner of the *Labour Listens* campaign. Neither of these initiatives proved successful and neither have had much abiding influence.

The Policy Review's importance lay not just in its role as a vehicle for the examination and restatement of Labour policy. It also provided what Shaw calls a 'symbolic function', which was to 'create the impression of a party willing to listen and eager to keep abreast with the times' (Shaw 1989, 2) . For some involved with the Review, notably Sawyer, consultation was not purely symbolic. The Review had the potential to shift the focus of policy-making decisively towards the Party's grass roots. *Labour Listens* became the bearer of such ambitions, and its failure was itself symbolic of Labour's inability effectively to involve its membership and support.

The focus of Labour's policy-making system has always been Annual Conference. Conference itself was dominated by trade union votes and was frequently cited as the clearest example of trade union dominance of the Party (Minkin, 1991, 279). This argument would hold more weight if Conference provided an authoritative policy-making body which could not be ignored within the Party. Conference is also the only place where Constituency Labour Party representatives, those of the ordinary Party members, have any voice. Although CLPs were allocated seats on the NEC, these were almost exclusively populated by MPs who are the only nominees likely to be known by a wide enough selection of members or delegates to get elected. Other positions on the NEC were allocated to the trade unions and women members. The latter are elected by the whole of Conference, and therefore effectively by the trade unions. So a significant proportion of NEC seats were controlled by the trade unions through Conference, though it should be noted that trade union votes are far from being a monolithic block. Nor would it be sensible to suggest that trade union nominees for the NEC simply reflect the views of their respective unions (Minkin, 1991, 26–7).

The NEC is charged with the day-to-day running of the Party, ensuring that Conference decisions are carried out, and organising Conference itself. It is the NEC, elected by Conference, who provides the Conference platform which is occasionally defeated, to little avail. As the development of the Labour Party has shown, the NEC is far from being the decisive policy-making organ of the Party, despite incorporating the Party's Leader and Deputy Leader. In fact, there have often been periods of vitriolic dispute, particularly during Labour governments, between the NEC and those who effectively control the policies of Labour: the Parliamentary Labour Party (PLP) and particularly the Cabinet or Shadow Cabinet.

Though, of course, the policy-making interaction within the Party is far more complex than this structure of Conference, NEC and Shadow Cabinet implies (Shaw, 1994, 159), this does constitute the formal structure within which the Policy Review was muted and has operated. In the last two decades there have been a number of attempts to alter this structure, particularly the interrelationship of its parts, and provide more authority for one or other of its elements. These have included bringing the trade unions and NEC together, notably external to the Party in the TUC–Labour Liaison Committee or drafting of the Alternative Economic Strategy (Minkin, 1991, 424); attempts to award control of the manifesto to Conference (Seyd, 1987, 121–4); and the rise in importance of subcommittees of the NEC as a focus for left dissent in the late seventies and early eighties (Shaw, 1988, 205). The most significant of these in terms of the subsequent history of the Review were the attempts to bring NEC and Shadow Cabinet members together for policy-making purposes after 1983.

The Review itself was intended to transcend left–right debates over policy, as well as providing an authoritative policy-making structure. This is not to say that the Review structure was created with the idea of permanence in mind from the beginning, but it was formulated with existing perceived deficiencies in policy-making very much in mind. It was only natural then that, when it was perceived to have succeeded, it was considered a potential model for future policy-making.

Both the Review's formal structure and the approach taken to submissions and evidence highlight the problems for policy-making in the Labour Party and present implications for future changes. Parallel to the Review, the creation of the Institute for Public Policy Research (IPPR) was the result of perceptions of deficiencies on the left which were deepened by the review process. The role of the IPPR and its relationship with the Party will be considered in chapter 6 when the work of the Commission on Social Justice, under the auspices of the IPPR, will be examined.

The Review's Formal Structures

The Policy Review was organised into seven distinct areas by the NEC, each of these areas had its own terms of reference and policy review group (Labour Party, n.d.a). Whilst coordination of the Review as a whole was to be conducted by the Campaign Management Team, chaired by Tom Sawyer (Shaw, 1989, 6), the division of responsibility itself pre-empted a number of possible debates.

No less than four of the seven groups dealt with different aspects of the economy. 'The democratic socialist approach to enterprise and ownership' was dealt with by a separate group to 'individual and collective rights' at work, which might be one reason why industrial democracy did not emerge as a serious issue for discussion. Similarly the 'distribution of income and wealth' was lumped in with 'taxation and social security strategies, low pay, pensions and family support'. This tended to reinforce historical Labour approaches of tackling the problems of economic inequality and residual poverty through income strategies, whilst ignoring wealth distribution. Whilst the Consumers and the Community group was charged primarily with considering 'responsible public services and more effective local government'; although the private sector was mentioned it seems something of an afterthought, the emphasis being placed upon consumer relations with the public services (Labour Party, n.d.a).

The responsibilities of the review groups were perhaps themselves designed to tackle the perceived 'burning issues' of the day, consumer responsiveness, ownership and markets, and beyond the economic issues those of democracy and the environment, concluding with an examination of defence and foreign policy, potentially the most controversial of all. It would be easy to read too much into these divisions of responsibility. I do not intend to suggest that these terms of reference prevented discussion of cross-cutting issues; there was clearly both scope and potential for such discussion, which to some extent did occur on a number of issues. Rather, I would suggest that this division of responsibility is indicative of a state of mind in the creation of the Review which was reflected in its deliberations. Firstly, it was believed that the Review should be about issues of contemporary debate and importance, that is that it should be an exercise in populism as much as in the creation of a lasting democratic socialist strategy. Secondly, the view was taken that certain aspects did belong together – ownership, for example, was separate from wealth, and in this the Review reflected established Labour Party practice.

The membership of the review groups was drawn predominantly from the NEC and Shadow Cabinet. Each group contained two joint chairs, or conveners, one from the Shadow Cabinet, one from the NEC. No less than three of the review groups, Productive and Competitive Economy, Consumers and the Community, and Democracy for the Individual and Community, had MPs holding both chair positions. This was a result of the position of MPs on the NEC: Bryan Gould, Jack Straw, and Roy Hattersley represented the Shadow Cabinet, while John Evans, David Blunkett, and Jo Richardson filled NEC places.

In fact, the inclusion of MPs from the NEC meant that in only two groups were MPs in a minority. These were the People at Work group, where the trade union majority was not surprising, and the Physical and Social Environment group, which might not have evoked the political interest of MPs, and where the putative conflict between the environment and employment may have led to trade unionists providing a majority of the membership. Only one group had parity between MPs and others, Economic Equality with three each of its six members. The other four all had a majority of MPs, the largest being Britain in the Modern World where no less than seven of the ten members were MPs, and one of the remaining three an MEP. This may be indicative of the perceived controversial nature of the foreign and defence issues to be dealt with by this group (Hughes and Wintour).

This PLP dominance of the review groups occurred despite the refusal by NEC MP members Tony Benn and Dennis Skinner to participate, and the presence of a number of coopted members from neither Shadow Cabinet nor NEC. It reflects the dominance of MPs in the top decision-making bodies of the Party, notably the Constituencies Section of the NEC. It is probably no coincidence that MPs were most dominant in the group perceived to be most controversial, and that trade unionists were themselves dominant in only two groups, one of which might be regarded as non-controversial and the other in which they had an obvious and particular interest. It is also probably no coincidence that the one possibly controversial group in which MPs did not dominate, People at Work, was the only group whose policy output created problems.

MPs have common interests, a common language and a self-identification not necessarily shared by the rest of the Labour Party. They are often suspicious of Party activists and fundamentalists and are more intimately concerned with electoral priorities. They are also more likely to wish to appease and be amenable to the Party leadership than the wider Party because of their Parliamentary experience. Electoral considerations were also in the minds of trade unionists, as Tom Sawyer made clear at a Fabian Conference in 1988 (Hughes and Wintour, 103).

In these circumstances it is not surprising that subsequent phases of the Review uncritically accepted the electoral aspirations of the Review's initial phase. Nor that it concerned itself little with the political aspirations of Labour's grass roots, except in so far as they coincided with these electoral concerns, and failed to deal in any convincing way with Labour's ideological disputes.

Despite this dominance of the review groups by MPs, there does not seem much support for those who wish to claim that the Review, and its consequences, represented a diminution of trade union power in Labour's policy-making. In fact the opposite seems the case. Prior to the Review the major formal policy-making bodies were Conference and the Shadow Cabinet with the NEC playing an interpretive and executive role. Cabinets and Shadow Cabinets were clearly dominant in this relationship. Trade union involvement was mainly through elections to the NEC. On particular issues occasional ad hoc groups, not dissimilar to the review groups themselves, would be formed, and these did contain coopted trade union members. However, these were largely instigated on the initiative of individual Cabinet or Shadow Cabinet members and had no formal position in the policy-making structure.

For a short time at the end of the seventies and the beginning of the eighties NEC subcommittees became significant. Though some trade unionists, Tom Sawyer being a prime example, were part of this process, it was a left rather than a trade union influence which was important here. A reorganisation of these subcommittees after 1983 removed this power base and increased central control over the workings of the NEC (Shaw, 1988, 254–5).

In such circumstances, whilst individual trade unionists may have had some say in Labour's internal policy-making this was neither formal nor coordinated. Before the Review, the most significant involvement of trade unionists in Labour's policy-making system came through activities which were expressly and necessarily external to the Labour Party itself. These included the Social Contract, the TUC–Labour Liaison Committee and the Alternative Economic Strategy (Minkin 1991, 116–33). Labour's Policy Review, for the first time, gave the trade unions' highest echelons direct representation at the heart of Labour's policy-making system.

A number of Trade Union General Secretaries, among them John Edmunds of the GMB, Rodney Bickerstaffe of NUPE, and Ron Todd of the TGWU, were coopted onto review groups. Previously the election of any Trade Union General Secretary to an NEC position, the one possible avenue of direct representation in the Party's internal policy-making process, was specifically proscribed by Labour's constitution. This is not to say that these individuals, and the executive bodies of trade union's generally, did not exercise considerable informal power. Their financial contributions to the Party, personal contacts within the Party, and positions as public figures in their own rights were far too significant to prevent it.

Given the unprecedented formal recognition through the review groups of these General Secretaries' legitimate seat of power at the centre of Labour's internal policy-making structure, the sacrifice of a proportion of trade union voting power at the largely impotent Annual Conference may have seemed a small matter. In this light, the Review process could be seen as a significant centralisation of power within the labour movement. The most important fraction of the Party effectively excluded from direct representation on the policy review groups were the Constituency Labour Parties, whilst the involvement of Trade Union General Secretaries occurred at the expense of the involvement of trade union delegations at Conference.

The Review also brought together the Party's secretariat, based at the Party's Walworth Road headquarters and responsible to the NEC, with the parliamentary-based secretariat of the Shadow Cabinet. This had an impact not just on the drafting of the review group's reports, but also in uniting the Party bureaucracy behind, and identifying them with, the aims and aspirations of the Shadow Cabinet and the electoral preoccupations of the Review. It minimised any prospects of institutional dissent between the two permanent bureaucracies of the Party, and could be seen as another centralisation of power excluding the wider Party.

It was also through the secretariat that Neil Kinnock's office exercised its formal influence. The secretariat of the Leader's office augmented the secretariats of the NEC and Shadow Cabinet by servicing the review groups. This provided an opportunity not only to keep an eye on the progress of the Review, but also occasionally to present ideas directly to a particular group. These included suggestions gleaned from letters sent to Kinnock's office from Party members and the general public, though this option appears to have been used sparingly.

Whilst the membership, terms of reference and secretariat of the review groups were given, these were not rigid. Members were coopted to deal with particular issues; this included individuals regarded as experts in certain fields. In addition some individuals, notably members of the Shadow Cabinet, were involved in the work of more than one group. Involvement of this kind was largely of an advisory nature and actual decision-making was restricted to a narrower group based on the initial membership.

One means by which a political strategy might have been imposed on the policy review groups was the ideological statement *Democratic Socialist Aims and Values*, examined in the previous chapter, but there was another:

The main mechanism for coordinating the work of the various PRGs was the Campaign Management Team. The CMT was chaired by Tom Sawyer (Shaw, 1989, 6).

The function of the CMT was largely administrative. It dealt with any potential disputes arising from overlapping responsibilities, or between the various participants, the Shadow Cabinet, the NEC, and Walworth Road. In most cases the work of the Review proceeded smoothly enough for the CMT to be largely redundant, but in Shaw's view it was 'less successful in imposing an overall political strategy on the groups' (Shaw, 1989, 6). This absence of a clear sense of direction suggested that suspicions of a hidden agenda – a calculated attempt by the leadership to impose a predetermined set of conclusions upon the Party – were misplaced (Shaw, 1989, 3).

This is true to the extent that the Review did not represent an attempt at Revisionism, nor was there necessarily a set of policy objectives at which the Review was designed to arrive. As it happens, the one area of apparent dispute involving a review group drew into question the role of the Leader's Office rather than that of the CMT. This was because the problem did not involve a dispute over responsibilities, or a conflict between review group participants, but rather seemed to involve a dispute over policy output. It has been suggested that the role of the Leader was generally more insidious than would initially appear to be the case:

> [Kinnock] designed each [review] group to ensure the kind of political mix which he believed would bring about the results he wanted, while ensuring that dissident views were fairly reflected. He also assigned a member of staff from his office (or rather Charles Clarke did) to ensure that the groups stayed on track. (Hughes and Wintour, 102)

This implies a more important role in 'fixing' the personnel of the review groups and a more interventionist role than the argument here assumes was necessary. Hughes and Wintour claim that 'Kinnock kept his eye on the groups, but kept his own hands off' (Hughes and Wintour, 102); whilst Shaw argues that this was 'probably a considered political move' (Shaw, 1989, 47).

There is another interpretation which is that Kinnock's lack of direct involvement merely reflected the fact that such involvement wasn't needed. The Review was largely populated by a number of individuals who had arrived at the same conclusions and opinions about the direction which Labour should take. These had been reinforced by the agenda-setting work of phase one and all that was needed following that was to allow the mechanism to work itself out.

The one exception to the otherwise universal appearance of like-minded harmony was illustrative:

> Only one of the seven review groups – 'People at Work', run by Michael Meacher, the employment spokesman – did not deliver the report the Party leadership wanted. The failure caused climactic tensions between Meacher, Kinnock's office and the leadership of the trade unions. (Hughes and Wintour, 143)

Hughes and Wintour go on to describe a curious tale of how Michael Meacher, able to prevail in this review group despite representing a 'minority of one' (Hughes and Wintour, 147), was browbeaten by Charles Clarke, Peter Mandelson, and Geoff Bish, amongst others, into providing a more acceptable report. The result, if Hughes and Wintour's version is accurate, was the bypassing of Meacher and his representation of the review group's opinions (Hughes and Wintour, 151–2). It seems strange that individuals closely associated with the Leader should have chosen to intervene in such an apparently direct manner given Kinnock's own hands-off approach, but the fact that this is the only intervention of this kind confirms that such direct intervention was largely unnecessary (cf. Hughes and Wintour, 166).

If Kinnock's personal aloofness was a political move as Shaw suggests, this situation raises questions about his method of leadership. If the Hughes and Wintour account is accurate it seems impossible to conceive that Kinnock could not have known what was going on. If he knew, then it appears he was willing to allow others to do his dirty work for him, at least in the context of the Review. If, on the other hand, he did not know of, or sanction, these actions it draws into question his ability to control those with whom he was most closely associated.

This raises the question of whether the Review's policy-making system was perceived as successful by the Party's leadership because it faithfully represented and balanced the disparate views within the Party, or because it managed to exclude views other than their own. The particular problems involved with the People at Work group are illustrated by the fact that soon after the completion of phase two Michael Meacher was replaced as shadow employment speaker by Tony Blair.

Consultation and Submissions

One of the most public aspects of the review process was the *Labour Listens* campaign. This was an important element in convincing the electorate that Labour was a listening party, interested in keeping abreast of the times. It was a conscious response to the initial polling information which had highlighted Labour's outdated image, as well as being an attempt to involve Labour supporters in a more participatory party. As such it had a rather schizophrenic nature. Having been lumbered with the dual function of providing both important input to the Review and a high profile public relations exercise, *Labour Listens* ended up doing neither well.

Part of the reason for this was the fact that responsibility for the campaign was uncertain. Both the Review secretariat and Peter Mandelson's presentation team vied for control of the project. The most important of the meetings organised under the campaign's banner doubled as discussion forums with public input, and as media events providing local photo opportunities. However, this was far from being the only reason why *Labour Listens* eventually provided little of worth.

Despite the abortive nature of the campaign, numerous meetings were organised around the country during its existence. Nearly every member of the various policy review groups was involved in them at one time or another. On each panel, at each meeting, were representatives of the NEC, the Shadow Cabinet and other leading Labour figures.

The meetings themselves fell into two broad categories. There were those with an invited audience in a particular locality, and those open to the general public. Both were victims of the perceptions, of public and politicians alike, concerning the nature of public meetings. Although they were organised to 'listen' to the opinions of the public and Labour supporters, those who came generally expected to be talked at rather than listened to. Occasionally the platform did not disappoint them.

Whilst *Labour Listens* was intended to gather the views of a local public and grass-roots Labour supporters, a parallel, though less publicised, consultation was taking place inside the Labour Party designed to obtain the opinions of members. This, too, suffered from lack of resources and provided disappointing results.

In fact this consultation process illustrated one of the major obstacles Labour has in communicating with its membership: the attitudes of Labour MPs, including the Party leadership, to Party activists (Seyd and Whiteley, 1992a, 40; Mitchell, 1987, 392). Whilst the Review was intended, by Sawyer at least, to provide a more authoritative voice in policy-making for Party activists, concerns about the 'unrepresentative' nature of the activist base persisted (Seyd and Whiteley, 1992a). Indeed the *Labour Listens* campaign was necessary precisely because of the 'unrepresentative' nature of Party members and their untrustworthiness in representing the Policy Review to a wider public.

Given Labour's perceived public relations success in the 1987 General Election, and the fact that internal Party consultation inevitably received less publicity than the wider *Labour Listens* campaign, it is perhaps also inevitable that it was not seen as such a great priority. To a large extent, the internal Party consultation demonstrated less imagination and took a far more orthodox form. Walworth Road informed CLP secretaries of what was happening, told them that responses were invited, and left it up to them.

The results of internal Party consultation demonstrated, even to those most in favour of wider participation, that:

> The Party just isn't in a position to handle proper membership participation in policy making. That's something we've got to face up to. (Sawyer quoted in Hughes and Wintour, 101)

The problems were structural as well as attitudinal, and resulted in changes in method and approach in this area of the Policy Review above all others.

As it became increasingly apparent that *Labour Listens* was proving a disappointment, so the reaction of constituency parties to the first phase Review document was 'all too often a mixture of mistrust, bewilderment and inertia' (Shaw, 1989, 15). It was hoped that distribution of these documents in June would promote discussion and debate prior to the October Conference.

For the Party bureaucracy this was a radical departure from usual practice. Previously, NEC policy statements were placed on delegates' seats the day before, or even the morning of, Conference debates. This barely gave a dedicated constituency delegate the chance to read them, let alone consult the constituency party or membership whose delegate they were.

It was probably also the case that the Review enthusiasts amongst the leadership, looking forward to the exciting prospect of a Labour Government, felt that the rest of the Party would share their enthusiasm for a chance to discuss what that Government might actually do. Who, under such circumstances could fail to be galvanised? If this was the expectation then it rapidly became clear that the answer was the Party's activists and membership.

Part of the reason for this was the mistrust that Party activists had of the central bureaucracy. Partly it was purely a result of the fact that constituency parties had no history of organising, nor the resources to organise, the dispersion and debate of detailed policy documents amongst its members. Receipt of such documents in June, and the fact that many constituency parties do not bother to hold meetings in August, provided at best three, and more likely two, monthly General Management Committee meetings in which the documents could be discussed, consultation of branches organised and constituency responses decided upon before Conference. Given the extra business Conference generates for constituency parties anyway, the dwindling number of Party activists, and the fact that the constituencies had never been consulted in this way on any regular basis, it is more surprising that Walworth Road expected a useful response than that they got none.

The problem wasn't purely one of constituency party organisation and resources:

> Part of the responsibility lay with Head Office and the NEC. No structural system for feeding local Party comments into the Review had been organised. (Shaw, 1989, 15)

Nor should Labour's administration be absolved from blame for failing to realise the time constraints and resource problems facing constituencies, but the fact is that the pace set for and by Walworth Road was dictated by the exigencies of the Review itself. In deciding the timetable for consultation the crucial factors were the workings of the groups and the possible timing of a General Election. The need to give constituencies time to consult, and assistance in consulting, their members was simply not a consideration, reflecting the traditional lack of concern in the Party hierarchy for the views of members.

Even when responses from individual members or constituencies were forthcoming they were frequently in a form which was difficult to fit into the Review structure. Nor was it at all clear how the review groups should assess such contributions. In quality and content they varied widely, and review groups were left to decide what weight to give to unstructured contributions from such Party sources in contrast to contributions originating from academic or interest groups which were well argued, to the point and tailored to fall into line with the responsibilities of the individual review groups. Assessment of the value of these contributions came down to personal interpretation. A general feeling was left, perhaps because the contributions were not related to the concerns reflected in the Review structure, that little or nothing of any value came from the first phase of consultation.

It was decided to tackle these problems in two ways:

> Firstly, all constituencies and branches were circulated with a political education pack. This included discussion sheets on each of the seven main policy areas listing key themes and problems; response sheets to be filled in and returned to Head Office; and guidance on how to organize discussions. Secondly, eight national policy forums were to be held (on each of the seven areas plus one on 'women's perspectives') to enable members 'to discuss the policy options being considered by the review groups' with members of the group in attendance. (Shaw, 1989, 15)

Both of these initiatives were largely dependent on trade union support. The political education pack was predominantly a trade union project, leaning heavily on the experience of encouraging membership participation in unions like NUPE. It was both financed and compiled by officials of unions affiliated to the Party. This was a sign that those within the union movement who wished to see greater membership participation believed the Party itself to be incapable of conducting meaningful internal consultation. Despite this the results were as disappointing as before (Shaw, 1989, 15).

It might be regarded as indicative that this consultation was seen as an exercise in the 'political education' of the Party membership. Some members might be forgiven for feeling that a consultation process should hardly involve the 'education' of those being consulted, and that this might point to the existence of a predetermined end state to which the participants needed to be 'educated'. In short, this may have reinforced existing prejudices against the Review amongst a significant proportion of the membership.

For whatever reason, the political education exercise failed to galvanise Labour members into active participation; neither did the national policy forums. Membership reaction to the latter may have been affected by the development of the *Labour Listens* campaign. The fact that this wider consultation had been seen as a greater priority than internal consultation, and was given prominence, may have led members to feel that once again their views were likely to be marginalised. Compared to the highly publicised local meetings organised for *Labour Listens*, the internal consultation process with one national forum for each policy area may have seemed a token gesture. Moreover, the turning of *Labour Listens* into a publicity exercise, and the structure of these meetings, which appeared to resemble those which all parties regularly organised with invited national speakers to talk at supporters, may have led members to conclude that the policy forums were likely to involve Party leaders telling delegates about the Review rather than listening to, and taking on board, members' contributions.

The forums were eventually cancelled in January 1989:

> The main reason for the cancellation was an acute financial crisis, but the savings were relatively small and were justified by the extremely small number of constituency delegates who had registered to attend. (Shaw, 1989, 15)

To a casual observer, it may come as something of a surprise that a party which sees meetings with a wider public in the *Labour Listens* campaign as a major publicity opportunity should invest so little time, money, energy and thought to the consultation of its own membership. In the context of the Labour Party this is merely a reflection of the mistrust between the leaders and the led. From the perspective of the leadership responsible for conducting the consultation process, the Party's small membership base makes the grass roots vulnerable to takeover by extreme and unrepresentative views. Curiously, the view that Labour's base is often unrepresentative thanks to a restricted membership is a perspective shared by both right and left within the Party (see, for example: Tatchell, chapter 1).

The Review vividly demonstrated Labour's lack of ability effectively to consult either its support in the country or its own members in any meaningful way. In the unlikely circumstances that the *Labour Listens* campaign and internal Party consultation had provided a plethora of responses and served to galvanise members, supporters and sympathisers into participatory action, neither the Policy Review nor the Party was geared to cope with such responses. The individual review groups could not have assimilated such a variety and wealth of submissions, nor did the Party have any real vision of what to do with this participation after its initial stimulation by the Review. Labour did not expect to galvanise its members or its supporters and that, in part, is why it failed in this object.

Instead the *Labour Listens* campaign was put down as a reasonably useful publicity exercise, whilst the review groups and the Party turned back to nicely predigested private polling to discern public attitudes. Internal Party consultation was virtually abandoned. This is not to say that the attempt to make Labour a more participatory party had no result, but the result it did have confirmed the Party's inability effectively to consult its own membership and entrenched paternalistic attitudes within the Party.

Another impact of the Review was in the area of Party publications, a side-effect of the desire to promote greater participation. In order to encourage participation, it was felt that Labour needed a publication which reached every single member, but it could not afford to produce another publication alongside the Party newspaper *Labour Weekly*, and the initially successful Party discussion magazine *New Socialist*. Both of these were sold to Party members and supporters who were not members. In effect they were read by only a fraction of the membership. It was decided to replace these two publications with a new publication to be distributed free to every member.

This led to the launch of *Labour Party News*. If the intention behind this move was to widen internal debate, it cannot be regarded as a success. *Labour Party News* has proved reluctant to print anything approaching criticism of the Party's leadership. Indeed, within two years of its launch *Labour Party News* underwent a facelift.

Apart from these ineffective attempts to consult Party members and supporters, there were two other important sources of submissions to the review groups. Interest and pressure groups submitted evidence to every review group, as did a number of academics and other interested individuals with specific knowledge in particular fields. Some of these were invited or commissioned by the review groups, other contributions were unsolicited. These, alongside the work of the Shadow Communications Agency, which had contributed much to the Review's phase one report *Social Justice and Economic Efficiency*, formed the basis on which the Review proceeded.

None of this was new to the Party. To this extent the workings of the review groups closely resembled those of various earlier policy-making groups, some of which had included both NEC and Shadow Cabinet members, that had characterised detailed policy-making in the Party for a number of years. The only new factor was the higher profile given to the canvassing work of the Shadow Communications Agency (Shaw, 1994, 137–9). In phase one this amounted to direct input, and their efforts became important again as the Review moved towards the conclusion of phase two and into phases three and four. Here private polling was used to assess the appeal of policy to the public and the best means of presenting the policy decisions reached.

Each review group was left to decide for itself how to approach its work. Submissions were invited from groups or individuals suggested by members of the review groups themselves, or occasionally from suggestions of the secretariat servicing the groups. Those asked to make personal presentations were suggested by the same sources, though they did include those whose written submissions had caught the eye of one or other of the group members.

The number of meetings held to hear, discuss and consider evidence submitted varied from group to group, as did the attendance at and participation in such meetings. In addition to meetings with those submitting evidence, some review groups organised meetings to discuss policy options with a wider audience invited from interested pressure groups. Again, such meetings were initiated by the review group members themselves.

Both the assessment and the nature of the evidence examined depended largely on the membership of the review groups. It was suggested in the last chapter that the Review was the creation of, and populated by, the mainstream group which formed around the leadership of Neil Kinnock. It is in the activities of the review groups that this observation becomes fundamentally significant. It is not suggested that the Review or its product derived from some kind of political conspiracy to do away with existing policies either because they were considered to have 'failed' or because they were considered to be the product of an unrepresentative and discredited hard left (cf. Shaw, 1994, 84). This group did not need to conspire together to arrive at common values, they had come together because they shared those values already. The desire for renewal determined attitudes towards the Review, the evidence to be sought, and perspectives on existing Party policy. To this extent the criticism of some in the Party that '[leadership] control over all key committees mean[t] that the outcome of the Policy review [was] predetermined' were correct, but this does not automatically mean that it was 'no more than a cosmetic exercise allowing the Party establishment to achieve its aim of pulling Labour to the right' (Shaw, 1989, 16).

The group which came together around Kinnock was driven together by external events. It was not simply based upon the right of the Party or the Party establishment. What made the Review a conservative, and not a radical, exercise was not the nature of this group, but rather its acceptance of pragmatic perspectives on policy and the primacy of electoral objectives.

It was these values which were reflected in the nature of the evidence taken, and in the assessment of the evidence received. It was these values which marginalised the views of members and supporters, partly because they were not organised with the priorities of the Review in mind. This said, it should be emphasised that nobody was excluded from participating in the Review process. All views were welcomed, but some were more welcome than others.

Evidence was taken from pressure groups affiliated to the Party and those who had no formal contacts. Affiliates were circulated about the Review in much the same way that constituencies were. Some were invited to make submissions, others submitted evidence on their own initiative. Occasionally affiliated groups organised parallel events helping them to formulate and publicise their submissions, but most had neither the resources nor the inclination for such an extensive initiative.

The most impressive contribution to the Review from any one such organisation came, predictably, from the Fabian Society. During the period of the Review, the Fabian Society remained the only organisation affiliated to the Party effectively able to provide a debating platform for Policy Review themes which remained independent of the organisation of the Review and the Party's leadership. Despite its lengthy association with the right of the Party, the Fabian Society has provided an invaluable forum for wide-ranging views over a considerable period of time. As such it again proved its worth during the Review.

Fabian pamphlets were published on a range of issues to be examined by the review groups. These were both instigated by the Society, and the result of individuals asking the Society to publish their contribution on a particular subject. They included contributions which attempted to rekindle debate on particular issues, as well as contributions to debates sparked by the Review. The Society also helped to organise meetings to discuss the themes of the Review and fostered debate in a way which no other group proved capable of emulating. The Fabian Society was able to involve and organise its membership in a way which had completely eluded the Party as a whole (Sawyer, 1989, 11). Despite all this, the influence of the Fabian Society's efforts was mainly apparent where it helped the leadership to consolidate its own preferred options, notably on defence policy.

Though many of the pressure groups consulted both internally and externally felt that they may have had some influence on marginal issues, few seemed to feel the central thrust of their concerns had been addressed. To some extent, the adoption of pressure group policies had presentational value. The largely friendly reception afforded by environmental groups to the Party's policy statement *An Earthly Chance*, for example, reflected the incorporation of many individual policies from such groups.

Another side effect of the Review was its stimulation of limited academic debate. This included the publication of two books of collected material, both on economic issues (Cowling and Sugden; Le Grand and Estrin). Advocates of the Review might claim that this indicates the radical and ground-breaking nature of the Review, but the fact that this debate was so limited, and short-lived, demonstrates the Review's fundamentally conservative nature.

The adoption of specific policy suggestions, or even attempts to stimulate further debate, appear to have been determined by two considerations: first, a view of whether there were presentational gains, and therefore presumably electoral ones, to be had from the adoption of a particular policy or strategy; second, whether the options appeared to clash with the common objectives of the Review or any other individual element within it. These considerations were, of course, judged within the context of the assumptions of review group members reinforcing these pragmatic and electoral considerations.

This probably accounts for both the lack of controversy in all but one of the review groups, and the view of many pressure groups that their opinions were of only marginal influence in the Review. It should be said that the marginal influence of pressure groups still appears far greater than the non-existent influence of Party members on the outcome of the Review.

The Future of Conference

Two characteristics of Labour's organisational structure need to be borne in mind here. Firstly, it is pluralistic, with policy-making powers distributed between the Annual Conference, the NEC, the Shadow Cabinet and the Party Leader. Secondly, it is confederal, with affiliated trade unions, at the time of the Review, controlling two thirds of the seats on the NEC and, via the mechanism of the block vote, 90 per cent of the vote at Conference. As a result, no major policy initiative can secure passage without trade union approval (Shaw, 1989, 7).

Despite the trade union dominance of Conference through the block vote, the policy-making role of Annual Conference was never the sole, nor perhaps the most important, of avenues for union influence. The domination of elections to both the Trade Union and Women's Section of the NEC, participation in the selection of Parliamentary candidates and the financial support of MPs, and participation in a number of joint policy-making initiatives have all been important. In addition trade unions have an independent role wielding economic power in the labour market, and trade union leaders exercise their own, imperfect, access to the mass media. From the arguments made above, the Policy Review has developed new avenues for trade union influence in Labour's internal policy-making structures.

MPs, another part of Labour's confederal structure, also have a variety of different points of influence. The Party Leader must be an MP, and MPs have privileged access to the Leader via their mutual membership of the House of Commons. MPs also populate the Shadow Cabinet, partly through election by the PLP as a whole, and occupy many seats on the NEC, most importantly for our discussion in the Constituencies' Section. Though disenfranchised at Conference, a matter of little relevance given the dominance of trade union votes, MPs retain their right to attend and to contribute to debates.

The two other elements of Labour's confederal structure do not possess such advantages. For Constituency Labour Parties and for affiliated organisations other than trade unions there is only one means of potentially influencing Party decision-making, and that is Annual Conference. Though seats on the NEC were allocated to constituencies, these are invariably won by MPs, the only nationally known potential representatives of membership views. At best this can only be regarded as an extremely indirect expression of constituency interests. Meanwhile affiliated organisations have only one seat on the NEC, and usually that is also taken by an MP.

Of course CLPs and affiliated organisations are well aware of the limitations of Conference. Any of their delegates who have attended Conference, or anybody who has heard a report back from a delegate, cannot fail to know them well. Nevertheless, Conference is of vast symbolic importance to these two, otherwise powerless, groups. Occasionally, it is true, these delegates could decide issues at Conference. When trade union votes were split, or unions were prepared themselves to vote against the platform, individual votes did make a difference, but this was rare. The importance of these pyrrhic victories, and of Conference itself, for constituencies and affiliated organisations was largely involved with the potential for embarrassment of the leadership on a public stage. As one interviewee put it to me: 'Conference is all about letting the rank-and-file let off steam and giving them a platform to express their views.' Occasionally, Labour's Conference has had importance as a real and effective means of challenging Labour's leadership. This has been most obvious in relation to proposed reform of the Party's constitution, notably Gaitskell's attempt to abandon Clause IV part 4.

It was not that CLPs or affiliated organisations receive, or expect, any direct influence over policy from Conference, but Conference remains the one place where the Party leadership, in the shape of the NEC, has to account for its policies and actions. It is a highly public platform for dissent and opposition and, as such, has enormous symbolic value in a Party where the vast majority of members are otherwise excluded from power and influence.

It was for this reason that proposed changes to the role of Conference in Labour's policy-making structure were so central to Party democracy. The Party leadership retained a sharp awareness of the inadequacies of Conference as a policy-making body. As Tom Sawyer has argued:

In reality Conference decisions are made elsewhere – in the union delegations, debating and deciding on how block votes are cast and which resolutions will be carried. The votes are lined up before the first speaker gets to the rostrum. (Sawyer, 11)

Partly, then, the problem was in the allocation of votes which awards so much power to the trade unions (Shaw, 1989, 17). Nonetheless, representatives at Conference, who have so little power, still afford it such importance that they spend long hours drafting and debating resolutions, scrutinising the Conference agenda, and mandating delegates. This demonstrates the significance of the symbolic role of Conference.

Apart from the highly weighted voting structure and the lack of effective debate provided at Conference there were also problems with Conference's policy output. The composite resolutions eventually voted on are cobbled together by Conference delegates in the weekend before Conference commences. This means that most of the resolutions voted on at Labour's Conference are hybrids of two or more other resolutions whose form depends on the negotiations of Conference delegates.

The result is that policy passed by Conference takes the form of resolutions which may contain a wealth of comment and instruction covering a variety of issues. It is quite possible that elements of these resolutions would not have been passed by Conference if they had been proposed separately. Voting may become a question of balancing the good and bad parts of a curate's egg composite resolution. This leaves the NEC with the responsibility of picking the good from the bad and assessing what Conference intended.

The curious aspect of these criticisms of Conference practice is that all are ways in which the Party leadership have managed to justify the marginalisation of Conference. The trade union block vote has remained predominantly loyal to the Party leadership and generally operated within unwritten 'rules' (Minkin, 1991, chapter 2). The agenda is under the control of the Conference Arrangements Committee which is usually also loyal to the leadership. Similarly, the composite nature of Conference decisions gives the leadership greater opportunity to sidestep embarrassing defeats by claiming that it was not what Conference intended. So why was the Party leadership interested in raising these criticisms of Conference? Was it a question of a benevolent leadership seeking to increase the power of the grass roots at their own expense?

Undoubtedly some who supported a participatory Party were interested in providing more power to the membership. For others it may just have been the intellectual rationalisation of an attack on an annual event which provided regular public embarrassment. The possibility of appearing to restrict trade union influence through the diminution of the block vote, and perhaps the marginalisation of Conference itself, was also appealing.

Conference's ability to examine the Policy Review itself was extremely limited. In effect Conference was afforded a purely negative role. Policy Review documents, including the three central reports *Social Justice and Economic Efficiency*, *Meet the Challenge, Make the Change*, and *Looking to the Future*, were all distributed to organisations delegating to Conference some months before Conference began. This was a departure from previous practice with NEC statements and was intended to encourage debate, but this was not the only departure from established practice:

> There was a justified protest ... on the first day of [the 1989] Conference, against the executive's ruling that the Policy Review documents could not be amended. (Hughes and Wintour, 199)

This left Conference with no chance to make positive changes to the crucial phase two reports, published in *Meet the Challenge, Make the Change*. All that was left was acceptance or rejection. Wholesale rejection would have left two years of Party strategy in ruins, Party policy in tatters, and the Party itself deeply divided and needing to pick up the pieces with a possible General Election looming in 1991. Acceptance was the only tenable position.

The decision to refuse amendments to these Policy Review reports also effectively ended serious debate. Those who would have wished to challenge parts, or sections, or even individual policies in the Review, were left with little of worth to contribute in this take-it-or-leave-it situation. The symbolic, as well as the actual, power of Conference had been usurped.

Though it was, no doubt, a great relief to supporters of the Review that potentially embarrassing reverses at Conference had been avoided, the decision to eliminate amendments was not taken predominantly for this reason. In fact, it would have been practically impossible to allow amendments at Conference and still to have retained the overall strategic sense of the Review. It was felt that, just as Party contributions to the review groups had been diffuse and impossible to absorb into the Review's final output, the same would be the case with amendments at Conference. Those who had worked so hard to develop what they took to be a winning formula were not prepared to see it dismantled piecemeal at a troublesome Conference.

This one decision gave total power over the Review to its own, specifically created, policy structure. It excluded Conference from any real say in the Review and marginalised Conference as a policy-making body from 1989 onwards. It also provided the starting point for potential changes to future Party policy-making.

From the conclusion of the Review's second phase the Review was widely perceived as a success. It was seen as having modernised Labour's entire policy output in two years, and it had apparently already provided electoral rewards in the elections to the European Parliament earlier in 1989. Not surprisingly, the Review was seen as the model for the development of a new, improved and more relevant policy-making system than the seemingly flawed and redundant Annual Conference.

Implementation of some of the changes envisaged began at subsequent Conferences, but more far-reaching changes were also considered. The proposals were contained in a Party consultative document *Future of Labour Party Conference* (Labour Party, n.d.e). Included were initial suggestions for altering the way in which speakers at Conference were chosen, the treatment of resolutions and amendments, and other changes which could be made 'within the existing framework of Conference' (Labour Party, n.d.e, 11). Also included was a further section detailing 'a more radical approach to policy-making' (Labour Party, n.d.e, 14–15).

After consideration of a number of options for the future of Conference this section suggested six changes:

1. a two-yearly policy-making cycle;
2. a rolling programme subject to amendment in the policy commissions or at Conference;
3. policy commissions dealing with detailed policy and amendments to policy;
4. rules revision Conferences every four years;
5. provision for reports on the NEC's stewardship and on organisational and campaigning priorities;
6. electoral mechanics dealt with away from Conference, on a two-yearly basis. (Labour Party, n.d.e, 15)

The inspiration for these proposals arose partly from a comparison of Labour's Conference structure with the organisation of other West European socialist parties (Labour Party, n.d.e, 10).

The most important of these proposals in terms of policy-making were those for a rolling programme and the setting up of policy commissions. The Policy Review presented a ready-made basis for any rolling programme, whilst the policy commissions would have important new functions including the sifting of amendments to the rolling programme to be debated at Conference (Labour Party, n.d.e, 14).

Conference was changed in two ways. Debates were structured into the same categories as the initial review groups, and resolutions were expected to develop and build on the existing work of the Review. It was also decided to reduce the power of trade union block votes at future Conferences, though they still provide the majority of votes cast (Shaw, 1994, 121–2).

The instigation of policy commissions presented the opportunity to develop involvement in Party policy-making:

> The special commissions could include representatives of the regional parties, affiliated organisations, Parliamentary Labour Party, British Labour Group, Labour local government, as well as the NEC, and ensure adequate representation of women, ethnic minorities and youth in this policy-making process – with the use of quotas if appropriate. (Labour Party, n.d.e, 15)

It was also seen as affording a focus for greater participation and more detailed discussion of policy amongst the Party's grass roots (Sawyer, 11).

Instigating a two-yearly cycle could provide affiliated organisations and constituency parties with the time they need to consider in depth their responses and attitudes to Party policy. Against this must be set the loss of the public platform of Conference and the possibility that, for the greater part of the Party, this will become another opaque and inaccessible structure.

This prompted three developments in Party policy-making. Initially the policy review groups themselves were retained with some alterations, such as the amalgamation of a number of groups into a new economic 'super review group'. There was also a movement towards external advisory groups, discussing and reporting on particular issues. The first was the Plant Commission on electoral reform whose membership included a number of Labour MPs, academics, and respected figures (Plant Commission, 107). The second, the Commission on Social Justice, had a membership drawn entirely from institutions and organisations external to the Labour Party (1993a, 37), and will be considered further in chapter 6. Finally, there was the creation in 1993 of the National Policy Forum, with subsidiary policy commissions, which acts as a non-voting advisory body (Labour Party News, 1995b).

These moves suggest a desire on behalf of the Party to deal with particularly important or controversial issues in a way which shows the Party as listening to outside advice, and which enables the Party to discount any advice given without appearing to be embroiled in internal dissent. Perhaps this demonstrates the perceived experiences of the external 'think tanks' associated with the Conservative Party during the Thatcher years.

For proposed changes to Conference to improve Party accountability, rather than central control, they would need to compensate for the draining of power from the public platform of Conference. This implies a shift of power towards Labour's grass roots and a move toward greater participation in policy-making. Yet the *Labour Listens* campaign and internal Party consultation were clearly the biggest flops of the review process, and to improve participation the Party would need to prioritise Party activists and members in a way that has never before occurred in the Labour Party and seems alien to its paternalistic mentality.

Since the Policy Review the reverse has occurred, with a greater centralisation of Party decision-making and marginalisation of the Party's grass roots. The Policy Review itself represented a largely opaque policy-making system, based on the policy review groups. The use of external policy-making forums and the creation of a National Policy Forum which receives little or no publicity excludes ordinary Party members and trade union affiliates in the same way. With a more acquiescent Conference, partly the result of tighter stage management, partly of a deep desire for a Labour government, grass-roots frustration is likely to grow.

The legacy of the Review appears to have restricted rather than extended accountability within the Party. It should be acknowledged that John Smith's battle to ensure Conference support for 'one member, one vote' at the 1993 Conference suggested a continued role and importance for Conference. Nonetheless, under current conditions the leadership does not appear to have much incentive to reverse the marginalisation of Conference. It seems possible that any effective change is more likely to result from the demands of the elements of the Party disenfranchised by the review process, constituency party membership, trade union members, and affiliated organisations, than from any initiative taken by concerned and benevolent leaders keen to limit their own powers.

Conclusion

The most significant development resulting from the Policy Review in terms of Labour's existing policy-making structure was the effective marginalisation of Annual Conference. This, and an impending General Election, was probably the reason why many commentators remarked on how tame Labour's Conferences became in the years after 1989. This resulted from the focus on the Review as a policy-making system and the decision in 1989 to refuse to allow Conference to amend the Review reports, thus effectively stifling debate.

Though the 1993 Conference did show some signs of renewed life this may prove a temporary abberation, at least until Labour comes to power. The permanent marginalisation of Conference would demand the creation of new policy institutions to take over much of Conference's present role. To some extent such changes are occurring within the Party. A National Policy Forum has been created, but its impact remains uncertain.

If Conference does become permanently marginalised within the policy-making structure this will remove the important symbolic nature of public accountability embodied within it. Whether this will diminish the accountability of Labour's leadership to its members and affiliated groups, as well as active and grass-roots trade unionists, will depend on the constitution of any alternative policy-making body. Whatever the resulting position, such institutions will need to award much greater power and responsibility to representatives of these disenfranchised groups if it is to replace the highly public arena of Party Conference and maintain a pretence of internal democracy.

The development of the Review's policy-making structures served to exclude ordinary Party members, affiliated groups and the majority of trade unionists from participation in policy-making, and from knowledge of how policy decisions had been reached. In compensation for the loss of a proportion of their Conference voting share, Trade Union General Secretaries gained an unprecedented position in Labour's internal policy-making machinery through the review groups themselves. This may have removed the need for them to organise and control their delegations to Party Conference in order to realise their influence.

These initial changes reflect a more deep-seated and long-standing problem within the Party, that of the complete inability of the Party's leadership and its central organs to communicate meaningfully with Party activists and members. The ability of Conference to provide a potentially embarrassing, largely ineffective, but extremely useful safety valve has been activists' and members' only compensation. Genuine attempts to use the Review as a means of creating a more participatory party have been entirely fruitless. Nor is there any obvious reason to suggest this will change with the formation of new institutions. In fact the trend has been in the reverse direction serving to exclude, rather than encourage, participation.

It is also open to question to what extent the Review's apparent success, and its ability to galvanise the higher levels of the Party, was a result of the elite consensus created in the Party which helped to bring a new loyalist group together around Kinnock's leadership. If this was a significant factor, then the durability of such effects is dependent on the Review's success in delivering the goods. This itself is dependent on two further factors: the legacy of the Review as an electoral strategy, examined in chapter 5; and the value of the Review's output as a basis for future Labour policy. This will be the subject of the next chapter.

Beyond these fundamentally important factors a number of other important elements emerge from the Review as a policy-making exercise. Probably the most successful element of the review groups was the tying together of the NEC and Shadow Cabinet, and their secretariats. This success itself may have been due to the existence of an elite consensus.

This relationship would have faced serious strains if Labour had been in a position to form a government. Labour Governments are frequently characterised by conflict and tension between the Cabinet, the PLP and the wider Party. If the structure of the Review had been maintained under such circumstances it might have required the subjugation of the NEC to the needs of a Labour Cabinet at the expense of the wider Party.

The smooth running of the Review does not seem to reflect skilful management on the part of the Leader, but rather the initial strength of the elite consensus. In fact the one area of real difficulty within the Review, though resolved, did not reflect well on the Leader's role.

Policy-making in the Review has clearly demonstrated Labour's inability to involve its wider membership and support. It might be suggested that this is not a problem of the Party but rather of the British political system within which it works (Taylor, 1993). It is certainly difficult to see how any Labour Government might be made effectively accountable to the Party and yet still be able to govern in the context of British democracy. What will be crucial for the future of any Labour policy-making system will be its ability to create and sell policies in an electorally appealing way, and to implement agreed policies with any future Labour Government. This in turn will depend on the quality of the policy arrived at and its relevance to the British political scene. It is this question, with regard to the actual output of the Policy Review, to which we now turn.

4 Economic Policy and the Policy Review

Introduction

The central purpose of the Review was, of course, to provide a base of new policy for the Party. This chapter will consider the Review's policy output, focusing on the economic policies and policy groups. This focus will enable a concentration in greater detail on the attitudes, changes and policies provided in this important policy area. Economic policy is interpreted in a wide sense allowing an examination of the interaction between different groups. This is a policy area of particular importance; it can be seen as a basis for other areas of policy (Whiteley, 16), and has been seen as an area of particular contention in the 1992 General Election (Sanders). As a policy area of consistent importance, examination of economic policy provides an opportunity to assess how genuinely innovative and radical the Policy Review actually was.

The central publications containing the Review's policy statements were *Social Justice and Economic Efficiency*; *Meet the Challenge, Make the Change* and *Looking to the Future*. These will be considered alongside *Opportunity Britain* which was published as a holding document in 1991 when it was clear a General Election would not occur early in that year.

During this period there were also a considerable number of policy statements developing the Review's reports in particular policy areas. These were intended as restatements of the Review's policy output to highlight commitments in particular areas. They added little to the main Review documents, and in order to ensure clarity only the main documents will be considered here. Given the Review's focus upon the electoral dimension these efforts can be seen as reaching their natural culmination in Labour's 1992 manifesto *It's Time to Get Britain Working Again* (1992a).

The four economic groups to be considered are: a Productive and Competitive Economy (PACE), which was the central economic group dealing with, amongst other things, ownership and trade and industry policy; the People at Work group, concerned with employment issues and particularly the collective rights of trade unions; Economic Equality, which examined the distribution of income and wealth, taxation and social security; and Consumers and the Community, which considered the public services. They will be considered through an overall examination of the policy statements themselves and through a more detailed consideration of a few representative policies. In addition some comparison will be made with previous Labour positions, particularly those expressed in the Party's 1987 election manifesto.

Social Justice and Economic Efficiency brought together the review group's initial reports which set the context for the consideration of policy options. The phase two reports, collectively published in *Meet the Challenge, Make the Change*, contained the substantive policy output of the Review. They exemplified the difficulty the Review faced in both creating a comprehensive policy programme, and at the same time popularising and promoting it with the electorate. *Meet the Challenge* proved far too long to be widely read, but was still well short of the all-embracing nature of *Labour's Programme 1982* (Labour Party, 1982), the Party's last previous attempt at a comprehensive policy statement.

The Policy Review approach clearly contrasted with that of the earlier policy statement. *Labour's Programme 1982* was clearly not meant as an electioneering document (Labour Party, 1982, 2). Another obvious distinction between the documents of 1982 and 1989 lay in their attitude towards the Party Conference, the *Programme* explicitly deferring to the greater authority of Conference (ibid.).

In terms of the policy output, the confusion over whether the Review was intended as a programmatic exercise setting Labour's long-term path on a different course, or a public relations exercise designed to boost the Party's electoral fortunes, had its effect. *Meet the Challenge, Make the Change* demonstrated this confusion. The way in which the reports were written and set out seemed clearly to be an attempt to sell the Review. The policies themselves seemed to have a clear eye on the activities of a Labour government which it was hoped would be elected in the early nineties. Perhaps this was not surprising given the concentration in phase one of the Review on discovering the economic, social and political landscape a Labour government would be faced with in the early nineties.

This provided *Meet the Challenge* with a distinctly electioneering bias, but if it was intended to sell the policy output to an audience beyond Party members it was a long and cumbersome document for this purpose. In fact much of this was due to the repetition of many of the justifications for policy outlooks which were first given in the Review's phase one documents.

Another problem which manifested itself in the phase two documents was the uneven responsibilities of the review groups. This particularly affected the report of the Economic Equality group. Much of their 'A Fairer Community' report merely referred to the work of other groups, because many of the responsibilities allocated to this group had clear overlaps with the work taken on by other groups.

One group, Consumers and the Community, had a rare passion for recommending new institutions and schemes. In fact, they managed to recommend twice as many as any other single economic review group and nearly as many as the other three groups put together (Taylor, 1994, appendix 4).

These problems were resolved in the phase three document *Looking to the Future,* and the following interim document, *Opportunity Britain.* These provided shortened, populist restatements of the Review's output and involved, in part, merging the reports of the groups before the drafting of the 1992 manifesto.

Opportunity Britain, was criticised by some commentators as containing nothing new. Labour's response to this was to observe that this criticism misunderstood the nature of the document and the review process. This was quite right. In fact *Looking to the Future* contained very little that was new, but it was a shortened, clearer and more accessible restatement of those policies from the Review regarded as the most immediate priorities. The public relations element was emphasised in the attempts to link policy document artwork with that for the Party Conference in 1990, to be followed up the next year when the *Opportunity Britain* cover design was used as the model for the Conference platform. Before the Policy Review reports are considered, an examination must be made of Labour's existing policy stance, as outlined in their 1987 manifesto.

Labour's 1987 Manifesto: Britain Will Win

Perhaps the most interesting aspect of the economic policies in the manifesto of 1987 is how little room they take up. Despite the clear priority given to economic problems in Neil Kinnock's introduction (Labour Party, 1987, 1) only two out of fourteen pages of the manifesto are devoted specifically to economic issues. In addition a further page of the two-page 'Priority Programme' and perhaps another page dotted around in different areas might be regarded as coming under the broad definition of economic policy adopted here. In all then no more than four pages, less than one third, of the manifesto is devoted to these issues.

It would be difficult and tendentious to try and read too much fundamental principle into a single policy statement such as a manifesto, but this does represent Labour's last significant policy statement before the Review process, and therefore provides an illustrative comparison.

As with the Review, *Britain Will Win* sought to portray Labour as on the same side as 'Britain's people'. Policies were already expressed as 'socially just', a term to be transformed in the Review to social justice, on both occasions this was linked to economic priorities, and, to some extent, 'efficiency' (Labour Party, 1987, 3).

The manifesto's section on economic affairs, interestingly entitled 'New Strength for Industry', contained proposals which were to reappear in the Review's reports. These included a British Industrial Investment Bank, to create a holding company for state owned industry called British Enterprise, and to 'strengthen the Department of Trade and Industry as the spearhead of this new national industrial strategy' (Labour Party, 1987, 6). In addition there was a proposal for an Adult Skillplan, with a youth version, the Foundation Programme, and a commitment to create Regional Development Agencies (Labour Party, 1987, 6). There were also interesting commitments to social ownership, to be administered by British Enterprise (Labour Party, 1987, 6).

The Party's 'Priority Programme' appeared early in the manifesto as Labour's programme for its first two years of government (Labour Party, 1987, 4–5). It contained three interesting aspects: firstly, a directly corporatist element with a call for the creation of a National Economic Summit (Labour Party, 1987, 4); secondly the manifesto was clearly prepared to provide concrete commitments of both a general nature and of a more specific and financial nature such as specific improved benefits for pensioners and increases to child benefit; finally, the 1987 manifesto included a detailed analysis of how the programme would be financed (Labour Party, 1987, 5).

Two other aspects of the manifesto also deserve mention. The first of these was Labour's Charter for Consumers (Labour Party, 1987, 14). The second was the section on 'Democracy in the Workplace' which dealt with trade union rights. Again, this section demonstrated a readiness to make commitments; in this case to significant alterations to Conservative trade union legislation, notably in the area of fair pay (Labour Party, 1987, 13).

There are both clear continuities and differences between the Review and Labour's 1987 manifesto. The structural framework appears very similar, whilst Labour appeared more prepared to make concrete commitments in 1987. It also moved away from support for the trade unions, and was more wary about providing hostages to fortune by the time of the Review. Significantly, both the manifesto and the Review seem to share a common approach to the economic problems of Britain.

The Phase One Reports

The central theme of Labour's economic strategy was set out in the first sentence of *Social Justice and Economic Efficiency*. 'Labour's aim is to develop a talent-based economy for the 1990s and beyond' (Labour Party, n.d.a, 3).

In essence this reflected a long-standing Labour analysis of Britain's economic ills. The belief in the need for improved investment in new technology and skills was probably most vividly expressed in Harold Wilson's evocation of the 'white heat of technology' in the 1960s (Elliott, 73). As then, Labour's commitment to technology had a distinctly technocratic flavour (Labour Party, n.d.a, 3), which itself reflected past Labour attitudes (Crosland, 14).

Another reflection of historical Labour commitments was the primacy given to industrial over financial concerns. This was most clearly demonstrated in the emphasis upon a 'medium-term industrial strategy' (Labour Party n.d.a, 4). This included explicit criticism of the predominant position of Treasury policy, another opinion which had clear parallels in Labour history.

The Policy Review and *Social Justice and Economic Efficiency* as its first substantive statement, were credited with giving expression to Labour's rediscovery of the benefits of the market, or, perhaps more grandly, providing the first statement of 'market socialism'. Yet the approach to the market adopted in *Social Justice* is far from straightforward, nor is it clear what role, precisely, government should play with regard to market forces.

The commitment to a 'medium-term industrial strategy' is itself part of this equivocation over the relationship between government and market. PACE claimed:

> it is in the nature of markets to undervalue the long-term investment necessary to produce high-quality education and training, or to carry out pure research and apply it through research and development programmes. (Labour Party, n.d.a, 4)

This seems anything but a wholehearted embrace of market forces. It reads more like an old-fashioned argument in favour of a mixed economy.

The equivocal endorsement of markets carried over into the examination of 'social regulation and social ownership' with proposals for a new category of 'public interest companies' for those serving 'the national interest' (Labour Party, n.d.a, 5). These companies would then be tightly controlled by 'regulatory authorities'. Nor was the extension of public ownership, including Morrisonian nationalisation, ruled out (Labour Party, n.d.a, 5).

There remained a noticeable lack of any underlying principles for the assessment of when 'social ownership' should be undertaken and which form should be considered under what circumstances. This reflected pragmatic considerations and the need to promote 'economic efficiency' (ibid.). This approach contained a distinctly paternalistic edge. Despite comments about 'workforce participation' or the 'potential role of regional institutions in bringing this about', it seemed clear that decisions on the nature of social ownership and regulation would be left to central government.

There were some clearer statements of intent within the report:

> At the heart of a rational economic policy must be a commitment to full employment and to the measures necessary to secure it. (Labour Party, n.d.a, 4)

Full employment was, in turn, strongly linked to lifetime training. This acknowledgement of the limitations of Keynesian demand management in achieving full employment may be regarded as merely realistic, but it clearly diluted government responsibility for its achievement. Instead this was to be achieved by improving skill levels in competition with foreign workers – employment in Britain seemed to equal unemployment elsewhere.

PACE also anticipated a return to government intervention in regional policy (Labour Party, n.d.a, 5). Nonetheless, policy was viewed almost exclusively from the point of view of the national economy. This reflected Labour's lack of a critique of the British state.

Given the intended consequences of the move to a European Single Market in 1992 and the proximity of this to an election expected in 1991, it was perhaps surprising that the international economy did not play a central role in Labour's thinking but instead was relegated to one section, out of eight, in the report. The European Community only merited part of this section. The preoccupation was with trade. In fact Europe was regarded as worthy of separate mention apparently because: 'Over half our trade is now with other members of the European Community' (Labour Party, n.d.a, 6).

Attitudes to Europe were another area of equivocation (Labour Party, n.d.a, 6). Whilst clearly committed to the European Community, the report, nevertheless, seemed to see the Community as an obstacle to economic policies in the national interest which must be overcome, rather than the context within which all Britain's future economic decisions must be made.

A comparison of the initial reports of the PACE and People at Work policy review groups demonstrates an interesting difference in approach to the first phase of the Review. Whilst PACE seemed content with generalised statements and agenda setting, People at Work set out a series of clear guidelines for policy and was prepared to make commitments to definite policy options.

This was reflected in the identification of seven objectives for Labour's policy. These were:

- to create an 'opportunity economy' in which every individual has the chance to develop and use their talents to the full;

- to provide all workers with clearly defined basic rights;
- to promote effective trade unions;
- to achieve genuine equal opportunities for all at work;
- to help bring about greater work satisfaction;
- to encourage effective employee participation;
- to provide a firm basis for partnership and cooperation between employers and workers (Labour Party, n.d.a, 10).

These statements in themselves were general, but each was followed by more detailed discussion. Here commitments to fairly specific policy objectives, or even specific legislation, were included.

With regard to the kind of economy with which a Labour Government would be faced, the predominant concern of the group appeared to be with the divided nature of the workforce. This would leave a 'core' of secure, well-remunerated workers, separated from a 'periphery' facing greater insecurity (Labour Party. n.d.a, 9).

The group's response was to concentrate on training and education to provide a more highly skilled workforce. Possible alternative approaches to unemployment, such as shorter working hours, alterations to the social security system or a more equitable distribution of income and wealth were not considered, perhaps because they largely fell outside the responsibilities of the group.

The one area where the People at Work group took a definite and more radical line was with regard to its attitude to trade unions and particularly its view of Conservative employment legislation. Though trade unions were still defended in respect of their contribution to economic efficiency, the general view of trade unions taken by the group was clearly a positive one (Labour Party, n.d.a, 13). Despite couching their defence of trade union rights in terms of the underlying theme of economic efficiency, which provided the key theme for the initial reports, it was in this area of policy that the group fell into conflict with the apparent views of Labour's leadership.

The group did not suggest a complete repeal of Conservative employment legislation, but did specify a number of its 'most objectionable provisions' for attention. Apart from the use of economic efficiency to justify their approach, the group, uniquely in this document, also set down historical precedent: 'Our basic approach was set out in our report *People at Work* in 1986' (Labour Party, n.d.a, 14). Whether the reference of the group's approach to policy statements dating from before 1987 was agreed with the leadership, or whether this formed a point of contention, is not clear. It may be that the leadership perceived the group as identifying itself with past Party conflicts, rather than using the potential of the Review to bypass these debates in the way the leadership felt was needed.

Apart from the seven general objectives listed above the group also detailed six further objectives with regard to employment legislation. These were:

- the extension of conciliation and arbitration procedures;
- workers' rights to include a right to involvement in their union's decisions;
- a review of the boundaries of lawful strike action to obtain a fair balance of power between employers and employees;
- protection of workers engaged in legal strike action against unfair dismissal by their employer;
- the restriction of the use of interim orders and injunctions by employers;
- 'a union must be able to remain in existence and work on behalf of its members' (Labour Party, n.d.a, 14–15).

The group was far from seeing trade unions as being the answer to all the ills of industrial relations, as the commitment to a right to involvement in union decisions and the section in its report on encouraging employee participation demonstrate. However, as was shown in the last chapter, its attitude was far stronger than Labour's leadership was apparently prepared to countenance.

In common with the People at Work group, the Economic Equality group set out objectives, or in this case aims. In contrast with People at Work these were far more vague and did not commit the group to particular policy outlooks or options. There aims were 'to banish want and poverty from Britain', 'fairness' and 'to enable people to be independent' (Labour Party, n.d.a, 17).

In the absence of any attempt at a definition of such concepts as 'independence' or 'fairness' these aims were little more than pious hopes. It was also interesting that four decades after the Second World War the banishment of want and poverty was still seen as an 'ambitious project'.

Nor was criticism made of the increasing use of 'targeted' social security in the 1980s. Indeed the group's approach sought to sidestep the issue of means-testing by arguing for: 'fewer people obliged to live on means-tested benefits' (Labour Party, n.d.a, 18).

It is not easy to take such statements seriously when the group failed to analyse why poverty continued in a country of considerable wealth and despite three lengthy periods of Labour Government in the postwar era. For the group poverty was merely associated with unemployment and low pay.

With regard to unemployment, the group suggested four areas which required attention: the regional imbalance in Britain's economy; discrimination on the basis of sex and race; disability; and the provision of child care to assist parents back into the workforce. Its contribution to poverty was not the only reason for abolishing low pay: 'it is also inefficient' (Labour Party, n.d.a, 18). In suggesting an examination of minimum wage legislation the group appeared to believe that both unemployment and low pay are problems for correction within the system, rather than intrinsic characteristics of the British economy.

The group's comments on national insurance read almost like advertising copy claiming: 'no private insurance can match the comprehensive cover public provision can give all society's members, irrespective of their circumstances' (Labour Party, n.d.a, 19). This views social security as some form of state-run insurance policy. The apparent comparison of state systems with commercial organisation was emphasised by the commitment to a 'user-friendly DHSS'.

Government control of social security therefore rested upon the fact that it was better able to run such services. This immediately opened social security up to the kind of criticisms levelled at state-run services and industries by the New Right over the past 20 years. In taking the line they did, the group appeared to have adopted the underlying assumptions of the New Right, that economic 'efficiency' should be the basis of choice, whilst failing to recognise, let alone contest, the arguments of the New Right concerning the inefficiencies of the state. This seems to be a central flaw with this whole phase of the Policy Review and may have contributed to Labour's inability to put their case effectively to the public.

This phase of the Review clearly committed itself to a progressive taxation system on the grounds of 'fairness' (Labour Party, n.d.a, 21). Both the principle of progressive taxation, and the empirical claim of its worldwide support were asserted without supporting evidence. Whatever the basis of these assertions they did not fit well with the fact that the shift in the profile of Britain's tax burden, away from income and towards purchase taxes, since 1979, had brought British taxes more in line with other European Community economies (Johnson, 110). Of course, it was this change which had helped to make Britain's tax system fundamentally less progressive in the 1980s.

Of the four policy review groups here regarded as concerned with the economic aspect of the Policy Review, without doubt the least convincing phase one report was provided by the Consumers and the Community group. This was precisely for the reason anticipated in the earlier analysis of the Review's ideological document *Aims and Values* (see chapter 2): the failure to resolve the philosophical tension between the individual and social provision.

It should not be surprising that this failure prejudiced the considerations of this group, as it was centrally concerned with the public services and individual accountability. In fact this dilemma was implicitly recognised within the group's report. No less than four of its seven pages are concerned with detailing changes in the British economy in the 1980s, although significantly there was a failure to address the ideological challenge to public service provision.

Once again, the much-vaunted commitment to the market was far from clear. In fact, it was in this area that the conflict between individual and society in the report was most obviously expressed:

> Only through the community can we regulate the market to prevent abuse, ensure fair shares for everyone – regardless of their wealth or status and provide the services upon which the whole of society depends for its well-being. 'The consumer' and 'the community' cannot be separated. (Labour Party, n.d.a, 25)

As an exercise in question begging, or perhaps avoidance, this statement has its merits. As a statement of principle it was less than clear.

Part of the group's problem was that its remit raised questions it could not adequately deal with because they were the responsibility of other groups. Two of these were particularly important. The first was public accountability and democratic control: 'We regard it as a priority to increase democratic consumer control in both public and private sectors' (Labour Party, n.d.a, 26).

Whether this was to be regarded as an introduction of the idea of consumer sovereignty through 'market forces', or an attempt to establish the kind of 'democratic consumer control' attempted by the Conservatives with the Community Charge was not clear. If the group was considering the structure of political democracy then the problem for it was that the structures of local and central government were the responsibility of the Democracy for the Individual and Community group.

The second problem was that already alluded to, the interface between the individual and the state, or in economic terms the relationship between market forces and collective provision. This was also dealt with by the PACE group in their consideration of enterprise and ownership.

This left the group in something of a no man's land considering accountability without democracy and individuals in the market divorced from questions of ownership, enterprise and government intervention. It was no wonder the group ended with few real conclusions.

The section which dealt with 'new attitudes, new expectations' with regard to public services again interpreted New Right, particularly Thatcherite, criticisms of state provision in purely pragmatic terms as a problem of under-investment (Labour Party, n.d.a, 26). This failed to address the quite reasonable observation that under-investment has been a factor for the public services under both Labour and Conservative governments. It also failed to recognise the deeper ideological critiques of public provision which in many ways Thatcherism represented.

It is impossible to be sure whether the group's blindspot concerning ideological criticisms of state provision stemmed from the essentially pragmatic approach taken by the group itself, indeed by the Review overall, or whether it was because the group lacked any basis upon which to make a considered ideological response. What was clear was that this failure was a constant and enduring theme throughout the Review.

The group suggested a series of pragmatic resolutions to redress the perceived deficit in consumer responsiveness in public services. They suggested information technology and new management methods would improve the quality and change the nature of public services (Labour Party, n.d.a, 28). Praise was made of the benefits of a public-enterprise culture whilst ignoring how this would affect the relationship between local and central government (Labour Party, n.d.a, 28). The group promoted the idea of democratic control of business (Labour Party, n.d.a, 29). Finally they asserted the principle of individual entitlement (Labour Party, n.d.a, 29). These approaches essentially redefined the relationship between public services and individuals, without addressing the central problems identified by New Right thinking.

The group's general approach to policy development was boiled down to 'three tests':

- does the service put the individual consumer at the centre of the picture?
- does it adequately reconcile any conflicts between different individual interests?
- does it serve and safeguard the larger interest of the community as a whole? How far does it reinforce the mutuality, cooperation and inter-dependence of a healthy and civilised society? (Labour Party, n.d.a, 28)

Here the problems of conflicting interests were at least recognised, on an individual if not on a collective level, and some basis for resolution was suggested in the third 'test': but who was to apply this test?

Once again the Review demonstrated the shallowness of its approach and its essentially pragmatic nature. Whilst this third test was put forward as the basis on which the group would decide between policy options in phase two of the Review, its wider application and importance was not clear.

The group made a commitment to quality which included the creation of a 'Quality Commission'; movement towards 'public service orientation' on the Swedish model; and the implementation of Labour's 'Charter for Consumers'. There was also a statement that choice must be limited by the 'ability to pay', and a brief and ineffective nod toward redistribution, but which again saw the group coming up against the responsibilities of others, in this case the Economic Equality group.

Perhaps the most interesting aspect of the group's report was the demand that government policy must embrace the private as well as the public sectors. Inevitably the relevance of New Right critiques was ignored, and the approach to the private and public sectors was different. Four priorities were set down for each sector. In the public sector:

- the setting of clear targets and priorities, for instance in service levels and safety standards;
- measuring user satisfaction, for example using opinion polling or 'panels' of local service users;
- involving users in planning, either directly or through voluntary and community groups;
- monitoring complaints, including specific feedback on tasks such as council house repairs.

In the private sector:

- 'social audits' for private companies;
- arbitration and complaints procedures;
- more resources for local authority inspectorates;
- creation of consumer and user 'shares' in these activities (Labour Party, n.d.a, 30).

This insistence on private sector inclusion is interesting. However, is it realistic? It immediately raises an obvious question: how would a Labour Government react if such conditions were to increase the costs faced by British industry and thereby adversely affect their competitiveness? Given Labour's history in government, and indeed the state of the British economy, the answer would not be likely to satisfy the consumer.

The result of this approach, failing as it did to deal with the underlying tensions between state and individual control, was effectively to leave decision-taking to the Government of the day. In essence, as with other economic groups, the public were asked to trust Labour's instincts to get things right. This might be considered a lot to ask.

The Phase Two Reports: Meet the Challenge, Make the Change

Perhaps the first thing to observe about the economic policies of *Meet the Challenge* is the avoidance of the postwar commitments to full employment, stable prices, economic growth and a long-term balance of payments equilibrium. The document only included statements of intent; it failed to address the question of what governments are economically capable or have a duty to provide. On unemployment the main economic group PACE comments:

> We made explicit in the first stage of the Policy Review our commitment to rid Britain of the scourge of unemployment. ...
>
> Merely setting a target for the reduction of unemployment is not, however, enough. If full employment is really to mean anything, to the individual or the national economy, it must mean the provision of jobs that people want to do, which are worth doing, and which are properly paid. Full employment in a modern economy will rightly reflect changing patterns of preference as to when, where and for how long people wish to work, but one thing is certain – it is the quality of jobs that matters, and not just their total number (Labour Party, n.d.b, 9).

In line with the concentration on economic efficiency in phase one of the Review, this was a predominantly economistic justification of the need for full employment. In seeking to stand on this ground Labour appeared to have undermined any justification for full employment, or indeed any other economic measure, on moral as opposed to economic grounds.

In fact this statement was not centrally about creating full employment, but rather about creating the economically efficient framework within which full employment would arise and in which individuals would have choice of employment. In curious contrast PACE complained of inflation that it 'hits the weak and defenceless most acutely', and 'increases inequality', as well as threatening investment and weakening international competitiveness (Labour Party, n.d.b, 14).

If it is to be claimed, as the Review at numerous points did, that Thatcherite policies were simply not economically efficient then this was an empirical question and open to empirical examination. This was attempted sporadically during the Review documents, but nowhere with any great conviction. It was certainly not shown empirically that Labour's policies would prove better in enhancing wealth, or income.

Just as there was no consensus style commitment to specific economic goals, so there was no simple restatements of the instruments of economic consensus, in particular demand management. Rather, the approach was far more supply-side oriented. The general goals of higher employment and lower inflation were to be achieved through improvements in British competitiveness and a more flexible labour market. The first of these was largely the responsibility of PACE, the second of People at Work.

The central analysis of PACE followed the phase one reports. It was asserted that the British economy pays too little attention to its industrial base; this in turn arises from an undue stress on the financial sector and short-term considerations in British government, alongside a poor investment record.

PACE proposed a Medium Term Industrial Strategy (MTIS) which would have 'the same centrality and continuity' as the Conservatives' Medium Term Financial Strategy (Labour Party, n.d.b, 10). Quite what was involved in this MTIS was not made clear in the PACE report, though it would be administered by a new 'transformed' Department of Trade and Industry (DTI).

The report's description of the new DTI was strong on generality and weak in detail. The new DTI 'will have an equal, if not superior status, to the Treasury'; it 'will be strengthened to become a powerhouse dedicated to raising the quantity and quality of investment in British industry, just as MITI has done so successfully in Japan'; it 'will develop a new proactive role providing continuity, consistency and commitment to the processes of economic development'; its 'task will not be to pick winners but to create the conditions in which winners can come through, an environment that nurtures wealth-creation in all its stages'; it 'will need to develop a close partnership with both sides of industry'; and 'it will leave to industry, private investment and the market those aspects of development which they are best at doing, but it will identify with industry and the trade unions the contribution which must necessarily be made by government' (Labour Party, n.d.b, 10–11). All this was stated even before the section in the report which dealt with the new Department.

Quite what all this meant and what specific duties, responsibilities and, most importantly, powers the new DTI would have was by no means clear. The report further claimed that:

> The DTI will not be concerned with detailed operational decision-making in industry but with strategic intervention in key sectors. It will not, therefore, become a vast bureaucracy, but will have at its heart a small team drawn not only from the civil service but also from both sides of industry and from academics with applied knowledge and expertise. (Labour Party, n.d.b,11)

The credibility of this non sequitur was not helped by the statement that:

Although the DTI teams [sic] will necessarily be organised on an industry-by-industry basis, they will be ready to work with and meet the needs of both the representative organisations of industry and with individual firms. (Labour Party, n.d.b, 11)

It is interesting to compare this generalised description of the 'new' DTI with the creation of the Department of Economic Affairs (DEA) under the auspices of George Brown by the Wilson Government of the late 1960s. Like the new DTI, the DEA was seen as in institutional competition with the Treasury. The DEA was also dedicated to giving priority to the industrial base, not least through improving levels of investment. The DEA was compared with the best practice elsewhere, though in this case usually with France and Germany, rather than Japan. The DEA was also interested in identifying with 'both sides of industry' the necessary role of government to be expressed through a National Plan. Perhaps most ironic of all if Labour had won the 1992 General Election then the likely first Minister of the new DTI would have been another G. Brown, this time Gordon rather than George. In fact the only thing the new DTI appeared to be missing was a National Plan, but maybe the Medium Term Industrial Strategy would have sufficed as an indicative planning mechanism.

PACE's commitment to investment, and particularly research and development, did not rest solely with the establishment of the new DTI and in this field they were prepared to set targets. The group called for 2.5 per cent of GDP to be devoted to civil research and development (Labour Party, n.d.b, 11).

The problem of investing in 'the leading edge of technology' was one for which PACE suggested another institutional solution. After commenting favourably on the provision of 'high-risk, high-tech investment through the National Enterprise Board', the report proposed the establishment of British Technology Enterprise which would evaluate investment proposals against 'alternative commercial' criteria, and establish new industries to be sold on to 'socially responsible' shareholders (Labour Party, n.d.b, 12).

It might cynically be suggested that we have now discovered why the DTI would not need to 'pick winners' – it would have had British Technology Enterprise (BTE) to do it instead. Certainly if the essential problem here was a lack of high risk finance then it is difficult to see why BTE had to become an owner of enterprises rather than simply a provider of high risk finance.

The concentration of PACE on research and development and its comments on 'the importance of science' again brought to mind Wilson's devotion to 'the white heat of technology', although here they were married to the basic ideas of productivity, competitiveness and economic efficiency. One of the most specific commitments in the PACE report was the surprisingly strong advocation of a national broad band fibre optic cable network. Despite protestations against the general principle of the DTI 'picking winners' it would appear that PACE felt that this was a winner even they could not resist.

The group also proposed a British Investment Bank to service a range of regional and local investment banks (Labour Party, n.d.b, 13). Once again the precise role of government in this initiative was far from clear. Nor was it clear whether these institutions would be driven from the centre, or, as implied in the wording of the report, from the local and regional centres.

The other major aspect of PACE's work was to examine public ownership. Interestingly, the clearest commitment to renationalisation of any privatised enterprise involved British Telecom (Labour Party, n.d.b, 12–13). This was linked directly to the commitment to a fibre optic cable network noted above. Pragmatic considerations of this sort dominate the report's discussion of public ownership.

The principle of public ownership was made explicit only with regard to 'the major utilities'. Here the report met a dilemma which it faced squarely: on the one hand leaving these utilities in private control was unacceptable, on the other returning them to public ownership 'cannot be a costless exercise'. The proposed solution was to increase government control gradually, perhaps by settling for purchasing voting rights without a share of the equity (Labour Party, n.d.b, 15). In the meantime the report proposed a regulatory framework which would involve establishing a Regulatory Commission for each, headed by a Public Interest Commissioner 'representing directly consumer interests as well as the national interest' (Labour Party, n.d.b, 15).

Whilst there was a discussion of the limitations of Morrisonian-style nationalisation and some suggestions for alternative models were put forward, the actual proposals for the major utilities did not seem a great step forward from what had gone before. In fact the role of consumer, worker and other interests was dealt with in more depth in other reports. Curiously, given the suggestion that the Policy Review represented a reassessment of Labour's attitude to the market, the final section of the PACE report concentrated on the formation of a planned energy policy. In its own words: 'The ideology of the "free market" is nowhere more misguided than in energy policy' (Labour Party, n.d.b, 16).

Perhaps the most novel aspect of Labour's economic strategy was the extensive intervention in the labour market proposed by the People at Work group in their report 'A Talent-Based Economy'. Whilst the chronic problems infecting the British labour market were acknowledged by PACE (Labour Party, n.d.b, 9–10), it was People at Work which was awarded the responsibility of dealing with training and it was through training that the Review addressed these problems.

Like PACE, People at Work tackled its brief through the creation of an institutional framework to administer policy in this area. In this case the framework consisted of a new training agency, Skills UK, administering a new 16-plus Traineeship Scheme to be financed by a National Training Fund.

Rarely in *Meet the Challenge*'s 88 pages were issues of accountability regarded as a cause for concern. Where existing practice was regarded as insufficient, then the general response was to introduce the voice of a few more organised concerns, notably consumer interests. However, it must be acknowledged that PACE, for example, did propose limited rights of information for workers in specific circumstances such as takeovers (Labour Party, n.d.b, 11 and 13). On the whole, though, individuals were seen as being best protected through their roles as consumers, notably through a network of 'Charters' setting out standards and rights to redress, particularly in the public sector.

Training would itself not be at the behest of the individual but would be state controlled. Training strategy would provide 'an opportunity to acquire the most marketable skills', and it would provide training 'needed nationwide to assist the smooth running of industry'. Those involved in training would not be free to choose the training they wished, rather they would be free to undertake the training government agencies deemed necessary for the good of the economy.

The group proposed two main training systems to be administered and financed through Skills UK: the Traineeship Scheme and the Opportunity Training Programme. Both represented substantial interventions in the labour market to improve flexibility, productive value and thereby industrial competitiveness.

Traineeships were designed as a replacement for the Youth Training Scheme, to provide a bridge between leaving school at 16 and full time work, and to provide a new system of vocational education breaking down the barriers between academic and vocational studies. Alongside the adoption of a more flexible five subject 'A' level, the Traineeships represented a more flexible entry into the labour market from the ages of 16 to 19, allowing a choice, either through higher and further education or through traineeships, for those without employment at 16.

This more flexible form of entry into the labour market was mirrored by the Review's strategy with regard to retirement. Here, in response to proposals before the EC to equalise the age of retirement the group proposed 'to make the period from 60 to 70 a decade of flexibility' enabling choice over the age of retirement rather than imposing a particular retirement age (Labour Party, n.d.b, 22).

Apart from greater flexibility of entry and exit from labour, the report also suggested means of loosening up inflexibilities within the market itself. In particular this involved measures to encourage women into the labour market through provision of child-care facilities, extension of employment rights to part-time workers and the development of 'career break' and 'returner' programmes.

With regard to the skills shortage and unemployment the report proposed an adult training scheme called the Opportunity Training Programme. This proposal saw the training as a means of solving the problems of the labour market and with it increasing employment opportunities, rather than as an opportunity for individuals to learn skills they regarded as worthwhile (Labour Party, n.d.b, 20).

This suggested a form of government planning for the needs of the labour market exercised through training programmes. Indeed, Skills UK was given the role of monitoring labour market needs (Labour Party, n.d.b, 18) and the Opportunity Training Programme would 'provide a solution to these complementary problems of supply and demand' (Labour Party, n.d.b, 20).

Some access to decision-making procedures was suggested through the establishment of workplace Enterprise Training Councils to monitor and guide training in particular enterprises. Once again access to decision-making was within the context of corporatist, or central and local government, structures as they have operated since the war. The individual can only participate through a trade union and through the workplace.

As elsewhere in the Review, funding was seen as a key issue. In this case the group proposed setting up a National Training Fund to provide allowances for the trainees and to finance training programmes through Skills UK. The discussions of finance in the Review were generally concerned to point out areas where major finance would be provided from sources other than central government. In this case the 'three primary sources' were to be a Training Investment Contribution paid by every employer, public expenditure on training, and European Community money for which Britain would bid (Labour Party, n.d.b, 21).

Taken together, and with the report's other proposals to increase training for those in work, these measures represented a serious attempt to tackle Britain's labour market problems. In particular, they represented an important response to the need for improved skill levels throughout the workforce. They also represented a significant intervention in the labour market by government and government agencies in a clear attempt to plan training for economic need. The report also proposed a National Advisory Body on Training to advise companies, unions, local authorities or the proposed Enterprise Councils on training, and the creation of a National Vocational Council to ensure recognised vocational qualifications, with the responsibility to guarantee the value and quality of vocational qualifications offered under the Traineeship scheme.

The only real problem with these proposals, apart from their finance, was the timescale involved. The report proposed a reform of YTS and Employment Training to cover the period whilst these proposals were phased in. This meant that Labour would have needed at least two periods of office to benefit from the improved employment prospects, productivity and competitiveness which was the object of the proposals. This was likely to be the case anyway given the four-year span of Traineeships, but if these were introduced quickly they might at least have improved expectations amongst young voters.

Employment legislation was the other major aspect of the People at Work group's remit. It was perhaps not surprising that the group's report in this area was a lot less convincing or radical than its position on training.

Despite the report's rhetoric concerning the creation of a 'partnership at work' between employers and trade unions, it was clear that the main thrust of policy in this area was concentrated on individual rights. The central embodiment of these individual rights at work was intended to be the Charter for Employees. This charter was designed to cover: health, safety and welfare; discrimination; 'family responsibilities', such as maternity and paternity leave and family leave days; unfair dismissal; representation through a trade union; and the commitment to a National Minimum Wage. This was an attempt to guarantee the employment conditions of all individuals whether unionised or not (Labour Party, n.d.b, 25).

A number of measures involved change in employment legislation; for example a review of legitimate secondary action and an end to sequestration. These were important concessions based on the idea that a balance was needed between the rights of organised labour and of employers, but they did not alter the fact that the central approach was individualist in nature. Organised labour appeared one area of the economy where the Review was prepared to see a weakening in organised interest representation, whereas in almost every other area interest representation was to be strengthened. In these circumstances it is difficult to see how individuals would be in a position to defend their putative employment rights.

Most of the Economic Equality report read more like a statement of intent than a statement of policy, a result of the already noted overlap of responsibilities with other groups. The exception came in their treatment of the taxation and benefit system. Here, changes were seen as an explicit device to achieve a more equitable distribution of income (Labour Party, n.d.b, 31).

The major attack on poverty was seen as operating through labour market intervention providing job opportunities and a National Minimum Wage set at an initial level of half male median earnings. Nonetheless, taxation had a role to play particularly in the short and medium term.

Despite the redistributional nature of the report's taxation proposals it was clear there would be no attempt entirely to redress the shifts of taxation made by the Conservatives, in particular the shift in the tax burden from direct taxes, notably income tax, to indirect taxes, notably VAT (Johnson, 141–2). Instead 'A Fairer Community' concentrated almost exclusively on direct taxation.

The proposals fell short of supporting a return to the higher tax bands of the seventies and before. It also did not bring back the additional premium for unearned income. However, more radical proposals were made with regard to National Insurance Contributions. The group proposed a new Social Insurance Scheme to replace National Insurance. The lower earnings limit would be replaced by a personal allowance, which, with the replacement of the main personal tax allowance with a zero-rate tax band, would go some way to tackling the poverty trap which many low paid fall into when they cross into the initial tax band and first National Insurance contributions. A new 20 per cent tax band was also proposed. Linked with the proposed removal of the National Insurance Contribution ceiling these were perhaps the clearest redistributional measures to which the Economic Equality group was prepared to commit itself.

The group also promised a crackdown on tax avoidance through loopholes and tax havens. The report quoted Inland Revenue estimates that '£5 billion is lost every year due to short staffing and high labour turnover among tax inspection staff' (Labour Party, n.d.b, 34). Quite what level of extra revenue the group anticipated netting from tackling these deficiencies was not stated, though the potential was significant, and so were the problems.

The group's strategy for the benefit system centred largely on building on the perceived success of the State Earning Related Pension Scheme (SERPS). Commenting on their proposed Social Insurance Scheme the group made significant claims:

> Labour offers a new contract between the individual and society. The social insurance we propose will provide greater security than any private insurance scheme can guarantee. Participation in it is not altruism, but self-protection. (Labour Party, n.d.b, 34)

It should be noted again that this statement followed a form which was familiar elsewhere in the Review, that is promoting public services as improved versions of private services. It has already been seen that the Review itself accepted criticism of the quality of public service provision, but one area where the Review apparently believed the public sector could improve on the private was in security of provision.

As with SERPS, the principle behind that of the Personal Pension Plan was one of levelling up benefits. It also proposed using the more 'flexible' age of retirement in the decade between 60 and 70 to offer a wider range of potential benefits and options tailored to individuals. The levelling up principle of gradually extending the best, non-means-tested benefits to a wider group, and bringing social security claimants out of poverty, was extended in other areas such as disability and long-term unemployment. There were also new benefits for the disabled and their carers (Labour Party, n.d.b, 37).

These were essentially long-term objectives and the report did not hide the fact that the full effects of the changes in benefit would take time to implement. In the short-term claimants would be dependent on means-tested benefits and the success of the proposed social security strategy was clearly dependent on success in wider economic policy areas (Labour Party, n.d.b, 37).

Although the other three groups occasionally found themselves involved in detailed policy proposals, they also all put forward some clear overall strategies in their area. In contrast the Consumers and the Community report, 'A Commitment to Excellence', was entirely dominated by piecemeal proposals with very few strategic shifts.

As was noted above, this group was fundamentally wedded to the creation of new government agencies and regulatory bodies. Some, such as the Higher and Continuing Education Council, were merely adaptations of existing quangos, but most were new bodies involving representatives of organised interests

The group seemed keen to emphasise its 'even-handed' attitude in dealing with the public and private sectors (Labour Party, n.d.b, 41). Despite this statement only one of sixteen named changes the group proposed, a national Food Standards Agency, was directed primarily at the private sector. What is more even here the agency would be responsible for setting nutritional standards in public sector institutions such as schools and hospitals. Indeed, most of the group's report was aimed entirely at the public sector.

Although purporting to be a consumer-centred approach the group can find no better means of guaranteeing consumer interests than through an extensive new regulatory and monitoring framework. A central initiative was the creation of a 'quality programme' for central and local government services to be administered by a Quality Commission which would replace the Audit Commission. In addition, there were proposals for a new Regulatory Commission for each of the public utilities, whether in public or private ownership, and for a Department of Consumer Affairs with a Minister of Cabinet rank.

However, most of the report's recommendations deal with health and education. In health they proposed: a new Health Quality Commission; a Health Technology Commission; a 'National Health Initiative'; and a Minister for Community Care. In education apart from the Higher and Continuing Education Council, partly replacing existing funding institutions for universities and polytechnics, proposals included: an Education Standards Council; National Schools Awards; Home Partnership Agreements; and a Return to Learn entitlement.

Here responsibility for the private sector rested entirely with the Department of Consumer Affairs. For the rest, the report concentrated on replacing narrow commercial calculations with social and 'quality' audits, the former covering public and private sector provision, the latter council services. It is remarkable that, given the political events of the 1980s, the report seemed entirely sanguine about public reaction to greater control of the private sector by public sector agencies. It was as if the Conservative emphasis on the need to curtail the power of the state either never happened or was completely irrelevant to Conservative electoral success. There was also no attempt to assess the effects of such changes on local and central government costs.

The Consumers and the Community report seemed to share a common fault with the other economic policy groups in phase two of the Review: the seed of a good idea, in this case the need for the community to judge provision of goods and services on more than purely commercial criteria, was applied in ways which were poorly thought out, largely populist, and ignored the ideological challenge of the New Right. The Review failed to provide a mechanism for resolving genuine conflicts of interest between given individuals and the community, or even between individuals. The ideas which were put forward merely replicated the kind of policies Labour was pursuing in the 1970s. This was in spite of the fact that the Review itself frequently talked in terms of a 'new partnership' or a 'new contract' between the state and the consumer, 'both sides of industry' or whatever it might be in the particular context.

Sometimes the Review talked about this in terms of 'market socialism'. The fact was, though, that the main aspects of the economic policy of the Review could easily have been adopted in the 1970s. The policy proposals were, if anything, even more interventionist than those employed previously. The major changes were due to considerations of pragmatism or electoral strategy. Nationalisation was downgraded because of the economic cost, but was replaced with a series of regulatory commissions and a statutory framework for the utilities. The 'transformed' DTI closely resembled the former DEA, the National Plan was replaced by a Medium Term Industrial Strategy, what was regarded as the best of the NEB was incorporated into the BTE and the public services found themselves hemmed in by a whole plethora of new institutions centring around a Quality Commission.

In other areas, redistribution would occur on the gradualist lines of the 1970s, using SERPS as the example. Taxation would become more progressive and seek to deal with the poverty trap, but would not be as progressive as it was in the seventies, and the benefit system would continue to be means-tested for the foreseeable future. We are perhaps entitled to ask what was so new here that it required the incorporation of a new epithet?

Looking to the Future

The most obvious refinement in *Looking to the Future* was to collapse the work of the seven review groups, and their subsequent reports, into five thematic chapters. The four economic groups provided the basis for two-and-a-half of these chapters, with the defence and foreign policy group and the democracy group having a chapter each and the environment group providing half a chapter. The first chapter, 'creating a dynamic economy', consisted basically of the work of the PACE group, with the Economic Equality group's work on taxation and the People at Work group's training proposals added in. Environmental policy shared the second chapter, 'bringing quality to life', with the local government and health proposals of the Consumers and the Community group. The third chapter, 'creating new opportunities', amalgamated the work of three groups: Consumers and the Community's ideas on education, People at Work's proposals for a Charter for Employees and on employment legislation and the social welfare sections from the Economic Equality group.

Most of the named changes which had been proposed in the phase two reports were maintained, though with some important modifications and changes of emphasis. From the PACE report only the commitment to a 'new' Department of Trade and Industry remained unscathed, and even here the policy seemed a lot less central (Labour Party, n.d.c, 18).

The Medium Term Industrial Strategy was no longer mentioned, nor was the promised Small Firms Policy Division of the DTI, though there was a section on policy toward small and medium sized firms. For the first time *Looking to the Future* made it clear that British Technology Enterprise would be a strengthened version of the British Technology Group (Labour Party, n.d.c, 14). The British Investment Bank became National Investment Bank shorn of the network of local and regional investment banks which it had been designed to service. Meanwhile the Regulatory Commissions for each major utility proposed in phase two were replaced by a single Consumer Protection Commission to cover them all (Labour Party, n.d.c, 17).

The main framework of the proposed training bodies remained intact with Skills UK, the National Training Fund and Enterprise Training Councils all retained, though the local and regional Skills agencies were now to be developed from existing Training and Education Councils (Labour Party, n.d.c, 12). Although trainees and opportunity training were both mentioned, neither was given the status of named schemes or programmes awarded in phase two.

Vocational training and the importance of recognised qualifications also seemed to be downgraded with no mention of either the National Vocational Council or the National Advisory Body on Training. In a later chapter the National Minimum Wage became the more convoluted national legal minimum hourly wage.

The Social Insurance Scheme was retained as a replacement for National Insurance but without its independent Commission (Labour Party, n.d.c, 35). Developments on SERPS were mentioned leading to a National Personal Pensions Plan (Labour Party, n.d.c, 37), whilst the commitments to both Disability and Carers' Benefit were restated (Labour Party, n.d.c, 36). In local government the Quality Commission (Labour Party, n.d.c, 24), Health Quality Commission (Labour Party, n.d.c, 28), and Education Standards Council (Labour Party, n.d.c, 30) all feature, whilst the proposal for a Department of Consumer Affairs was not mentioned.

The only other significant institutional development of economic policy was the proposal for Regional Development Agencies which were not mentioned in phase two of the Review (Labour Party, n.d.c, 16). It was here that the proposal for local and regional investment banks seems to have been incorporated, though it was not stated what their relationship, if any, would be with the newly proposed National Investment Bank.

These changes, with the single exception of the Regional Development Agencies, were more centralised than the phase two proposals and they follow more traditional lines. *Looking to the Future* also provided the first statement of what was to become a familiar formula in Labour's public relations up to 1992: 'We will not spend, nor will we promise to spend, more than Britain can afford' (Labour Party, n.d.c, 8). This was accompanied by promises to improve benefits 'as rapidly as resources allow' (Labour Party, n.d.c, 35). This was the case even with so-called priorities such as Child Benefit, though some clear cash commitments were made particularly with regard to pensioners.

With regard to taxation, on the other hand, it was stressed that most will not be losers. Changes such as the phasing out of married couple's tax allowance would be made 'in such a way that the amount of tax-free income received by a married couple will *not* fall in cash terms' (Labour Party, n.d.c, 9). A return to progressive income taxation was promised, but in the context of redressing the shift in the tax burden from higher earners to middle and low earners, not from indirect to direct taxation.

The more central consideration in phase three of what a Labour government could afford and when it would be legitimate to sanction government borrowing emphasised the fact that it was looking toward electoral strategy and refining the policy proposals for this purpose. This was also demonstrated in the greater emphasis given to economic policy areas such as the Exchange Rate Mechanism and inflation. Both were mentioned in the phase two reports, but both were given greater prominence and explanation in phase three (Labour Party, n.d.c, 7).

In the event the Conservative government decided to join the ERM before the General Election was called, but this statement makes it clear that Labour would have probably taken the same course, and, although there was some criticism of the rate set against the Deutschmark at the time of ERM entry, would have found it difficult to enter at a rate significantly below that agreed by the Conservatives, if only because of the possible effects on market sentiment.

Reference was made to the pragmatic reasons for ERM entry, claiming possible benefits with regard to exchange and interest rate stability and inflation (Labour Party, n.d.c, 7). However, no mention was made of the potentially adverse effects on employment, or of the essentially deflationary policies ERM entry entailed, or the possible effects on Labour's public spending programme.

The statement made no bones about the fact that the long-term anti-inflation effects of the ERM were based on its ability to maintain relative costs in the European Community (Labour Party, n.d.c, 10). If the Review's analysis of Britain's poor productivity and investment was correct, then this meant that British inflation would be tackled by lowering the relative wage rates of British workers in comparison to their European counterparts, unless Labour's strategy for improving productivity and investment proved phenomenally successful.

Despite this obvious implication the very next paragraph promised to halt the deterioration in pay and conditions experienced in the public sector under the Conservatives and to develop 'fairer more rational ways of settling pay and conditions' disputes (Labour Party, n.d.c, 10). This seemed clearly at odds with the 'market discipline' approach of ERM entry.

The renewed prominence of the ERM and inflation control through the ERM was a return to the dominant concern of finance as opposed to those of production. A Labour government could easily find itself in a similar position to the 1960s, effectively abandoning policies for industrial rejuvenation and social welfare, which were not in essence dissimilar to those proposed in phase two of the Review, in favour of the protection of a weak pound.

The idea of 'charters' was mentioned in *Social Justice and Economic Efficiency,* developed through *Meet the Challenge* and finally refined in *Looking to the Future.* The two 'charters' which survived into phase three from the economic groups were the charter for consumers (Labour Party, n.d.c: 23) and the charter for employees (Labour Party, n.d.c, 33).

The major contribution of the 'charters' appeared to be as a guarantee of clear and reliable information on consumer and employee rights, although they also included means of redress for failures in performance. 'Charters' may also be another sign of the more European attitudes adopted in the Review. So, for example, the 'charter for employees' was explicitly linked with the European Social Charter (Labour Party, n.d.c, 33). Essentially this contractual approach was a paternalistic one based on the granting of 'rights' to individuals guaranteed by a benevolent state. Once again the possibility of genuine conflicts of interest, perception or approach was ignored.

The commitment to bringing BT back into public ownership because of its technological importance was restated (Labour Party, n.d.c, 14). A commitment to make water companies a priority for nationalisation, perhaps to give more substance to the campaign against water privatisation, was added (Labour Party, n.d.c, 17).

Phase three marked a return to the primacy of financial economic measures over those stimulating production and investment, and measures to tackle social injustice. *Looking to the Future* also provided a clearer statement on the position of trade unions (Labour Party, n.d.c, 34–5). It provided clearer statements on the Review's attitude towards such issues as: secondary picketing, 'permitted only where the second employer is directly assisting the first employer to frustrate the dispute' (Labour Party, n.d.c, 34); and the closed shop, 'whilst recognising the freedom not to join a trade union in the Charter, we fully support and advocate 100 per cent trade union membership at the workplace' (Labour Party, n.d.c, 35).

The one departure in this area from phase two was the proposal for an Industrial Court which will 'deal with the whole area of industrial disputes' (Labour Party, n.d.c, 34). Headed by a High Court judge, the Court would include expert industrial members and replace the Employment Appeal Tribunal.

Phase three represented a considerable alteration in emphasis from the phase two reports. It was both more cautious and less ambitious, removing the more radical elements of an approach already based on established priorities. It might be said that this was only to be expected given that phase two was intended as a re-examination of Labour's existing policies, whilst phase three was the first step in a wider promotion and refinement of the proposed policy options in the run-up to a General Election. This may be, but phase three nonetheless established a clearer return to the priorities of the sixties and seventies in Labour's practice of economic policy. Though this trend was already apparent in phase two, its development in phase three was clear with *Looking to the Future* representing a document of less radical force and intent than those produced under Wilson and Callaghan.

Opportunity Britain

In his introduction to *Opportunity Britain* Party Leader Neil Kinnock confirmed the nostalgic, fundamentally conservative, approach of the Policy Review. In his view Britain's underlying system seemed fine. Our manufacturing produced great companies, scientists, inventors, designers and committed workers; our broadcasting and arts deserved admiration; our welfare state was worthy; even our political democracy was essentially sound and to be admired (Labour Party, 1991, i). Kinnock's comments, and the Review as a whole, give the distinct impression that all of Britain's economic ills can be blamed on a period of rogue government since 1979. The Review completely failed to acknowledge or respond to the nature of Britain's long-term economic decline, and the Thatcherite response to it. Essentially the Review returned to the very policy approaches which led to the economic problems of the seventies, inspired Thatcherism, and which helped to give the Conservatives three successive election victories.

By 1991 the Review had been making headlines for two years and the election still seemed some way off. As a consequence *Opportunity Britain* suffered because it lacked direction, had no essential function, and had nothing new to say. In many ways it was simply a rehash mainly of *Looking to the Future* with occasional elements of *Meet the Challenge* reintroduced. Its format was the same as the phase three report, although there was some attempt to deal with current policy issues and to take on board changes which had happened during the Review process. There was also an attempt to play to Labour's perceived strengths and give priority to electorally strong issues.

Opportunity Britain did restate some of the commitments of phase two which had been left out of phase three. These appeared mainly to have been items where public attention had been focused on a particular issue by events. One example of this was the restatement of the proposal for a Food Standards Agency (Labour Party, 1991, 17), which probably was included following some well publicised food scares.

Another development in the document was a greater integration of the work of different Review groups, notably the incorporation of environmental issues into areas such as the economy (Labour Party, 1991, 10), but on the whole phase four merely continued the trends apparent in phase three. Mention of the DTI was dropped altogether, whilst a specific inflationary target, related to other European Community countries, was announced (Labour Party, 1991, 11). Social security improvements were narrowed further, with greater qualifications over resource availability and fewer specific cash commitments. An explicit statement of the source of new resources for public spending was incorporated: 'The results of economic growth – the national dividend – will provide new resources for public investment' (Labour Party, 1991, 13).

Another charter was reintroduced, this time for patients (Labour Party, 1991, 18), and the tying of industrial relations policy with Europe was made explicit again with the promise to introduce legislation on sympathy action in line with other European countries (Labour Party, 1991, 39).

The one sense in which *Opportunity Britain* was clearly an electorally oriented document was the fact that it gave priority to those policies thought to be Labour's strongest suit. This demonstrated the fruits of Labour's use of public surveys to promote the Review. The survey responses may also have had some effect on the continuing trend to caution and circumscription of policy options. Each chapter of the phase four document showed an ordering designed to play Labour's strongest cards early on. The three chapters gave prominence in turn to training, health and education. Training and education in particular were presented as central to Labour's vision of the future and linked to Labour's past achievements, particularly in the creation of the NHS (Labour Party, 1991, 33).

Phase four was intended as a period in which to publicise and promote, and this was attempted by giving priority to Labour's stronger electoral issues in a better written document which brought policy proposals up to date. However, the document failed to provide either a statement which offered anything to entice or excite interested observers, including the media, or a format which might reach a wider audience. The contents of the document were substantially those of previous Review documents: in this case, if anything, less radical and more pedestrian than its predecessors. Meanwhile the document was still long, 56 pages, and did not contain a contents page or an index to allow the casual reader to quickly find their area of interest.

Labour's Manifesto 1992

It would be difficult for anyone to describe *It's Time to Get Britain Working Again* (Labour Party, 1992a), Labour's manifesto for the 1992 General

Election, as a radical document. In fact it was a cautious, often pedestrian, document which had been shorn of nearly everything original, ambitious or adventurous which arose from the Policy Review. The one thing it certainly had inherited from the Review was a set of electoral priorities.

Neither of these facts should surprise given the electoral nature of the Review as a whole, and the extent to which it was guided by sample surveying, the effects of which were clear in this manifesto. They were clear in the fact that perceived electoral strengths, such as education and health, which were given priority in phase four were afforded chapters of their own. They are also clear in the fact that the policy contents of the manifesto were restricted in tone and approach, particularly where it comes to making clear financial commitments.

It might be argued that, by relying on sample surveys and opinion poll data, Labour had devalued the duty of a political party, particularly an opposition political party, to persuade its audience, rather than merely to seek to tailor its policy priorities to the public's perceived opinions (Dunleavy, 129). Certainly there seems some mileage in the view that in pruning its review to meet public sensibilities, as suggested in polling data, Labour developed policies closer to those of the existing Government.

The substantial labour market intervention to promote skills promised in phase two had been slimmed down to a 'Skills for the '90s fund, with an initial budget of £300 million, to upgrade the training of those in work' (Labour Party, 1992a, 10). Skills UK and its network of local and regional offshoots is reduced to a commitment to retain Training and Enterprise Councils (Labour Party, 1992a, 13). The general commitments to the option of training for all 16-year-olds, and improved training for the unemployed and those in work were maintained, though with less ambitious targets, but the mechanisms designed to achieve them had virtually disappeared.

Specific cash commitments were restricted to improvements in child benefit and on basic pensions, while the move towards a progressive income taxation system amounted to no more than the addition of a 50 per cent rate on incomes over £40 000 a year. Initiatives such as the Quality Commission, replacing the audit commission, and the Health Quality Commission were retained, as was the National Investment Bank now 'operating on strictly commercial lines' (Labour Party, 1992a, 13).

Apart from being drastically pruned, Labour's training commitments were also specifically linked to employees' rights (Labour Party, 1992a, 13). Once again the stress in employee rights was on an individually based approach and associated with Europe (Labour Party, 1992a, 13).

On the whole the manifesto continued the trend of caution and restricted commitments noted in the successive policy documents. The state-centred approach observed in the earlier Review documents was much less in evidence, at the expense of sacrificing any realistic attempt to improve the position of such concerns as consumer interests.

The general effect was that the manifesto was left proclaiming that Labour would manage the economy, with its current set of priorities and concerns, better than the Conservatives. This shift of economic policy closer to existing practice, combined with the stress on economic efficiency as the basis for the Review, enabled the Conservatives calmly to adopt significant aspects of Labour's proposals. Most notable of these was their adoption of 'charters', albeit on an entirely promissory rather than a statutory base. This in effect was what the 'charters' had been reduced to by phase four and it led directly to the abandonment of 'charters' by the time of publication of Labour's manifesto. Perhaps even more celebrated was Norman Lamont's introduction of the 20 per cent income tax band, proposed in the Policy Review up to phase three, in the Budget immediately before the General Election.

Conclusion

Overall this consideration of the four economic groups indicates the clear weaknesses in the Review's structure and practice. In phase one underlying assumptions about service provision and the role of government were not discussed. Rather they were merely taken from Labour's historical positions, a fact only effectively recognised in the Consumers and the Community group's discussion of historical values. On the other hand there was only one attempt to situate current policy against the background of Labour's existing policies. Indicatively this was the one area where policy differences occurred during the Policy Review process, over the People at Work group's discussion of employment legislation.

This tends to confirm the argument of previous chapters that the Review was intended to transcend the policy disputes of the late 1970s and early 1980s. However, the 'new' policies only represented a break with the past if the comparison is with the years since the mid-1970s. In fact, the phase one reports of the economic review groups clearly demonstrated the Review's pragmatic context. This in turn was a major reason for their failure to address the problems of public service provision which were raised by the challenge of Thatcherism in the 1980s and, more generally, for the complacent and ultimately unconvincing nature of the phase one reports of the economic groups.

In many ways the economic policies of *Meet the Challenge, Make the Change* resembled closely the actual practice of the Labour Governments of the 1960s and 1970s, and the policy proposals of 1987. Whilst it is true nationalisation took a back seat, this was for reasons of pragmatism rather than principle. Planning was also no longer a feature, but here Labour's practice in the sixties and seventies was far from its rhetoric, and in the seventies in particular it might be suggested that Labour had little intention of actually following through its promises on planning agreements once in government.

There were, of course, new initiatives and in many areas a different emphasis, but these had all been handled in a way with which earlier Labour Governments would have been at home. There were two significant exceptions to this observation, and both, like the term 'market socialism', had been borrowed from abroad. It is noticeable that three countries were cited as precedents for the adoption of economic policy in the Review, Germany and Japan presumably because of their economic success, and Sweden, presumably more because of the longevity of its Social Democratic government.

From Sweden the Review, developing on the 1987 manifesto, gained its taste for government intervention in the labour market, and particularly the emphasis on training, and its desire to justify all its policies with reference to economic efficiency. It is perhaps ironic that Labour turned to Sweden for important elements of its economic policy and presentation at just the time when Sweden's Social Democratic hegemony appeared to be unravelling.

There may have been a desire here for Labour to open up into a more European socialist perspective. This might have been one reason for the second departure, the concentration on individual rather than collective rights at work. It may also have manifested itself in the stress laid on consumer interests by the economic groups as a whole and on Consumers and the Community in particular. With 1992 approaching rapidly this might have been seen as a politically necessary, as well as electorally desirable, step to take.

If this was so then it is curious that the underlying strategy of the economic policy, particularly with regard to employment and competitiveness, was so narrowly nationalistic. Undoubtedly this was true of socialist parties in other countries, but some acknowledgment of the international problems of employment and demand faced by the European and world economies might have proved a greater awareness of the country's problems.

Economic policy was central to the challenge of Thatcherism to Britain's postwar consensus. Economic policy was also fundamental in the General Election of 1992. It was therefore both unfortunate and predictable that Labour's failure to grasp either the significance of the ideological position of the New Right, expressed through Thatcherism, or to provide an adequate response, should be most clearly manifested in its economic policy.

The fundamentally cautious, conservative and unambitious nature of Labour's economic policies were the result of its pragmatic approach. This in turn derived from the lack of a clear ideological alternative. Faced by a

Conservative Government forced into cautious pragmatism because it was seeking to defend what some regarded as the historic gains of Thatcherism whilst dealing with an economy in recession, and with a Leader who was attempting to maintain the Thatcherite hegemony of Party loyalty whilst simultaneously stamping his own identity on the Party, it was perhaps unsurprising that the Parties' policies were seen as so similar – similar enough indeed for the Conservatives to adopt two of Labour's policy proposals: charters and the 20 per cent income tax band. Perhaps most significantly, Labour itself had rejected the 20 per cent income tax band as being too radical for the current economic climate.

The essential problem for Labour, and the reason for its comprehensive failure, was related to Jones and Keating's argument on Labour's attitude to the state. The populism of Thatcher rested explicitly on the relationship between individual and state. Thatcherism claimed to have altered the balance of power between individual and state in favour of the individual. The freedom of Thatcherism was not a freedom from; individuals were not to be protected from fear, poverty, want or anything else, they were to be self-reliantly free to do, at least in the economic sphere. In the words of John Roemer, individuals were 'free to lose' (Roemer).

Thatcherism expressed itself as the alternative, perhaps the only possible alternative, to the state-dominated paternalism of the postwar years. This state-centred approach had itself been intimately associated with the Labour Party through the initial work of the Government of Clement Attlee. It was the breakdown of this approach, and the consensus it engendered, which led to the triumph of Thatcherism in 1979. It has been Labour's failure to find an alternative left-wing approach, or indeed even conceive of the need for one, which has maintained the Conservatives in power since.

The Review exemplified this failure more clearly than any other political event since 1979. As an attempt by Labour, in part, to overcome its outdated image, it eventually served only to underline the nature of that image. Whilst there was clearly an attempt in phase two to concentrate on individuals as the basis of policy, particularly with regard to consumer affairs and employment legislation, these ideas were developed entirely within the context of Labour's acceptance of the state. As Jones and Keating point out, this acceptance of the state was characterised by an uncritical belief in the state's neutrality (65).

The defence of individuals was seen as a job for the state. Individuals were to be granted rights, set down in charters and implemented by the state through Departments, Ministers, Commissions or legislation. For the most part individuals would participate in the institutions through third parties, representing their interests. In some cases their interest would merely be mooted as a consideration, such as the consumer interest to be considered by utilities or through the social and 'quality' audits which would automatically take care of public interest issues. Individuals themselves would only be empowered through the use of state power.

Of course, Thatcherism required state power too: the economic freedom of individuals must be protected from the incursions of those who are effectively excluded from the exercise of this freedom, but in the context of the direct empowerment of individuals in the economic sphere at least, Labour's Review must be seen as a return to the state paternalism of the postwar period. Furthermore, where fundamental problems with the economy exist these were to be addressed by substantial state intervention, most obviously in the labour market and skills training, but also in investment.

As the Review progressed and these state-centred approaches were placed before the public, a curious process occurred. The further the Review went on, and the more Labour gained responses to its proposals through sample surveys and opinion poll data, the more it became clear that state intervention and individual liberties guaranteed through the state would be electoral liabilities. As a result they were shorn from the policy documents as the Review moved forward. Each successive document in the Review process promised less state intervention and less institutionally backed guarantees than its predecessor.

It also became clear that one resentment resulting from this lack of faith in state-centred approaches was the cost of the state, made visible through taxation. For electoral purposes Labour decided to rein back on its spending promises, particularly with regard to social welfare programmes, and stress that expenditure would only be increased as economic growth allowed. Some of the economic priorities of the Conservatives, particularly with regard to inflation, were also adopted. This locked the Labour manifesto into the short-term, institutionalised financial responses to inflation which the Conservatives were pursuing.

Even within their Review documents, up to and including the manifesto, Labour recognised that a more sensible response to inflation was through medium- and long-term action to improve investment and productivity. Nonetheless they felt it impossible to avoid the trap of promoting the defence of the pound's exchange rate parity in the ERM. It is interesting to note that the policies to defend the pound pursued by the Conservative Government in the months following the election drew comparison from 'one prominent Conservative MP' with the 1960s:

> To learn what will happen, all you have to do is turn to the sterling crisis of 1967 and substitute Callaghan for Lamont and Major for Wilson. (Observer, 30/8/92)

Shaw has argued that the changes in the Review's policy positions after phase one were inspired by the ease with which the first phase review groups report, *Meet the Challenge, Make the Change*, was steered through the 1989 Conference. According to Shaw this led the Party leadership to conclude that it had been too circumspect in its approach and that it could push through its preferred options more rapidly than had previously been believed (Shaw, 1993). It seems unlikely that the final, rather anodyne, results of the Review would have generated the initial enthusiasm amongst the majority of the Party's elite if this had been a clear aim from the outset. It is suggested here that the changes reflected the fact that an approaching election, and Labour's opinion surveys, increasingly highlighted the inconsistencies in the Review's approach. These in turn reflected the fact that the Review did not come to terms with the deeper problems affecting the Party.

The Policy Review was always likely to throw up an economic contradiction for Labour in the sense that it would demonstrate the need for long-term action to reverse Britain's relative economic decline, but this would have to be set against the short-term desire for re-election. In the event Labour was only interested in divesting itself of its recent policy history; it found itself unable to break out of its postwar economic policy straitjacket. Both long-term and short-term policies were dominated by the state-centred mentality which had proved triumphant in the postwar period. When it became clear that the electorate no longer regarded these as credible in the long-term, Labour was thrown back on maintaining the position of the British state in the short-term. The manifesto was an electorally orientated, short-term document underpinned by no long-term economic strategy. It was perhaps not difficult in these circumstances for the electorate to reject it.

5 The Electoral Strategy

Introduction

The Party's Policy Review was primarily an electoral strategy geared toward the 1992 General Election. The analysis which has been undertaken here argues that the Review was far more than just an electoral strategy. It was interested in transforming the Labour Party in a far longer perspective than this. Nonetheless, its immediate objective was to help Labour to victory at the General Election initially expected in 1991. It is the Review's failure in this objective which is the subject of this chapter.

To consider the Review's electoral effectiveness its strategy for attracting voters must be considered. An assessment can then be made of its achievements in this regard. These achievements are considered both in terms of changing public attitudes toward the Party itself and toward the Party's Leader up to and including the 1992 General Election.

Strategy and Objectives

The Review's policy base, the subject of the last chapter, constitutes only one aspect of the Review, if the most obvious. The Review had many objectives, the most important and fundamental being to win the 1992 General Election. As such, its wider intentions, of restating Labour's ideological base and of creating a new policy-making machinery, say a great deal about Labour's perception of its own electoral failings.

Clearly the Review was intended to present the appearance, and in some ways actually have the effect, of addressing far more fundamental problems than merely finding the right policy mix to appeal to the electorate. After all, Labour had presented policy statements of many different kinds before.

Taken overall, the root and branch nature of the Review was intended to give the appearance of a party breaking with its past. Most importantly, as far as policy was concerned, this meant the immediate past of left-wing dominance in the early 1980s, but it also meant a symbolic break from the historic concerns and values of the Labour Party. This suggests that the Review was not merely concerned with issue voting, with presenting electable policies, but that it also saw its historic form of party identification, based largely on class, as being redundant.

To put this simply, there were two main elements in the message which the Review was intended to convey to the electorate: first, that the Labour

Party had a set of clearly defined, alternative policies to the Conservative Government; second, that it was competent to form a government and see those policies through.

The first message was contained in the policies of the Review itself. These policy prescriptions were reinforced and informed by Labour's extensive survey and polling data. Given this reliance on polling it should come as no surprise if analysis of survey data from the 1992 General Election shows a public perception that Labour had become more moderate, and more in line with the policy positions of the electorate (Heath and Jowell, 201–3). Labour put a lot of effort into achieving precisely this aim. Any gains from appearing more 'moderate' might need to be balanced against the perception that Labour was too similar to the Conservatives.

This feeling might have been reinforced by the fact that in 1992 Britain was in the midst of a recession and Labour's most significant difference from the Conservatives on economic management was over the importance of training. This was hardly a policy likely to affect the economy in the short-term and its achievement was likely to be dependent on Labour's success in bringing the economy out of recession. In such circumstances the electorate may well have opted for the party which was likely to do least damage to its personal finances in the short-term.

The analysis of the British Election Survey (BES) data for the 1992 General Election (Heath, Jowell and Curtice, 1994) includes the first direct consideration of the effects of the Review itself. The main focus is on the Review as a policy statement, although some consideration is also given to the effect of the Review on Labour's image (Heath and Jowell).

The consideration of policy effects follows former BES studies (Heath, Jowell and Curtice, 1985) in considering the relationship between voters' perceptions of Party policies and their perceptions of their own policy preferences (Heath and Jowell, 191). Heath and Jowell conclude that the changes in Labour's perceived position and the policy preferences of voters provided Labour with a gain of 1.1 per cent of the vote in 1992 (Heath and Jowell, 201).

Heath and Jowell acknowledge a number of problems with their analysis. One example is their claim that the Policy Review cannot account for the perceived shift of Labour to the right on unemployment as this was not a major theme of the Review, but they link unemployment with inflation and inflation was both a main theme of the Review's economic policies, and, with the advent of recession, was the subject of public debate. It is also not clear that causality runs in the way Heath and Jowell assume. It could well be that those voting Labour were more likely to associate themselves with Labour's policies.

Whilst Heath and Jowell's assessment of the electoral effect of the Review is challenged here, a definitive resolution of this debate would require a full analysis of the electorate's position on salient voting issues over the period in question. Such a study would be a large task and would itself have difficulty providing unambiguous answers, particularly given the second aim of the Review: to promote Labour as a competent Party of Government.

This second aim was pursued in a number of ways. Firstly, the Policy Review was intended to demonstrate strong leadership within the Party. If the aim of the leadership was purely to get rid of policies which were regarded as electoral losers, and to replace them with policies which were perceived as being more to the liking of the electorate, this could have been achieved using Labour's existing policy system. Using Annual Conference for this purpose, or simply developing policy under the auspices of the Parliamentary leadership, might have provoked renewed internal strife within the Party. The Policy Review was a mechanism designed to ensure policy outcomes were achieved in a way which carried enough authority to take the majority of the Party with it, and to sidestep public acrimony.

Secondly the Review was intended to show Labour as more in touch with ordinary people than the Conservative Government; to portray Labour as a 'listening' party. This was the main intention behind the highly public *Labour Listens* campaign. It was also important in the presentation of policy outcomes as moving away from the 'outmoded' Labour image of the past, more towards the 'centre ground' which was perceived as being the ground of the moderate British electorate.

Heath and Jowell claim that image effects of the Review accounted for 2.3 per cent electoral gain, and that this was over and above the policy effects discussed earlier. This means that:

> When combined together ... the direct and indirect effects of the Policy Review account in large part for the actual gains which Labour made at the centre's expense in the 1992 election. (Heath and Jowell, 203)

This view is not shared here. Heath and Jowell's analysis of the Review as an electoral strategy is certainly an interesting one, but the evidence considered in this chapter suggests other factors are responsible for Labour's improvement.

Labour's image relates to another aspect of the Review, that of presenting Labour as a modern Party, relevant to the problems of today. This was really an attempt to build upon the image and presentational achievements of the 1987 General Election. It was a reaction to the feeling that the public perceived Labour as being a party of the past, a consistent finding in Labour's private polling both during and before the Review.

This informed the attempt to formulate a new ideological basis for the Party in *Democratic Socialist Aims and Values*. It also fed into the presentation of the Review to the electorate and helped define the wide scope the Review was given as an agent of modernisation for Labour. Any analysis of the electoral effects of the Review which concentrated predominantly on its policy effects would thus be incomplete. The wider aim of changing public perceptions of Labour as a party was integral to the electoral strategy of the Review.

By changing the image of Labour and presenting it as a modern, forward-looking party, the Review was designed to create a new generation of party identifiers. This was reinforced in the early part of the Review by initiatives specifically aimed at young voters, such as *Red Wedge*. The Review sought to present Labour as throwing off the bonds of the past, discarding its historical obsessions and providing a new sense of direction. Finally, the concentration on economic policies, and the fact that taxation became a major cause of concern during the 1992 election campaign, clearly indicated the fact that Labour's leadership wished to be seen as economically competent and sound.

The Electoral Effects of the Review

As mentioned earlier, the Review involved a number of phases leading to a General Election, expected in 1991 at the earliest. Phase 1 saw the publication of the background documents in 1988, phase 2 resulted in the publication of the full policy group reports in the lengthy *Meet the Challenge, Make the Change* in 1989. Phase 3 involved a year- or two-year-long refinement and promotion of the policy output leading to a General Election. As it happened this was spread over more than two years with the publication first of *Looking to the Future* in 1990 and then *Opportunity Britain* in 1991, leading to Labour's 1992 General Election manifesto.

Publication of these documents, and the associated publicity it promoted, was designed to allow time for debate at each phase before Labour's Annual Conference, but this was not the only consideration. The phase 2 document in particular, *Meet the Challenge, Make the Change*, was deliberately published to coincide with the 1989 European elections and thereby have maximum publicity impact. In fact, Labour's good performance in these European elections was perceived by those involved in the Review as an indication of an early success for the Review's electoral intentions.

Relying on the European elections as a measure of the Review's electoral successes is far from adequate for the purpose of analysis here. Instead I shall first examine changes in Party popularity since the Review was established. Subsequently, I will look at the 1992 General Election itself.

As can be seen from Table 5.1 and Figure 5.1, Labour's appeal varied greatly over the period from July 1987 to December 1990. The table and figure present averages of the last five opinion polls in each month. What must be considered in this context is not the absolute level of those registering an intention to vote Labour, but rather the trends over time.

Labour's rating fluctuated between a low of 33 per cent in August 1987 and a high of 54 per cent in March 1990. As the figure clearly shows, following a trough in late 1987, Labour's poll ratings bumped along between 35 and 40 per cent until May 1989 when they rose above 40 per cent for the first time since the General Election and remained there for the next 18 months. These statistics provide clear evidence for those wishing to argue for a strong electoral effect for the Policy Review. May 1989 was both the month of the elections for the European Parliament, and the publication of *Meet the Challenge, Make the Change*. For supporters of the Review in the Party this was an obvious indication of the Review's success, and the period from May 1989 to October 1990 was certainly the highpoint of the Review in terms of its influence on Party thinking.

However, whilst these figures show a clear improvement, the beginnings of which certainly coincided with the publication of the Review's first substantial output, correlation is not cause. Alongside the Review, another considerable factor in Labour's electoral improvement was the problems of the Conservative Government. European integration and the Poll Tax were both considerable handicaps to the Conservatives in this period and it is probably no accident that Labour's decline from its rating highs at the end of 1990 coincided with the election of a new Conservative Party leader.

As Figure 5.2 shows, Labour's fortunes closely mirror those of the Conservatives during this period. Labour's biggest electoral advantage, 24 points in March 1990, coincides precisely with the Conservative low point and Labour's lead disappears eight months later following the election of John Major as the Conservative Party leader.

Whilst these observations should not be entirely surprising, after all Conservative electoral weakness must contribute to any Labour lead in the polls, the closeness of the coincidence strongly suggests that either Conservative weakness was due to Labour's strength, or conversely Labour's strength was due to Conservative weakness. Given the Conservatives' problems and the fact that Labour's lead was reversed following the election of a new Conservative leader, the evidence suggests that the most important factor during this period was public perception of the Conservative Government, and not, at least to the same extent, perception of the Labour Opposition.

Table 5.1: End of Month Averages for Voting Intentions
% intending to vote for each party, don't knows excluded from % base

	Conservative	Labour	Others	Labour Lead
1987: June	43.0	32.0	20.0	−11.0
July	47.6	32.5	17.5	−15.1
August	47.6	34.0	16.0	−13.6
September	48.5	33.5	15.0	−15.0
October	48.3	34.5	14.0	−13.8
November	47.9	34.5	15.0	−13.4
December	47.1	35.5	14.5	−11.6
1988: Jan	46.1	37.0	15.0	−9.1
February	45.0	38.0	14.0	−7.0
March	45.7	37.5	15.0	−8.2
April	43.2	39.5	14.0	−3.7
May	44.6	39.5	13.0	−5.1
June	46.0	38.5	12.5	−7.5
July	45.2	40.5	12.5	−4.7
August	47.1	35.0	14.0	−12.1
September	45.1	38.5	13.5	−6.6
October	45.5	37.5	13.5	−8.0
November	43.7	38.0	14.0	−5.7
December	44.0	35.5	15.0	−8.5
1989: Jan	45.5	36.6	13.9	−8.9
February	40.7	38.7	15.4	−2.0
March	41.3	38.9	14.3	−2.4
April	40.2	39.0	15.0	−1.2
May	41.5	41.5	12.0	0.0
June	36.6	45.0	9.0	8.4
July	36.7	43.3	9.2	6.6
August	37.2	43.9	9.2	6.7
September	37.0	43.4	9.2	6.4
October	37.8	47.8	7.4	10.0
November	36.5	47.1	9.3	10.6
December	38.1	46.3	9.3	8.2
1990: Jan	36.0	47.1	9.3	11.1
February	34.0	50.0	9.0	16.0
March	30.0	52.8	9.2	22.8
April	30.0	53.0	9.1	23.0
May	34.0	49.5	8.1	15.5
June	36.0	49.7	7.4	13.7
July	36.0	49.3	8.4	13.3
August	35.0	48.7	8.4	13.7

continued

	Conservative	Labour	Others	Labour Lead
September	37.0	46.7	11.1	9.7
October	34.0	47.7	12.9	13.7
November	37.0	44.5	11.1	7.5
December	44.0	42.1	9.1	−1.9
1991: Jan	44.4	41.2	9.2	−3.2
February	44.7	40.9	9.4	−3.8
March	41.0	38.5	15.5	−2.5
April	39.0	40.3	13.8	1.3
May	37.1	42.0	16.9	4.9
June	37.0	42.4	15.8	5.4
July	38.6	42.8	14.5	4.2
August	38.8	41.3	14.9	2.5
September	39.0	40.0	15.0	1.0
October	40.0	40.0	14.0	0.0
November	40.0	40.0	13.5	0.0
December	40.1	40.0	13.5	−0.1
1992: Jan	40.2	40.0	13.0	−0.2
February	40.0	40.0	15.0	0.0
March	39.0	40.5	19.0	1.5
April	43.0	37.7	16.5	−5.3
May	44.9	36.9	14.9	−8.0
June	44.0	37.0	14.7	−7.0
July	42.1	40.5	13.9	−1.6
August	41.0	42.0	13.5	1.0
September	38.3	41.9	15.8	3.6
October	34.1	46.7	14.2	12.6
November	32.0	49.2	14.5	17.2
December	33.5	46.0	16.0	12.5
1993: Jan	35.5	44.6	14.8	9.1
February	34.3	46.7	14.2	12.4
March	32.2	47.0	16.2	14.8
April	32.0	46.3	17.5	14.3
May	27.3	45.3	23.3	18.0
June	27.8	43.8	24.0	16.0
July	24.5	43.0	26.5	18.5
August	26.0	44.0	28.7	18.0

Source: Sanders. Monthly average of Gallup, ICM/Marplan, Harris, MORI and NOP polls.

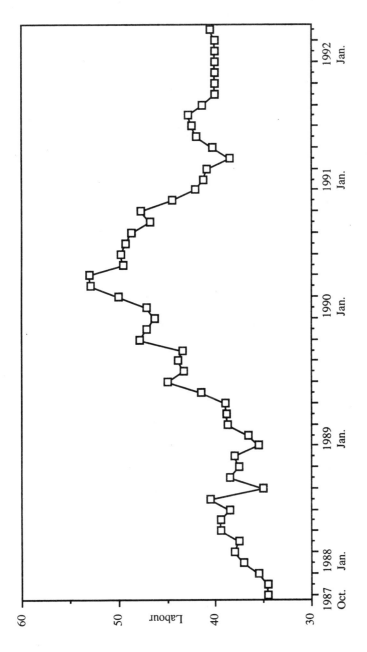

Figure 5.1: Labour Voting Intentions
Oct. 1987 to March 1992

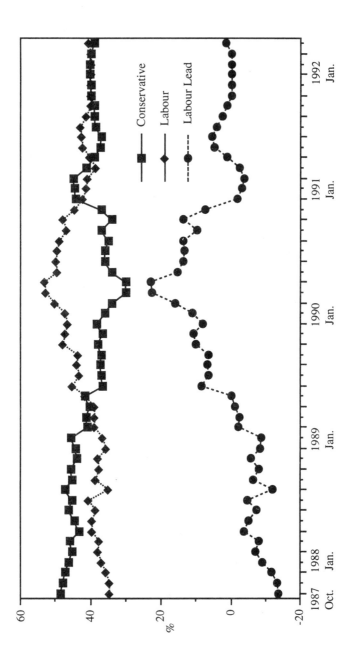

Figure 5.2: Labour and Conservative Voting Intentions and Labour Lead Oct. 1987 to March 1992

110

Nonetheless, this evidence suggests that as a result of the Review the electorate was prepared to consider Labour as fit for government again, given the coincidence of Labour's rating upturn with the publication of phase 2 of the Review. It might be that the Review, though not a sufficient condition for the election of a Labour government, was a necessary one. This may have something to do with the Review's attempts to provide a new image for Labour. Any effect the Review had in this period was not because it ditched 'unpopular' policies and replaced them with 'popular' ones, but because of the means by which this was achieved. The electorate may have been impressed by: the appearance of strong leadership afforded by the Review, or of an apparently united Party; a perception that Labour had a new sense of direction, or had ditched its old one; or a belief that Labour actually had a programme for government which might be carried through. It is impossible to determine which of these were important, or indeed if any were, without far more sophisticated data to analyse.

As far as one aspect of the Review, the attempt to promote the concept of a strong leadership, is concerned, there is some evidence available. This was an important aspect of the Review, tied up, as it was, with the promotion of Neil Kinnock as an electoral asset, and following on from the perceived electoral and Party gains, made through the confrontation with *Militant*.

We can consider the effect of the Review on perceptions of the Party leadership by examining the popularity of the Party's leader, Neil Kinnock himself. Table 5.2 shows the approval rating of Neil Kinnock and Margaret Thatcher up to November 1990 when Thatcher was replaced by John Major, and between Major and Kinnock from December of that year.

The general trends observed for the parties are replicated for the leaders. Whilst Kinnock's rating remained negative throughout this period, his position relative to the Conservative leader moved from deficit to advantage around May 1989, just as did the position of Labour relative to the Conservatives. Once again the peak in the Kinnock lead comes in early 1990. However, most dramatic of all is the change between November and December 1990, when a 33-point lead over Margaret Thatcher in November 1990 is followed by a 46-point deficit to John Major.

Just as with the Party ratings, Kinnock's lead owes as much to disapproval of Mrs Thatcher as it does to Kinnock's own improved position. However, the overwhelming message of this table is that neither leader is particularly popular, but for a period of some 18 months Margaret Thatcher was even less popular than Neil Kinnock, and by some distance. Once Thatcher was replaced the advantage was lost.

Popularity is one thing, though, but what about competence? Did Labour's Policy Review convince the electorate that its leadership was competent to

Table 5.2: Party Leader Ratings (positive response minus negative response)
Question: Do you think (X) is or is not proving a good leader of the (Y) party?

	Thatcher/Major	Kinnock	Kinnock Lead
1987: July	−1	−10	−9
August	−4	−19	−15
September	−5	−18	−13
October	8	−11	−19
November	−1	−13	−12
December	−2	−9	−7
1988: Jan	0	−18	−18
February	−6	−17	−11
March	−11	−24	−13
April	−16	−11	5
May	−9	−8	1
June	−11	−13	−2
July	−12	−24	−12
August	−4	−35	−31
September	−5	−29	−24
October	1	−23	−24
November	−5	−29	−24
December	−6	−36	−30
1989: Jan	−7	−32	−25
February	−11	−30	−19
March	−15	−30	−15
April	−13	−24	−11
May	−13	−17	−4
June	−19	−13	6
July	−25	−12	13
August	−24	−15	9
September	−23	−13	10
October	−29	3	32
November	−35	−4	31
December	−31	−1	30
1990: Jan	−29	−5	24
February	−36	−7	29
March	−47	−5	42
April	−49	−5	44
May	−43	−10	33
June	−40	−11	29
July	−35	−8	27
August	−31	−9	22
September	−30	−1	29
October	−32	3	35
November	−43	−10	33
December	22	−24	−46

continued

	Thatcher/Major	Kinnock	Kinnock Lead
1991: Jan	29	−16	−45
February	40	−12	−52
March	32	−15	−47
April	25	−20	−45
May	15	−14	−29
June	11	−12	−23
July	15	−16	−31
August	18	−18	−36
September	21	−21	−42
October	16	−11	−27
November	12	−18	−30
December	10	−23	−33
1992: Jan	7	−24	−31
February	6	−23	−29
March	2	−19	−21

Source: Crewe, Norris, Denver and Broughton (ed), 1992 and Gallup Political Index

lead Britain? Perhaps one measure that might be considered here is whether Kinnock was seen as a potential Prime Minister.

Table 5.3 shows the ratings of Neil Kinnock and Margaret Thatcher as the best person for Prime Minister between October 1987 and October 1990 and of Major and Kinnock since then. There is a clear contrast between this table and the earlier statistics we have examined.

The May 1989 improvement seen in the two other sets of statistics is nowhere near as prominent here. Kinnock still languished well behind Thatcher as 'the best person for Prime Minister' until January 1990 and failed to achieve a substantial and sustained lead over Thatcher, even during her lowest ebbs of popularity. The swing back to the Conservatives following the replacement of Thatcher by Major is, once again, dramatic and immediate.

Figure 5.3 shows that Neil Kinnock's rating as a Prime Minister in preference to Margaret Thatcher was consistently lower than his approval rating relative to Thatcher. From a trough in December 1988 and January 1989, both measures begin to improve; May shows a continuation of this trend, with no great change or acceleration. In fact both measures level out in July before a renewed leap forward in October, around the time of Party Conference.

Another way of considering these variables is through multivariate analysis. All three of the indicators mentioned above: Labour popularity, Kinnock's Prime Ministerial rating and Kinnock's Party Leadership rating, were subjected to separate multivariate analysis using a single lagged endogenous

Table 5.3: Best Person for Prime Minister
Question: Who would make the best Prime Minister?

	Thatcher/Major	Kinnock	Kinnock Lead
1987: Oct	54	23	−31
November	51	25	−26
December	53	24	−29
1988: Jan	53	26	−27
February	53	24	−29
March	39	20	−19
April	40*	20*	−20
May	41*	20*	−21
June	42*	21*	−21
July	43*	21*	−22
August	44*	22*	−23
September	45*	22*	−23
October	46	22	−24
November	48	20	−28
December	45	18	−27
1989: Jan	45	19	−26
February	43	20	−23
March	42	20	−22
April	41	24	−17
May	44	25	−19
June	39	32	−7
July	39	29	−10
August	40	29	−11
September	39	28	−11
October	37	31	−6
November	35	33	−2
December	36	33	−3
1990: Jan	33	34	1
February	33	33	0
March	28	38	10
April	31	32	1
May	28	39	11
June	38	37	−1
July	35	36	1
August	41	35	−6
September	36	35	−1
October	33	38	5
November	43*	31*	−12
December	52	24	−28
1991: Jan	48	28	−20
February	51	24	−27
March	56	23	−33

continued

	Thatcher/Major	Kinnock	Kinnock Lead
April	45	25	−20
May	46	26	−20
June	40	30	−10
July	42	25	−17
August	42	28	−14
September	46	22	−24
October	48	24	−24
November	40	29	−11
December	42	25	−17
1992: Jan	45	23	−22
February	48	22	−26
March	41	25	−16

Source: Crewe, Norris, Denver and Broughton (ed.) 1992 and Gallup Political Index.
Note: * figures interpolated in months when relevant question was not asked.

variable model. For the purposes of this analysis the effects of the Review were tested from the publication of *Meet the Challenge, Make the Change.* As I have suggested above, this was the phase of the Review which those involved seemed to feel had most impact. What justification was there for their beliefs?

Dummy variables were used to test first the immediate effects of the Policy Review, then any effects in following months, and finally other potential explanatory factors were controlled for, particularly aggregate personal expectations. The previous month's ratings were also controlled for throughout.

Table 5.4: Policy Review (PR) Monthly Effect on Labour Popularity (LAB)

Regressor	Coefficient	Standard Error	T-Ratio[Prob]
C	3.3704	2.0364	1.6551[.104]
LAB(-1)	.91735	.049031	18.7098[.000]
PR1(5/89)	2.3528	1.8909	1.2443[.219]
PR2(6/89)	3.5594	1.8878	1.8854[.065]
PR3(7/89)	−1.3514	1.8969	−.71241[.479]
PR4(8/89)	.80813	1.8906	.42746[.671]

Note: Dependent variable is LAB. 58 observations used for estimation from 87M7 to 92M4
Lagrange multiplier test: CHI-SQ(12) = 6.9914[.858]
Ramseys's RESET test: CHI-SQ(1) = 1.0512[.305]
Heteroscedasticity: CHI-SQ(1) = .48804[.485]

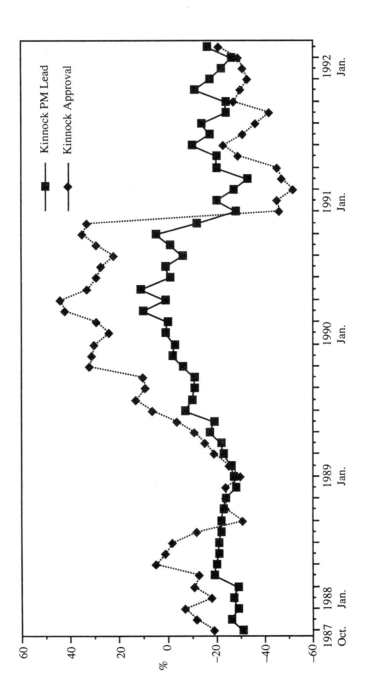

Figure 5.3: Kinnock Approval and Best Prime Minister Leads Oct. 1987 to March 1992

Table 5.4 shows the consequences of adding a series of dummy variables (PR1–PR4) to a simple lagged endogenous variable model of Labour popularity (LAB). The coefficients on PR1 (B=2.35 for May 1989) and PR2 (B=3.55 for June 1989) suggest that Labour popularity did increase by almost 6 percentage points in the spring of 1989. However, neither of these effects was significant at the .05 level and both 'decayed' fairly rapidly (see the discount rate of B=.91 indicated by the coefficient of the lagged endogenous variable, LAB(-1)).

Table 5.5 shows the consequences firstly of retaining only PR2 in the model (on the grounds that it was the only dummy that nearly achieved significance) and, secondly, including a term for personal expectations as suggested by the Essex model (Sanders, Ward and Marsh). As the table shows, when controls for expectations are made, the significance of the PR dummy appears even weaker.

The model suggests, quite simply, that the Policy Review added, at most, 2.5 percentage points to Labour's popularity in the spring of 1989 but that this effect decayed rapidly and had virtually disappeared by the end of the year.

Table 5.5: Policy Review (PR) and Economic Expectations (PEXP) Effect on Labour Popularity (LAB)

Regressor	Coefficient	Standard Error	T-Ratio[Prob]
C	12.7789	2.4285	5.2621[.000]
LAB(-1)	.67358	.061030	11.0369[.000]
PEXP	−.16180	.031402	−5.1526[.000]
PR2	2.4875	1.5618	1.5927[.117]

Note: Dependent variable is LAB. 58 observations used for estimation from 87M7 to 92M4
Lagrange multiplier test: CHI-SQ(12) = 12.5818[.400]
Ramsey's RESET test: CHI-SQ(1) = 1.4224[.233]
Heteroscedasticity: CHI-SQ(1) = .082087[.774]

If the Review failed significantly to affect Labour popularity, what of its effects on public perceptions of the Party leadership? Table 5.6 shows the effects of the Policy Review on the percentage of the electorate that thought Kinnock would make the best Prime Minister. The large and significant coefficient at PR2 indicates that some 7 percentage points rise in Kinnock's ratings in June 1989 might be attributed to the Review. However, this effect then gradually discounted (at a rate of .84 per month) thereafter, and had certainly disappeared by the time of the 1992 General Election.

Table 5.6: Policy Review (PR) Monthly Effect on Kinnock Prime Minister Rating (KINPM)

Regressor	Coefficient	Standard Error	T-Ratio[Prob]
C	3.8593	2.1725	1.7765[.082]
KINPM(-1)	.84376	.079932	10.5560[.000]
PR1(5/89)	.89034	3.3413	.26646[.791]
PR2(6/89)	7.0466	3.3374	2.1114[.040]
PR3(7/89)	−1.8598	3.3637	−.55289[.583]
PR4(8/89)	.67152	3.3410	.20099[.842]
PR5(9/89)	−.32848	3.3410	−.098316[.922]
PR6(10/89)	3.5153	3.3373	1.0533[.298]
PR7(11/89)	2.9840	3.3543	.88961[.378]

Note: Dependent variable is KINPM. 56 observations used for estimation from 87M11 to 92M6
Lagrange multiplier test: CHI-SQ(12) = 14.6657[.260]
Ramsey's RESET test: CHI-SQ(1) = .017397[.895]
Heteroscedasticity: CHI-SQ(1) = 2.6060[.106]

Table 5.7 shows that this effect remains even when the non-significant variables are removed from the model reported in table 5.6.

Table 5.7: Policy Review (PR) Effect on Kinnock Prime Minister Rating (KINPM) After Two Months

Regressor	Coefficient	Standard Error	T-Ratio[Prob]
C	3.8838	2.0709	1.8755[.066]
KINPM(-1)	.84684	.075642	11.1953[.000]
PR2	6.9453	3.2171	2.1589[.035]

Note: Dependent variable is KINPM. 56 observations used for estimation from 87M11 to 92M6
Lagrange multiplier test: CHI-SQ(12) = 9.1113[.693]
Ramsey's RESET test: CHI-SQ(1) = .15691[.692]
Heteroscedasticity: CHI-SQ(1) = 3.3204[.068]

Table 5.8 shows the effects of applying controls for aggregate personal expectations. The results suggest that expectations affected Kinnock's Prime Ministerial rating as well as Labour's popularity. Once these effects are considered, it is clear that the impact of the Policy Review falls even further. In table 5.8 the Review added only 5.7 points to Kinnock's rating in June 1989.

What all of this suggests is that, over and above the negative effects of aggregate personal expectations, the Policy Review did affect Kinnock's PM ratings, temporarily. For at least a time, voters seem to have considered Kinnock as looking more like PM material thanks to the Review and may even have considered Labour's leadership as looking more like a potential Government. Unfortunately, as we saw in relation to tables 5.4 to 5.6, these changes in voters' perceptions of Kinnock did not make them more likely to vote Labour.

Table 5.8: Policy Review (PR) and Economic Expectation (PEXP) Effects on Kinnock Prime Minister Rating (KINPM)

Regressor	Coefficient	Standard Error	T-Ratio[Prob]
C	7.0736	2.1943	3.2236[.002]
KINPM(-1)	.70766	.086193	8.2101[.000]
PEXP	−.13708	.052935	−2.5895[.013]
PR2	5.7271	2.9790	1.9225[.080]

Note: Dependent variable is KINPM. 54 observations used for estimation from 87M11 to 92M4
Lagrange multiplier test: CHI-SQ(12) = 10.4533[.576]
Ramsey's RESET test: CHI-SQ(1) = .078422[.779]
Heteroscedasticity: CHI-SQ(1) = 2.0308[.154]

A different relationship can be seen in our final measure of popularity, Kinnock's rating as Party Leader. As table 5.9 shows, the most significant, and sizable effect occurs not in month two, but in month six. In month six Kinnock's leadership rating improves by a dramatic 17 points, and although the decay is once again rapid (B=.78) the effect continued for some time, though not long enough to affect the outcome of the 1992 General Election. When isolated from the other dummy variables the effect remained broadly unchanged. As table 5.10 shows, however, when personal expectations are controlled for, both the level and significance of the effect diminishes.

Two reservations should be noted with regard to this finding. First, the analysis in tables 5.9 and 5.10 is based on significantly fewer observations – 44 as opposed to 58 for Labour popularity and 56 for Kinnock's PM rating. Second, and more importantly, there is an obvious alternative explanation for the improvement in Neil Kinnock's personal rating. Month six brings the data up to October 1989, the month of Labour Party Conference, and this was a particularly peaceful, amicable, and perhaps successful Conference for the Party leadership. The effect may have been due more to the sense of unity emanating from Labour's Conference rather than the

Review itself, though the Review may have played its part in creating the impression of unity.

Table 5.9: Policy Review (PR) Effect on Kinnock Leadership Rating (KINPL)

Regressor	Coefficient	Standard Error	T-Ratio[Prob]
C	−4.1207	1.8784	−2.1937[.035]
KINPL(-1)	.78527	.10096	7.7783[.000]
PR1(5/89)	5.9673	6.4244	.92885[.359]
PR2(6/89)	4.4704	6.3691	.70189[.487]
PR3(7/89)	2.3293	6.3726	.36552[.717]
PR4(8/89)	−1.4560	6.3774	−.22830[.821]
PR5(9/89)	2.8999	6.3676	.45541[.652]
PR6(10/89)	17.3293	6.3726	2.7194[.010]
PR7(11/89)	−2.2351	6.6368	−.33677[.738]

Note: Dependent variable is KINPL. 44 observations used for estimation from 87M8 to 91M3
Lagrange multiplier test: CHI-SQ(12) = 12.4667[.409]
Ramsey's RESET test: CHI-SQ(1) = .023558[.878]
Heteroscedasticity: CHI-SQ(1) = .020875[.885]

Table 5.10: Policy Review (PR) and Economic Expectation (PEXP) Effect on Kinnock Leadership Rating (KINPL) After Six Months

Regressor	Coefficient	Standard Error	T-Ratio[Prob]
C	−6.4065	1.8351	−3.4912[.001]
KINPL(-1)	.69726	.090634	7.6932[.000]
PEXP	−.21546	.092900	−2.3193[.026]
PR6	13.2998	5.9262	2.2329[.031]

Note: Dependent variable is KINPL. 44 observations used for estimation from 87M8 to 91M3
Lagrange multiplier test: CHI-SQ(12) = 8.9600[.706]
Ramsey's RESET test: CHI-SQ(1) = 1.2282[.268]
Heteroscedasticity: CHI-SQ(1) = 1.0205[.312]

So what does all this tell us? This analysis suggests that the effects of the Policy Review were largely concentrated on Neil Kinnock's personal rating amongst voters, with no significant knock-on effect on Labour's popularity as a whole. Even the effects that the Review had on Kinnock's personal ratings were not consistent. There was an effect on public perceptions about Kinnock's ability to lead the country two months after the publication of the phase two Review documents. It could be argued that this might have resulted from the need for time to absorb the detailed policy statements and their implications before voters could make a calculation on the policy issues involved. However, there is an alternative explanation, and one which I believe makes more sense.

The phase two Review documents were deliberately published early to coincide with the 1989 European Elections. Labour did particularly well in these elections and it seems unlikely that the public had had enough time to absorb the lengthy phase two documents before the elections themselves. The general effect of an apparently successful manoeuvre on the part of the Party leadership, and the press coverage of its improved position following its European electoral success may have presented the Party as clearer contenders for Government. The voters were, therefore, more likely to see Kinnock as a potential Prime Minister, on the back of recent success, and evaluate him accordingly. The effects of the Review were indirectly rather than directly felt. It is also important to note that none of these effects was stable, all show rapid deterioration, and none could have lasted long enough to make a significant impact on the General Election of 1992.

From the perspective of the supporters of the Review the apparent effects were enough to keep hope alive. Firstly, there was the success of the European Elections following closely on the heels of the publication of the phase two reports. Then there was the improvement in Kinnock's rating as a potential Prime Minister the following month, possibly remedying a perceived weakness in Labour's public appeal (Hughes and Wintour, 62). The October Party Conference was peaceful and provided another boost to Kinnock with an improved Party leadership rating, and through all this the Party's general popularity was improving, whilst the Conservatives were going down.

As has been shown, the Party's performance had little to do with the Review, and any Review effects had worn out by 1992. This might help to account for the change in attitude to the Review output, as 1992 approached, which led to the emasculation of the central economic policies published in phase two and the establishment of a 'safer', more conservative alternative, closer to the Government's line and perceived economic orthodoxy.

How can apparent effects on Kinnock's popularity be squared with no apparent effect on the Party as a whole? I would suggest that the public saw the Review as being the creation of the Party leadership, as being intimately associated with Kinnock and his leadership. To some extent this was precisely the intention. Mandelson had said: 'the elements of this ... strategy are democratic constitutional change, reorganisation, policy renewal, and leadership enhancement' (quoted in Hughes and Wintour, 4).

From this perspective the Review might be judged a resounding success. It did enhance Kinnock's position, his role, and his image as Party Leader, and potential Prime Minister, but that is all it did. Why did such an exercise, enhancing the position and image of the Leader, fail to have a significant knock-on effect on the Party's position and image?

A number of possibilities could be suggested. Kinnock personally performed poorly in Labour's private polling before the Review, and the Review might have provided nothing more than a chance to address that weakness and put Kinnock on a par with his opposite number for a while, rather than suggest Kinnock as a better alternative. It might be that voters evaluate Party Leaders and Parties separately and that the style of the Review impressed them with Kinnock's ability to push it through the Party, but that they were less than impressed by its content. A final possibility is that although voters were impressed by the Review and by the presentation of the Party they were less convinced Labour would carry through its proposals in government.

The 1992 General Election

The General Election must be regarded as the ultimate test of the Policy Review's electoral influence because the Review was undertaken with this election in mind. Winning European elections and improving opinion poll ratings are all very well, but in the British political system control of the central government structure remains the real prize.

Parliamentary elections are not confined to General Elections, and a number of by-elections occurred during the period from 1987 to 1990, when the Review might have been having its most significant effect. Details of these by-elections are given in Table 5.11.

It is difficult, and dubious, to draw conclusions from such intermittent data. Nonetheless, Labour's two most impressive victories, at the Vale of Glamorgan and Mid-Staffordshire, both occurred in the year following the publication of the Review's phase two documents. Before this Labour had lost votes on their General Election performance at both Pontypridd and Richmond, a feat not repeated outside of Scotland until the Eastbourne by-election, and there the Liberal Democrats had clearly been the main challengers to the Conservative incumbent in 1987.

For the advocates of the Review, Labour's two gains from the Conservatives in these by-elections were merely further proof of the efficacy of the Review itself and the general revival of the Labour Party under Neil Kinnock. This view was not reflected in the 1992 General Election. However, perhaps the most startling feature of the General Election was not the result itself, but the unprecedented errors in the opinion pollsters' prediction of the outcome.

Table 5.11: Parliamentary By-elections, 1987–1990

By-election Constituency	Date	Voting Shares% Con Change	Lab Change	Result	Final Maj.
Kensington	14/7/88	–5.9	4.9	Con hold	815
Glasgow Govan	10/11/88	–4.6	–27.9	SNP from Lab	3 554
Epping Forest	15/12/88	–21.4	0.3	Con hold	4 504
Pontypridd	32/2/89	–6	–2.9	Lab hold	10 794
Richmond (Yorks)	23/2/89	–24	–6.9	Con hold	2 634
Vale of Glamorgan	4/5/89	–10.5	14.2	Lab from Con	6 028
Glasgow Central	15/6/89	–5.4	–9.9	Lab hold	6 462
Vauxhall	15/6/89	–10.2	2.6	Lab hold	9 766
Mid-Staffordshire	22/3/90	–18.4	24.4	Lab from Con	9 449
Bootle	24/5/90	–11	8.5	Lab hold	23 517
Knowsley South	27/9/90	–6.3	4.3	Lab hold	11 367
Eastbourne	18/10/90	–19	–3.8	Lib Dem from Con	4 550
Bootle	8/11/90	–10.9	11.5	Lab hold	19 465
Bradford North	8/11/90	–22.7	8.9	Lab hold	9 514
Paisley North	29/11/90	–1	–11.5	Lab hold	3 770
Paisley South	29/11/90	–1.3	–10.1	Lab hold	5 030

Source: Crewe, Norris, Denver and Broughton (ed.), 1992.

Table 5.12 shows the error in the final polls of the four major polling organisations. All the polls were conducted in the two days before the General Election, but none managed to get close to the final result. In fact, the consistency and scale of the prediction errors amounted to the worst ever opinion poll performance.

Butler and Kavanagh suggest six possible factors explaining this difference: possible errors in the sampling frame; inaccuracies in the electoral register, perhaps affected by the operation of the Poll Tax; a higher rate of refusal to disclose voting intention amongst Conservative as compared to Labour voters; systematic lying; a greater willingness to turn out and vote amongst Conservative than amongst Labour voters; and a late swing from Conservative to Labour on the day of the election.

Table 5.12: 1992 General Election Final Polls

	Con	Lab	Lib Dem	Other	Con Lead	Error
MORI	38	39	20	2	−1	8.6
NOP	39	42	17	2	−3	10.6
Gallup	38.5	38	20	3.5	0.5	7.1
ICM	38	38	20	4	0	7.6
Result	42.8	35.2	18.3	3.7	7.6	

Source: Butler and Kavanagh 1992

Butler and Kavanagh can only ascribe a total of 5.5 per cent of the possible error to these causes (145). What is more, their analysis does not indicate a committed and enthusiastic electorate. If Conservative voters were more inclined to refuse to admit their voting intentions, but also more inclined to turn out and actually vote than Labour voters it does not suggest any great pride in voting Conservative. Similarly, the failure of those who intended to vote Labour actually to do so does not suggest a great commitment to Labour voting. Any sizable late swing from Labour to the Conservatives reinforces this image of intending Labour voters.

Nor was it just the predictive polls which were wrong, so were the exit polls conducted after voters had actually voted. Whilst the exit polls were certainly closer to the final result the consistency of their error is surprising (Butler and Kavanagh, 145).

Whatever the definitive explanation of the polls' failure, these observations strongly suggest that whichever way people eventually voted in 1992 there was a lack of commitment to, and enthusiasm for, their chosen party. This situation should be more worrying to the party which lost, in this instance Labour, as it clearly indicates a failure to convince the electorate of their electability despite a Government over which the electorate appear to have severe reservations. It might be asked: if the Opposition cannot win under these circumstances when can it win?

In their immediate post-election analysis of two separate surveys both Curtice and King (1992a) discovered impressive swings to the Conservatives on policy issues from the period before the General Election to the period after. Both showed immediate swings on a range of issues, in King's case 14, to the Conservatives. This is reflected in the data reported in table 5.13.

Whilst we might expect a winner's bonus for the Conservatives as people re-evaluate their impressions of the policies which will now be adopted by Government, such a consistent swing in such a short period of time is impressive. It might be suggested that the electorate saw the election, and the Conservative victory, as justifying their beliefs and opinions and legitimising those things for which they actually voted on 9 April 1992, but were not prepared to enthusiastically embrace the day before.

Table 5.13: Pre- and Postelection Survey Findings on Perceptions of Conservative as Preferred to Handle Policy Issues (Conservative preference lead: Conservative 'best' – Labour 'best' %)

	Survey 7–8/4/92	Survey 10–11/4/92	Shift to Con
Environment	–4	5	9
Europe	20	33	13
Transport	–21	–13	8
Taxation	12	20	8
Homelessness	–28	–15	3
Law and Order	12	22	10
Inflation	15	29	14
Unemployment	–22	–16	6
Defence	30	41	11
Strikes	18	27	9
NHS	–25	–17	8
Education	–14	–6	8
Pensions	–18	–9	9
Women	–15	–7	8

Source: Sanders, 1992; Gallup.

Both before and after the General Election, the Conservatives fared better on economic issues, inflation, taxation and strikes, and Labour fared better on 'caring' and social issues, unemployment, health, pensions and homelessness. At the end of the day it appears that the economic issues were the more important factor.

The election result itself also provides some food for thought. The first observation that needs to be made is that Labour's current electoral task is far greater than it would at first appear. This becomes clear when we compare Labour's percentage vote with the number of seats won.

From these figures we can see that, despite polling 7.5 per cent more of the vote than Labour, the Conservatives were left with a small overall majority. Curtice and Steed calculate that it would have taken just 1,233 voters in 11 marginal constituencies to have changed their mind for the Conservatives to have lost their overall majority (Curtice and Steed, 351).

Table 5.14: Percentage Votes Received and Seats Won Oct. 1974–1992

	Con. Vote %	Seats	Lab. Vote %	Seats	Lib., etc. Vote %	Seats
Oct						
1974	35.8	277	39.2	319	18.3	13
1979	43.9	339	37	269	13.8	11
1983	42.4	397	27.6	209	25.4	23
1987	42.3	376	30.8 ´	229	22.6	22
1992	41.9	336	34.4	271	17.8	20

Source: Butler and Kavanagh 1992

The extent to which this misrepresents Labour's position is nowhere better illustrated than in Curtice and Steed's own comments.

> The 1992 election was a disaster for the Labour Party. They were as much as 7.6% of the vote (in Great Britain) behind the Conservatives, making it the fourth election in a row at which Labour were 7% or more behind the Conservatives. The last four results stand in stark contrast to those of the 1950–74 period. Then the most by which Labour trailed the Conservatives was by 4.2% in 1959. Only once did any election see a lead larger than 5% for the winning party – in 1966 when Labour led by 7.5%.
>
> Yet so far as seats in the House of Commons are concerned, the outcome was relatively close. The Conservatives won just 336 seats, sufficient to give them an overall majority of 21. This is a smaller majority than that secured by the Conservatives in 1955, 1959 or 1970 – or indeed by Labour in 1966. The only postwar Conservative government to have enjoyed a smaller majority was Winston Churchill's in 1951. But the Conservatives won 1.6% less of the vote in Great Britain than did Labour.
>
> The election result therefore presents a major paradox. How could a result that was so substantial in terms of votes appear so close in terms of seats? (Curtice and Steed, 322)

One point is obvious in these comments and the above figures. Any belief that Labour has been made 'electable' by the Policy Review, or anything else, is unsustainable. Labour is still in deep electoral trouble.

Labour managed to get so close in terms of seats, when they were still so distant in the percentage vote as a result of a unique aspect to the 1992 election: its proportionality. This was observed by Curtice immediately after the election. Labour received a higher proportion of seats than its percentage vote merited, within the British electoral system; but if we exclude the Liberal Democrats and the Scottish Nationalists (SNP), the distribution of seats between the two main parties was almost identical to the proportion of the vote won by each.

Table 5.15: Seats and Votes Won 1992

| | All Parties (UK) | | Excluding Lib Dem and SNP | |
	% Votes	% Seats	% Votes	% Seats
Conservative	41.9	51.6	52.2	53.5
Labour	34.2	41.6	42.6	43.2
Liberal	1.9	3.1		
SNP	1.9	0.5		
Others	4.1	3.2	5.1	3.3

Source: Curtice/The Guardian 1992

This proportionality of the 1992 election, and the failure of Britain's first-past-the-post system to award its traditional winner's bonus of extra seats to the Conservatives, was a surprising and unprecedented aspect of this election. It resulted from a differential marginal swing, as Curtice and Steed have pointed out (Curtice and Steed, 332).

Curtice and Steed attribute this phenomenon partly to the geographical concentration of marginal seats in regions where Labour did particularly well, though it must be asked whether Labour did particularly well in these regions because they did well in the marginals, or well in the marginals because they were in these regions.

However, one of the most important aspects of this swing was that it was disproportional, thus creating the elections proportionality:

[The marginal swing] was not concentrated in those seats where it would have most effect. Amongst those seats where Labour started off within 8% of the Conservatives the swing was –3.9%, whereas in those where they were between 8 and 16% behind the swing was –5.5%. Indeed, the swing was highest of all (–6.3%) in those seats where Labour were more than 16% behind the Conservatives and which were thus not apparently marginal at all. (Curtice and Steed, 333)

The implications of this disproportionate marginal swing on the ground are perhaps most easily illustrated by considering two constituencies, Norwich North and Ipswich, in the same geographical region. In Norwich North

Labour failed to win the seat by a few hundred votes on a swing of 7.6 per cent, whilst in Ipswich Labour squeaked home in one of the most marginal seats in the country on a swing of just 1.1 per cent.

Whilst it would be stupid to read too much into the results in two constituencies, the patterns pointed to by Curtice and Steed suggest that these trends were being repeated throughout the country. Labour was achieving a greater swing in the least marginal constituencies, and a lesser swing in the most marginal.

Table 5.16: Differential Voting in Norwich North and Ipswich 1992

	Con.	Change	Lab.	Change	Lib Dem	Change	Swing
Norwich North	43.3	–2.6	42.8	12.6	12.9	–11	–7.6
Ipswich	43.3	–1.1	43.8	1.1	11.4	–1.2	–1.1

Source: Butler and Kavanagh 1992

There may be many reasons for this differential swing to Labour, In the case of Ipswich and Norwich North it might be noted that Labour's advantage in the Norwich seat stemmed mainly from a squeeze on the Liberal Democrats which brought their vote close to that already existing in Ipswich. The point here is not to provide a definitive explanation of the pattern of voting on 9 April 1992, but rather to see what these patterns might tell us about the defects of the Policy Review's electoral strategy.

Once again, these figures do not suggest a positive Labour vote. Rather, as Curtice and Steed argue (332–7), they imply tactical voting for Labour on the part of the electorate; that is a vote which is against the Conservatives and not for Labour. Even so, the electorate is only prepared to vote tactically up to a point. The Liberal Democrat vote was less easy to squeeze for potential tactical defectors where it was lowest, in other words in precisely the seats where Labour was likely to be closest to the Conservatives.

If these observations are correct then a number of points follow. The first is that this vote can hardly be regarded as solid. Just as Labour gained votes not because of its popularity but because of Conservative unpopularity, it could see them disappear as rapidly should the Conservatives' fluctuating popularity pick up, however briefly, or should another challenger appear more credible. Secondly, tactical voting has not brought Labour electoral victory. It may have provided it with an unusually close-run thing in seats on the proportion of votes won, but it did not bring overall success and may well not be repeated at a future election.

Perhaps what should give Labour most cause for reflection is the thought of whether a government elected on the back of such a highly negative vote would have any authority to tackle the radical programme Labour claimed was needed and claimed to have provided in the Policy Review. The one thing that the 1992 General Election demonstrated was that if the Conservatives are an unpopular Government, Labour was even less popular as a replacement.

What part did the Policy Review play in all of this? It appears that, to the extent that it continued to have any electoral effect at all by 1992, its effects were largely to make Labour appear less beyond the pale to potential Liberal Democratic defectors than was the case previously. What the Review emphatically did not do was to rejuvenate Labour's positive constituency. That is to say, the Policy Review and Labour's electoral strategy in 1992 managed to persuade electors to turn to them as a potential alternative to the Conservatives, but not as a party in their own right.

The 1992 General Election was essentially about the Conservative Party, Conservative policies and Conservative government; Labour gained because the Conservatives were unpopular. The alternatives to the Conservatives were seen not in the light of their own strengths, but in the light of Conservative weaknesses. All Labour can claim for the Review is that it put fewer people off voting Labour than in 1983 and 1987.

This is reflected in another measure of public perceptions of the Labour Party, perceptions of Party 'extremism'. Table 5.17 shows responses to a Gallup poll question which asked respondents their reactions to the statement that: 'Labour has become too extreme'.

These figures show a massive jump from a rating of Labour as somewhat extreme to a far more moderate rating between April and September 1989, the period of the publication of the phase two reports, and the period of interest to us here. This said, it must also be observed that these figures do not lend themselves to the same kind of statistical analysis we have undertaken with the measures of Labour popularity and public perception of Neil Kinnock. This is because the observations are both small in number and very irregular.

It certainly appears that the Review had an effect in convincing the public that Labour had become less 'extreme'. This view forms the basis of Heath and Jowell's analysis of the effects of the Review on Labour's image (Heath and Jowell, 202). Considering BES data for the General Elections of 1983, 1987 and 1992, they claim that perceptions of Labour were substantially the same between 1983 and 1987, but showed dramatic improvement to 1992. The Gallup data reported above provides a more complete, and complex, picture. Perceptions of Labour 'extremism' had been improving since the 1987 General Election, and with the exception of the 1987 General Election period itself, for some time before that. This might be the result of the public perception of the realignment of the Party firstly under Michael Foot, and then under Neil Kinnock. The Review could have been perceived as a product of that realignment.

Table 5.17: Perception of Labour as 'Extreme', 1983–93

Date	Agree(a) %	Disagree(b) %	a–b
Nov, 1983	60	31	29
Jan, 1984	62	26	36
May, 1984	58	34	24
Sept, 1984	62	28	34
Jan, 1985	65	27	38
Apr, 1985	57	34	23
Sept, 1985	59	33	26
Jan, 1986	60	30	30
Apr, 1986	57	34	23
Sept, 1986	49	44	5
Jan, 1987	53	37	16
Apr, 1987	67	24	43
Sept, 1987	56	35	21
Sept, 1988	49	44	5
Apr, 1989	48	40	8
Sept, 1989	29	61	−32
Sept, 1990	28	61	−33
Jun, 1991	31	61	−30
Aug, 1991	35	55	−20
Jan, 1992	35	57	−22
Apr, 1993	21	65	−44

Source: Gallup

Whilst this, in itself, may be a desirable result, a democratic system which depends on the prospects of one Party, with an Opposition apparently incapable of winning positive support for a distinctive programme of its own, hardly appears to provide the electorate with real choice. The message of the 1992 election for Labour appears to be that they are currently a weak and inadequate party whose apparent electoral gains may well prove more illusory than real.

Conclusion

Examining the results of the 1992 General Election it is difficult to escape the conclusion that as an electoral strategy the Policy Review was a failure. Certainly, if its intentions were to help Labour rebuild its constituency by increasing the proportion of the electorate who are Labour Party identifiers and who see the Labour Party as their Party, there is no evidence from 1992 to suggest any positive results. Indeed, the data suggests quite the opposite. Labour's vote in 1992 appears to have been overwhelmingly negative, aimed at bringing the Conservative Government to an end. The 1992 Labour voter seems to have been less interested in bringing a Labour Government about.

Heath and Jowell disagree with this view, claiming that the Review was in large part responsible for the improvements Labour achieved in 1992 (Heath and Jowell). Nonetheless they raise substantial doubts about the ability of this kind of electoral strategy to achieve the gains Labour now needs to obtain electoral victory. Basing their analysis on the belief that the Review was intended to move Labour's policies towards the centre of British politics, they observe:

> Heath and Paulson have estimated that, according to the Hotelling/Downs model of rational voting, Labour would have gained only 5 percentage points even if it had moved as far as it reasonably could towards the centre. (Heath and Jowell, 206)

Ignoring the possible effects of a more dramatic shift towards the centre by Labour on the Party itself, it would appear that if this was the Party's objective in the Review it was doomed to failure. Moreover, Heath and Jowell's analysis suggests that such a strategy, by itself, could not bring victory at the next General Election either.

This all seems a far cry from the initial launch of the first substantial product of the Review, *Meet the Challenge, Make the Change,* in 1989. Then Labour's polling figures immediately improved and so did Labour's electoral fortunes both in the European elections of that year and in subsequent by-elections. It appeared to supporters of the Review that the electoral corner had perhaps been turned and Labour had persuaded the electorate of its electability.

The Review had attempted not only to provide a new set of policies for Labour, conveniently ditching perceived vote losers along the way, but was also intended to present a new image for Labour. It aimed to provide an image of a Party with a strong, determined and skilful leadership, yet in touch with the people; a Party distancing itself from its redundant past and providing itself with a new direction and meaning.

Both the structure and the content of the Review concentrated on those areas of policy which were perceived as having particular electoral relevance. Economic policy was a main focus because of the perceived need to move away from Labour's concentration on nationalisation and towards market solutions, and because the economy was seen as particularly important electorally, a view apparently reinforced by the 1992 election results. Beyond this the Review concentrated on perceived electoral weaknesses, such as defence and foreign policy, and on developing policy in potentially vote winning areas, such as the environment.

In all this the Review was much more than simply a vehicle for introducing new policies or getting rid of old ones. The Review itself contained a message for the electorate. It wasn't just what Labour was doing that was important, but the way it was being done. It is not a coincidence that those who saw Neil Kinnock's leadership as creating a 'new model party' looked mainly to the workings of the Review for their evidence (Hughes and Wintour).

So why did the Review appear to have such a significant effect in 1989, but such a reduced effect by 1992? The first thing to say is that it is by no means clear that the initial improvements in Labour's polling and electoral fortunes in 1989 were wholly or substantially due to the Review. The Conservative Government had their own problems, over Europe and the Poll Tax, and were presiding over an economy in decline. The significance of these problems, and their association with Margaret Thatcher is reflected in the dramatic change in polling fortunes on her replacement by John Major in December 1990.

It should also be remembered that Labour polled consistently higher in the 1992 election campaign than its eventual vote. When it came to voting for a government the British electorate was not as prepared to commit itself to Labour as the opinion polls suggested. This was also reflected in the personal ratings of Neil Kinnock in 1989 and 1990. Although he was much more approved of than Margaret Thatcher, there were not many who were prepared to reflect this in their willingness to see him as preferable as Prime Minister.

Nonetheless, many of Labour's improvements in this period can be traced back to the publication of the phase two Review reports in May 1989, timed to coincide with the European election campaigns. It is at least plausible that the initial favourable reaction to Labour's Review was a factor in these improvements, so why were they not sustained?

The first factor here is the timing of the Review. The Review was intended to contribute to a Labour election campaign and a Labour manifesto in 1991, the earliest possible date at which the Labour leadership thought the Conservatives might go to the polls. In the event the election did not come until April 1992 and the Review may simply have run out of steam by this stage.

Another possibility is that the electorate became disenchanted with the Review and its contents as they became more aware of what it actually contained. This is a very difficult argument to disprove, but one problem with it is that the content of the Review itself changed over time. By the time Labour's General Election manifesto was written the economic policies it contained bore little resemblance to those contained within *Meet the Challenge,*

Make the Change (see chapter 4). This presents another possibility, that the electorate was less inclined to support Labour's policies contained in the manifesto than it was those in the earlier Review documents.

The changes in policy over time were intended to eradicate policies and approaches which were perceived as vote losers and to introduce policies which were believed to be more acceptable to the electorate on the basis of Labour's private polling and survey data. Could it be that Labour got it so wrong as to actually move away from vote winning policies and towards policies which eventually cost them the election?

Again this is an argument which it would be difficult to disprove. However, it seems unlikely that many in the electorate would have been aware of the detailed changes in Labour's policies over time, or would have spent time reading the lengthy phase two reports in the first place. What the electorate may have been aware of, through press coverage and Conservative attacks, was that Labour's policy was changing and that the Review had not provided a firm foundation to future policy in the way intended.

In other words it may not have been the policy changes in the Review themselves which put Labour voters off, but what these changes said about the other electoral messages contained in the Review. Establishing a comprehensive set of policies which are then whittled away over the years does not seem the action of a strong leadership, but rather one which is unsure of its position and uncertain what stance it should take up. Similarly if the Review reflected a Labour Party listening to its supporters and voters, what did that say about the changes after its publication? Was Labour really prepared to stand by what its supporters wanted, or would it renege on its policies as previous Labour Governments had done?

Moreover, the ability and willingness of Labour to tinker with, indeed to change wholesale, the initial policies of the Review did not suggest that Labour was either more reliable than it had been in the past, or that it had clearly established a new direction and meaning for itself. The fact is that these changes exposed the pragmatic heart of the Labour Party, and of the Review, and showed the Review to be little more than an exercise in winning votes, to which the Party and its leadership only appeared committed in order to, and to the extent that it did, win votes.

In other words it is Labour's very pragmatic history and philosophy which has stimulated the mistrust of the electorate. Unless Labour is able to shake off this mistrust and establish a clear, principled alternative to the current philosophy of Conservatism it will be electorally dependent on an anti-Conservative, rather than a pro-Labour, electorate. This, it must be said, hardly seems a great basis for governing a country with the developing problems of the British state.

Part 2:
Beyond the Policy Review:
The Move to Modernisation

6 The Commission on Social Justice

Introduction

*ditched old policy
but didn't offer new
use*

After the 1992 General Election the Party was left with a problem. The Policy Review had been widely perceived as an excellent mechanism for ridding the Party of embarrassing policy commitments, such as unilateral nuclear disarmament, but less effective at providing a positive agenda for a future Labour government (Seyd, 1992, 85). In particular the Party's taxation policy was seen as an electoral weakness serving to alienate 'middle income' voters.

To have repeated the exercise of the 1987–92 period would have served to underline the failure of the Review and would have been restricted by all the limitations of the process which had been clear first time around, besides which the Party was now faced with a leadership election following the resignation of Neil Kinnock as Party Leader immediately after the General Election. Clearly the new incumbent would want to stamp a distinctive identity on the Party rather than relying on the approaches of predecessors.

Ahead of the contenders on this score was Bryan Gould, who was proposing a number of distinctive policy options and had strong views on future policy directions. In contrast John Smith's appeal was based on his managerial competence. He was seen as providing a 'safe pair of hands' not policy dynamism. Smith's advisors were concerned with creating a means for providing a positive policy platform which Smith could then advance to counter Gould's appeal.

Fortunately a model for an alternative means of policy discussion already existed in the form of the Plant Commission. The Plant Commission had been created by the Party a year or so before the General Election to consider the issue of proportional representation. The Plant Commission was intended to allow deeper consideration of a complex issue, notably with regard to the benefits of alternative systems of proportional representation, and to remove this debate from the pressures and tensions of policy-making within the Party. This had been achieved by setting up the Commission independently of the Party and with a membership predominantly from individuals not actively involved in the Party. In fact, as an independent body, it was even able to invite membership and contributions from Liberal Democrats.

Following this model some of Smith's advisors argued that proposals for a Commission on tax and benefits policy would boost Smith's leadership campaign. Robin Cook suggested that this should be broadened to a Commission on Social Justice, thereby tying it to a crucial concept within the Policy Review process and suggesting a continuation with the reformism of Neil Kinnock's leadership. One catch still remained: whilst the Plant Commission had attracted little publicity, and anyway fed into an existing and long-standing debate, a Commission on Social Justice would be far more visible, particularly if it undertook widespread consultation. How could such a Commission be created yet remain obviously independent of the Labour Party?

The solution was to invite the Institute for Public Policy Research (IPPR) to create and oversee the work of the Commission. It was believed that this would allow a more open, less restrained debate, whilst also allowing Labour to distance itself from any contentious proposals which emerged. Crucial to this model was the existence and work of the IPPR which itself had been created during the Policy Review period and was, to some extent, a product of the changes of this time.

The Institute for Public Policy Research

Through the period of the Review only one organisation associated with the Labour Party proved capable of providing an effective debating platform for themes raised by the Review. This was the Fabian Society (see chapter 3). Whilst other groups which might have provided such a platform existed, all were limited and of dubious utility. Whilst some internal pressure groups undoubtedly promoted useful debate on single issues, there was no organisation with a wider scope to examine the broad policy outlook, other than the Fabian Society. For many associated directly with the Labour Party or with the wider political left, this was unacceptable. It certainly appeared in sharp contrast to the Conservative Party which could call on the services of the Adam Smith Institute, the Institute for Economic Affairs, the Centre for Policy Studies, or any of a number of other groups for the discussion, and floating for public reaction, of policy options.

The view that a 'think tank' of the left was needed grew. As Tom Sawyer, the originator of the Policy Review itself, observed:

> The Tory Party contracts out their policy-making to [external] organisations ... Nobody in the Labour Party would suggest this, but they have an important role that has to be understood and accepted by the Party. (Sawyer, 11)

The creation of the Institute for Public Policy Research (IPPR), in 1988–9, was the result. Amongst its founder members was former Kinnock advisor, and later one of Labour's 1992 General Election team, Patricia Hewitt.

The precise relationship between the IPPR and the Labour Party has proved uncertain. So far the IPPR has provided a base for discussions and debates for a variety of policy issues of interest to the left. This has resulted in a number of reports exploring alternative options in policy areas. The IPPR's publication policy has not been determined by the concerns of the Labour Party, and they have been prepared to publish work clearly at odds with established Party policy.

The Commission on Social Justice (CSJ) was something of a departure, involving a closer association with the Labour Party than was the case before. This, and the related discussions on the role of the left (Miliband, 1995), provided a potential model for the future of the IPPR which would clearly mark it out from internal Party organisations like the Fabian Society. The future of the IPPR and its relationship to the Party may be influenced by the impact of the CSJ report on Party policy, and the interest of the Party's current leadership in pursuing semi-independent discussion of policy issues.

The Commission on Social Justice

The independence of the Commission was a condition of IPPR involvement in the project. This fitted in well with John Smith's own intentions and Smith's personal involvement was limited to agreeing the terms of reference and membership of the Commission with IPPR and the initial launch. Following this initial set-up the Commission ran itself.

A 16-strong membership was agreed, under the chairmanship of Sir Gordon Borrie. The most obvious bias was an academic one with six of the Commission coming from this background. None of the Commission represented current Party interests, though there were one or two former Party insiders, notably Hewitt herself who became Deputy Chair. Margaret Wheeler, UNISON's Director of Organisation Development, represented the only trade union involvement. Other places were occupied by representatives from the Asian Resource Centre in Birmingham, the Royal Association for Disability and Rehabilitation, and the Low Pay Unit, a Fellow of the British Psychological Society, the Chairman of Northern Foods, an economist from the Institute for Fiscal Studies and the Very Reverend John Gladwin providing a religious perspective (CSJ, 1994, x–xi).

There was clearly an attempt to create a 'balanced' membership, that is to say one which did not reinforce perceptions of labour movement bias. The lack of substantial trade union representation, the inclusion of a respected clerical figure, representation from an ethnic group, and from 'enlightened' business demonstrated the concern to move away from any class-based approach and to promote the idea that the Commission represented 'all the people'. The academic representation was presumably intended to provide intellectual authority and legitimacy to the final product, whilst the inclusion of an economist from the Institute of Fiscal Studies addressed Labour's concerns over its taxation policy.

The terms of reference for the Commission, agreed between John Smith and the IPPR, set a clear framework for the Commission's work. As with the Policy Review, social justice was unequivocally linked to 'the economic well-being of individuals', and the Commission was charged with the responsibility of looking at the relationship between social justice and 'other goals, including economic competitiveness and prosperity' (CSJ, 1994, 412). The terms of reference gave the Commission a flavour distinctly similar to the Policy Review, charging it to consider changes in economic and social life in the last 50 years, and to analyse public policy on employment, taxation and social welfare with regard to allowing individuals to live free from want, to enjoy the fullest possible opportunities, and to the creation of a fairer and more just society (ibid.). Whilst this framework did not necessarily prevent the Commission from exploring wider economic and social issues, given the mainstream membership of the Commission it is probably not surprising that the terms of reference were interpreted in this fashion. This, in effect, meant that the Commission accepted uncritically the economic and social framework on which postwar British governments had operated.

The Commission was charged with considering 'the principles of social justice', 'the relationship between social justice and other goals', 'the failure of public policy to reflect [social and economic change]', 'the demands the[se changes] will place on government', to 'analyse public policies', and 'to examine the contribution which such policies could make to the creation of a fairer and more just society' (ibid.). The Commission was therefore faced with the task of considering the policies existing government structures could adopt and what demands these would make of existing structures. Given the failures of the Policy Review, and of traditional Labour Party approaches to consider the inadequacies of the British state as a mechanism to address social inequality, this was crucial to the Commission's deliberation.

The final contribution of the terms of reference to the work of the Commission was to provide a historical dimension. Not only was the Commission asked to 'probe' social and economic changes 'over the last fifty years', but also 'to survey the changes that are likely in the foreseeable future' (ibid.). Of course the period chosen was far from accidental, considering that changes since the Second World War provided a neat political opportunity for the Commission's report to be presented as a timely update of the principles of the Beveridge Report, in much the same way that the Conservative Government had presented their market-based reforms of social security and the National Health Service. Another benefit was that it, once again, restricted the work of the Commission to traditional Labour Party approaches, identified with the changes introduced under Clement Attlee's postwar Labour Government. Any interest in considering the earlier lessons of the interwar period, or those of the last century, and in comparing Keynesian economic and Beveridge style social welfare approaches with earlier market systems was, therefore, abandoned. As a result the perceived failings of the postwar Keynesian system were examined in isolation.

Much of the direction in which the Commission was led by its terms of reference bore resemblance to the workings and approaches adopted in the Policy Review. This resemblance was carried into other areas of the Commission's work: submissions and consultations, the structure of the report, and its conclusions.

The work of the Commission can be divided into four broad phases. In the first a small number of individuals formulated a framework within which the Commission could operate, providing both a process of consultation and a timetable. The second involved the Commission in the discussion of the nature of the concept 'social justice' and can be roughly equated with the ideological aspects of the Policy Review. The third phase divided the Commission into three panels, akin to the policy review groups, in which substantive discussion of policy options, consultation and initial drafting took place. The full Commission continued to meet occasionally during this period to provide an overview of developments. The final phase brought the panels back together for final drafting and publication, and might be seen as similar to the final phase of the Policy Review leading up to the 1992 manifesto.

The first phase acted as a preliminary to the convening of the Commission. Patricia Hewitt, David Miliband and the Commission's two researchers set out the framework for the Commission's work. They decided on the objectives for the Commission to meet and then, with the help of a process designer, formulated the means of meeting these objectives whilst involving the greatest number of people possible. The objectives set for the Commission in this process phase, and later reflected in the terms of reference, were to provide a vision of Britain's future, an idea of how to obtain this vision, and to formulate the policies necessary to take Britain in that direction.

The success of this preliminary work, and the process tree which emerged from it, was reflected in the fact that in about 18 months the Commission published 2 interim reports, 13 discussion papers, an income distribution poster, and produced a video; conducted 11 'outreach visits'; and received written and oral submissions from over 400 sources, not counting the consultations conducted within the Labour and Liberal parties and amongst the trade unions (CSJ, 1994, 400–18). The problem for the Commission, as with the Review, was how to assimilate this volume and variety of information.

Submissions and Consultations

Written and oral submissions were received from academics, interest groups, business, MPs, educational and other institutes, and individuals. In addition the Commission distributed a number of consultation papers and a discussion pack, created with the help of the Trade Union Education Department in Manchester, to Labour and Liberal Democratic Party branches, trade unions, and community groups. This built on the experience of the Policy Review and provided a structured response to key questions facing the Commission. This allowed the Commission to receive responses which were targeted at the issues they were considering and in a format that could be easily digested. On the other hand, the questions addressed, and to some extent the structure of the answers received, were set by the Commission itself. Furthermore the responses to this consultation were collective in nature, the questionnaires becoming the subject of branch discussion and agreed reply. This meant that the character of the response was often still difficult to interpret.

Given the number of academics on the Commission it was likely that submissions from academics, and to a lesser extent those of pressure groups, businesses and MPs, were more likely to be speaking the same language. Those of ordinary members and individuals were unlikely to be informed by the same debates and concerns. To this extent the Commission shared the problems of the Review in consulting ordinary individuals. However, whereas the Review's *Labour Listens* campaign proved little more than a cosmetic public relations exercise, the Commission's 'outreach visits' proved far more influential.

The 'outreach visits' may have been intended as an attempt to demonstrate the Commission's desire to reach beyond the confines of the politically involved and of the South East. Whether or not they were intended as essentially a public relations exercise, the 'outreach visits' made a big impression on the Commission members. This was particularly true of the first 'outreach visit' to the Easterhouse estate in Glasgow in February 1993. Whilst the Commission members were well aware of the statistics and theories of deprivation and poverty in Britain, this firsthand experience of the lives of estate dwellers provided a significant culture shock, one which remained with the Commission through their deliberations. It also invested the evidence of the community action group Family Action in Rogerfield and Easterhouse (FARE) with particular weight. The message the Commission took from this first 'outreach visit' was that these individuals did not want open-ended state support, but wanted the resources to provide for themselves. This was translated by the Commission as a desire to see state-sponsored employment rather than a more radical challenge to the involvement of the state in the lives of individuals.

This consultation process was conducted by the three panels, coordinated at monthly meetings of the full Commission. The three panels covered Services and Communities, Money and Wealth, and Work and Wages. Membership of these panels was largely self-selecting with Commission members simply opting for the panel to which they felt most closely aligned. The panels conducted their own consultation, and digested the consultation responses. Initial drafts were brought together in the panels and, eventually, these were amalgamated in the final stage.

The final restriction on the nature of submissions and consultations was that they were based on the published work of the Commission to that point. These related to a philosophical discussion of the nature of social justice (CSJ, 1993a), an analysis of social and economic change (CSJ, 1993b), or various discussion documents considering specific policies related to this discussion (CSJ, 1994, 413–4). The Commission, by its nature, was unable to provide a finished product for critical analysis until the report was published. This meant that at least one academic who submitted a written report to the Commission later criticised its overall structure and assumptions (Townsend).

The Concept of Social Justice

However, before the consultation phase the Commission turned its attention to the nature of social justice. This second phase of the Commission's work had two main objectives. The first was to provide the Commission with a working idea of its central organising theme; the second, and equally important, was to provide a confidence-building mechanism for the Commission members. This was necessary not just because the Commission membership needed a better understanding of each other, but also because of the suspicion amongst some members of the Commission that they might be used to provide a front for promoting policies favoured by the Labour Party leadership, and John Smith in particular.

This phase owed a great deal to the contribution of Professor Bernard Williams, and resulted in the publication of an interim report (CSJ, 1993a) and formed the introduction of the report itself (CSJ, 1994, 15–22). The introduction summarised the discussion of the earlier interim document, *The Justice Gap*, as defining social justice 'in terms of a hierarchy of four ideas' (CSJ, 1994, 17):

> First, the belief that the foundations of a free society is the equal worth of all citizens, expressed most basically in political and civil liberties, equal rights before the law, and so on. Second, the argument that everyone is entitled, as a right of citizenship, to be able to meet their basic needs for income, shelter and other necessities. ... Third, self-respect and equal citizenship demand more than the meeting of basic needs: they demand opportunities and life chances. ... Finally, to achieve the first three conditions of social justice, we must recognize that although not all inequalities are unjust ... , unjust inequalities should be reduced and where possible eliminated. (CSJ, 1994, 17–18)

The question-begging nature of these ideas, for example over what basic needs actually means, was tackled through the further explanation included in the introduction and the creation of 'four propositions on social justice', which were intended to bridge the gap between the concept of social justice formulated by the Commission and the need for a pragmatic guide for government. These will be considered below, but it is worth spending a little time considering the 'hierarchy of ideas' outlined above.

The approach of the Commission represents a departure from that of the Policy Review regarding social justice inasmuch as it gives priority to political and civil rights. The Review defined social justice in economic terms, albeit linking economic equality to the pragmatic interests of efficiency (see chapter 2). In fact, although the Commission sees certain economic rights as guarantees for political and civil rights, it too links economic equality with pragmatic considerations:

> One important question is how far such a vision of social justice can coexist with economic success, or even with economic survival, in a competitive world. Social justice is indeed an ideal in its own right, but we believe in addition that the economic success of our country requires a greater measure of social justice. ...
> At the same time, it is also true that we cannot have social justice without a decent measure of economic success. (CSJ, 1994, 18)

In this approach the Commission manages to compound the problems faced by the Review over this issue. Firstly, what comprises 'economic success' is neither discussed nor defined. Instead, existing measures of 'success' such as growth rates are generally taken for granted. Secondly, the comments regarding the importance of 'economic success' to the creation of social justice provide a real dilemma. What comes first: social justice or economic success? Is it necessary to curtail social justice in order to obtain 'success'? If so exactly what level of social justice, if any, should be regarded as a minimum? Finally, the point made earlier regarding the Policy Review needs to be repeated here. If social justice is necessary for 'economic success' then the presence or absence of social justice is an empirical matter. If there is 'economic success' then there is social justice, but this comes back to the first point: what is 'economic success'?

This problem is not helped by the failure of the Commission's 'hierarchy of ideas' to define minimum standards provided by 'basic needs'. Nor is the concept of 'equal worth' defined or defended, and consequent ideas such as 'self-respect and equal citizenship' are presumably deemed to flow from it without any need for elaboration. In fact, the Commission's defence of inequalities is itself crucially undefined and fails to identify the criteria for determining what represents 'just' inequalities.

The Commission used their 'hierarchy of ideas' as a basis for 'four propositions on social justice':

1. We must transform the welfare state from a safety net in times of trouble to a springboard for economic opportunity. Paid work for a fair wage is the most secure and sustainable way out of poverty.
2. We must radically improve access to education and training, and invest in the talent of all our people.
3. We must promote real choices across the life-cycle in the balance of employment, family, education, leisure and retirement.
4. We must reconstruct the social wealth of our country. Social institutions, from the family to local government, must be nurtured to provide a dependable social environment in which people can lead their lives. Renewal must come from the bottom up as well as the top down. (CSJ, 1994, 20–1)

What is striking about these four propositions is how easily they fit with the priorities of the Policy Review. As was shown in chapter 4, education and training policies were given particular prominence in the Review, new policies to provide 'pathways out of poverty' and new opportunities 'across the life-cycle' were presented, as was the need for employment to be one of these pathways, and all of this was seen as contributing to the country's social wealth. This is a little surprising considering the fact that this phase of the Commission was designed to build confidence amongst the Commission members that there was no hidden agenda which Labour's leadership was attempting to use the Commission as a front to promote. If the Commission was not being driven by a hidden agenda, why were its propositions on social justice so similar to Labour's priorities as expressed in the Policy Review?

It is not argued here that the Commission members were secret dupes of a hidden agenda: there is little evidence to suggest this is true. As with the Policy Review itself, the fact is that there was no need for any hidden agenda as the membership of the Commission shared a broad consensus of opinion with the members of the policy review groups with regard to the principles which were needed to take forward the idea of social justice. To some extent this was a factor of the selection of the Commission members, with preference being given to those who were likely to be broadly sympathetic to Labour's reformist agenda, and partly a factor of the similarity of approaches between the Commission and the Review – the use of social justice as an organising theme itself demonstrating this similarity. How representative this might be of a wider consensus is difficult to judge, but it is argued here that this is a shared approach of an intellectual elite rather than an approach representing Labour's core support, members or voters. The Commission, like the Review, interpreted the submissions they received in line with this existing consensus.

It might be argued that the Policy Review and the Commission pursued similar concerns because this was the direction in which the problems they addressed led them. To a certain extent this is entirely true, from the perspectives adopted by their respective memberships. This is essentially the question which is posed in this work. The answer suggested here is twofold. Firstly, if this is the case both the Policy Review and the Commission have sought to deny this inevitability by proposing policy agendas which did not fit well with their professed underlying principles. Secondly, these approaches assumed the effectiveness of the British state as an administrator of radical policy, which, it is argued here, has been precisely the reason why postwar Labour governments have proved disappointing to their supporters.

The propositions noticeably say nothing about the economic means needed to achieve these ends. Whilst this may be an attempt to update Beveridge, it lacks the Keynesian economic policies to support a comprehensive welfare approach. Some discussion of the economic assumptions and expectations of the Commission would have been useful here, as would a recognition that social structure, for example the nature of the family, may itself be dependant on economic circumstances. The closest the Commission comes to this is in the arena of employment, where employment is seen as a necessity for social justice.

Finally, it is difficult to see the precise relationship between the 'hierarchy of ideas' put forward as the basis for the concept of social justice and the four propositions. For example, why are education and training so important, and what kind of educational policy does the social justice concept dictate?

What do terms like 'the family' mean, why are they important, and what is government's relationship to them? On the face of it, at least, there is no apparent reason why such propositions could not lead to some very authoritarian, unequal, and, for many, unjust solutions.

Following this brief introduction, concentrating on the concept of social justice, the structure of the Commission's final report followed a three-part format. Part one provided a state of the nation examination of 'the UK today', part two contained two chapters addressed to diagnosis and prescription respectively, and part three, by far the greater part of the report, examined policy options in five areas: education, employment, welfare, social policy and taxation. Consideration will now be given to the analysis of the problem and the general response provided in parts one and two.

The Investor's Approach

Parts one and two of the report provided a more detailed look at the problems faced and outlined the Commission's favoured response. Part one was given over exclusively to an examination of the evidence the Commission had collected regarding the changing nature of Britain and its social consequences. Whilst much of this was a collection of data and statistics submitted to the Commission or collected by the Commission's research staff, the approach to this material is illustrative of the Commission's assumptions and beliefs.

The most obvious feature of this chapter was its deliberate association of the Commission's approach with that of the Beveridge Report 50 years earlier. This was emphasised by the structuring of the chapter into five sections based on Beveridge's 'five great evils' of want, idleness, ignorance, squalor and disease (CSJ, 1994, 28). These were linked, in turn, to the priorities of the Commission. Want was linked to 'the goal of financial independence', idleness to the 'prize of fulfilling employment', ignorance to the 'opportunity to learn', disease to 'the chance of good health', and squalor to the 'need for a safe environment'.

The clearest restriction of this approach is that it limited the Commission to the general concerns of Beveridge, in line with previous practice of postwar Labour governments. Any wider discussion of state form, or economic approach was precluded. This constraint was made even more apparent by the concentration on social indicators to describe the problems of Britain. This diminished the strength of the Commission's arguments on two fronts.

Firstly, there was no discussion of the possibility that greater social inequality may have led to greater economic success. This, of course, impacts on welfare. The Commission agreed: 'in many respects, almost everyone living in the United Kingdom today is better off than their grandparents were' (CSJ, 1994, 27). This improvement has been, at least partly, the result of general economic improvements in standard of living and income, which is why the Commission linked welfare with economic success. The subsequent failure to discuss whether social inequality has contributed to economic success is thus crucial to the Commission's analysis.

Compounding this is the fact that conventional measures of economic success were not questioned, despite the concentration on wider social and environmental measures of Britain's shortcomings. The Commission's analysis might have had greater force had alternative measures been considered. The inadequacy of conventional economic measures of welfare, particularly economic growth, has been a major concern of environmentalists since the 1960s (Mishan; Meadows, Meadows and Randers; Douthwaite; Anderson). The failure to consider these possibilities meant that the Commission missed a real opportunity to formulate a new concept of welfare based more strongly on social and environmental concerns.

The final point of interest in the Commission's 'state of the nation' chapter is the use of class as a basis of analysis. The focus on inequality naturally led to an interest in economic divisions, and this came over most clearly in the Commission's discussion of health. The Commission recognised the strong links between ill health and class in Britain, repeating a number of statistics for infant mortality, heart disease, and even traffic accident fatalities which show strong positive correlations between illness and poverty. A link was also drawn between illness and greater levels of inequality in society (CSJ, 1994, 42–6). Despite these observations, class was not seen as a crucial factor in itself with regard to welfare, indeed the Commission argued that class was not a factor in infant mortality in Sweden (ibid., 43). In this way the Commission noted the importance of class with regard to health, perhaps the most basic aspect of welfare, yet sidestepped the conclusion that this implied the necessity for a class-based political response.

Given these observations the diagnostic chapter of part two of the report presented some contradictory aspects. It suggested Britain had become the victim of three 'revolutions': economic, social and political. The description of these 'revolutions' was particularly interesting:

> The economic revolution is a global revolution of finance, competition, skill and technology in which the United Kingdom is being left behind. ...
>
> The social revolution is a revolution of women's life-chances, of family structures and of demography. Although social change has been faster and gone further in the UK than in most other European countries, public policy has failed to keep up. ...

The political revolution is a challenge to the UK's old assumptions of parliamentary sovereignty and to its growing centralisation of government power; it involves a fundamental reorientation of the relationship between those who govern and those who are governed. (CSJ, 1994, 64–84)

On the surface of it these diagnostic attitudes appear to answer many of the problems outlined above. The description of the political 'revolution' faced is particularly promising. Unfortunately this promise was not lived up to in the detailed consideration of these 'revolutions'.

The general feeling given by the report's diagnosis was of Britain as a victim of wider social, economic and political change, which the state had failed to react to through, it would seem, no real fault of its own. Increasing economic globalisation was presented as the most significant of the changes. This was regarded as a change which Britain must come to terms with, and a change which dominates social and political transformations.

This was reinforced by evidence drawn from international sources with surprisingly little attention given to considerations of Britain's particular economic problems (CSJ, 1994, 64–77). One exception came towards the end of the section with a very interesting illustrative example:

At Southampton Container Terminal (SCT), TGWU dockers were locked in a bitter dispute with employers who were demanding a pay freeze, longer working hours, and job flexibility while threatening compulsory redundancies. A few hundred yards away, at Southampton Cargo Handling (SCH), TGWU dockers were their own employers, the result of an employee buy-out organised by the union three years earlier. Facing intense competition in an overcrowded industry, one firm was trying to compete by cutting costs and subcontracting, the other by engaging every employee in the drive for higher quality. (CSJ, 1994, 76)

The report links this contrast with a wider contrast between 'old' and 'new' approaches to industrial production. Whilst suggesting that the UK economy has failed, at least in part, because it has not encouraged 'new' organisational structures, the report did not consider whether this was the result of economic and political structures in Britain. As a result the report's diagnosis fails to explain Britain's particular economic problems over the past 100 years or so, exemplified by relative economic decline (Gamble, 1995; Coates; Pollard; Bacon and Eltis).

The other observation which should be made about this example is the fact that it implies that 'common ownership', in this case employee ownership through their trade union, may be important in helping to create the 'new', participatory forms of industry for which the Commission called. Perhaps unsurprisingly the Commission did not take this point up, and within months the Labour Party itself was amending its own commitment to common ownership, as will be shown in the next chapter.

The Commission's discussion of the social 'revolution' concentrated on three aspects: the changing roles of women and men in the economy and society, class changes, and demographic changes. The change in women's position in society was linked to changing family circumstances. Apart from highlighting the burden undertaken by many women faced with shouldering the main share of work and domestic responsibilities, the Commission's response was to highlight the need to involve men more in domestic relations.

The Commission's discussion of class change was also disappointing and lacked real direction. Whilst discussing the nature of class change, and dismissing talk of 'classlessness', the Commission argued that British society is marked by 'social exclusion'. The Commission suggested that:

> The UK remains a society corrupted by inequities of class, which intersect with those of gender, race and disability; but the nature of these inequities, and their implications, are changing. (CSJ, 1994, 82)

This may well be true, but does not tell us much about the significance of these class divisions. Some analysis of the changing importance and relevance of class divisions would have strengthened the Commission's case. Some discussion of the way in which class and other social divisions 'intersect' and their importance for class politics would also have been useful.

The Commission's discussion of demographic change concentrated exclusively on the growing elderly population. The focus was on the social burden that this growing elderly population represents. Whilst it is important to note that this will be the case, more central consideration of the basis on which the elderly receive support, their contribution to the community, and how political and social changes will affect the role of the elderly would have helped to put this problem in perspective, particularly with regard to social justice.

The most disappointing section of this diagnostic chapter was its discussion of political change. Although in opening remarks to its consideration of political change the Commission talked of a challenge to political sovereignty, of the growing centralisation of political power, and of a need for fundamental reorientation, the detailed discussion failed to take up any of these issues. Instead, in a section entitled 'reinventing government', the Commission considered the problems of public administration, and suggested, without real discussion, that the demands on government were growing. This, of course, implies a need to restrict the scope of the public sector. The following section involved itself with a discussion of 'political leadership'. Essentially this added nothing to the approach of Labour's Policy Review. The Policy Review asserted the need for a new 'partnership' between public and private sectors, and that a change in political leadership, from Conservative to Labour, was all that was needed to address Britain's problems.

The failure of the Commission to consider deeper problems, and more radical solutions, in their diagnostic phase bore implications for the subsequent proscriptions contained in chapter 3 of the report. In particular the failure to consider the contribution of Britain's political and economic institutions, and their activities greatly restricted the Commission's diagnosis. In its prescriptive chapter the Commission considered the relative merits of three 'futures', or to be more precise three potential approaches to social and economic policy. No further alternatives were examined. In fact the purpose of choosing the three alternatives considered seems to have been to head off political criticism. The first 'future', 'the investors' future', was the Commission's preferred option; the second, 'the deregulators' future', was intended to stand for the approach of the Conservative governments of the 1980s and 1990s; whilst the third, 'the levellers' future', represented the preferred approach of Labour's left-wing.

The chapter started with a 'pen portrait' of each of these 'futures':

Future 1: Investors' Britain — ~~furnmed open~~

The Investors believe we can combine the ethics of community with the dynamics of a market economy. At the heart of the Investors' strategy is a belief that the extension of economic opportunity is not only the source of economic prosperity but also the basis of social justice. The competitive requirement for constant innovation and higher quality demands opportunities for every individual – and not just an elite – to contribute to national economic renewal; this in turn demands strong social institutions, strong families and strong communities, which enable people to grow, adapt and succeed. Unlike the Deregulators, who would use insecurity as the spur to change, the Investors insist on security as the foundation of change; but unlike the Levellers, the Investors achieve security by redistributing opportunities rather than just redistributing income.

Future 2: Deregulators' Britain — ~~Cons. approach~~

The Deregulators dream of a future in which dynamic entrepreneurs, unshackled by employment laws or social responsibilities, create new businesses and open up new markets; in which there is no limit to how high earnings at the top will rise – and no limit to how low wages at the bottom will fall; in which the market widens and deepens its influence; and in which ... 'every business relationship is a one night stand'. It is a future of extremes where the rich get richer and the poor get poorer, and where the rewards for success are matched only by the risks of failure. Economically it depends upon the unceasing drive for competition through the ever-cheaper production of what we already produce; socially it relies upon the reduction of public services and public spending. Politically, it is built on a logic of centralisation and exclusivity, destroying publicly accountable institutions that stand between law-making government and individual decision-making in the marketplace.

Future 3: Levellers' Britain – labs left - wing

The Levellers are concerned with the distribution of wealth to the neglect of its production; they develop policies for social justice independent of the economy. Their strategy is founded on the idea that we cannot use economic renewal and paid employment as the basis for a socially just future. The Levellers share many of the aspirations of the Investors, but they have different strategies to achieve these ambitions. Theirs is a strategy for social justice based primarily on redistributing wealth and incomes, rather than trying to increase opportunities and compete in world markets. The Levellers believe that we should try to achieve social justice through the benefits system, rather than through a new combination of active welfare state, reformed labour market and strong community. (CSJ, 1994, 95–6)

These descriptions are worth quoting at length because they provide a digested outline of the Commission's preferred approach to social policy and its defence of this against other potential strategies. The first striking aspect of this is that it resembled the earlier postwar consensus over social policy in the 1940s and 1950s. This was based around the use of demand management to create growth, which could then be used to reduce inequalities; a mixed economy of public and private provision (Peden, 157–67); and was advocated by Conservatives like Macmillan (Dutton, 28 and 53), and Labour figures such as Crosland. In essence the Commission's approach was to create the kind of 'middle way' which had been characteristic of postwar Britain until the advent of Thatcherism.

middle way favoured

The difference in the 1990s is that the 'extremes' between which the 'middle way' ploughs its furrow have been redefined. This led the Commission to reject redistribution of income through the tax and benefits system, advocated by Crosland as a part of the earlier 'middle way' consensus (ibid.), as part of the 'levellers' option, and to express its preferred option in terms of 'opportunity' and 'life chances' reflecting the 'deregulators' concern with choice. Whilst the Commission might, justifiably, claim that its favoured policies promoted redistribution in practice, this was not reflected in the definition of its approach. What the Commission failed to do was to consider the effectiveness of any of these approaches. The 'middle way' appeared to be advocated above all because it was the middle way.

This was exemplified by a number of assumptions made by the Commission. The failure of the levellers to concern themselves with economic effectiveness was assumed rather than argued. It also appeared to contradict the Commission's own earlier assertion of the iniquitous economic effects of inequality. Once again the Commission's argument was undermined by its failure to outline the criteria to determine when inequality is acceptable and justified.

Deregulators, too, are entitled to similar criticisms of the Commission's approach. Whilst the Commission favoured an approach of creating 'opportunity' they contrast themselves with deregulators as providers of security rather than the insecurity of deregulation. There are two clear problems with this assertion. Firstly, what 'opportunity' was the Commission interested in? If it involved the opportunity to create wealth and income to be enjoyed by the individual then surely this implies inequality, change, and, thus, insecurity. For 'deregulators' this is an unavoidable part of the creation of wealth and income in the first place, a creation which can then benefit everyone. Secondly, characterising the alternative view as 'deregulator' implies that the Commission assumed that security and equality requires regulation. Who will undertake this regulation? What form will it take? If it is to be state regulation of the levels of income and wealth enjoyed by individuals how does this approach differ from those attempted, and failed, in the postwar consensus?

One prominent 'leveller' has complained that the Commission's description of this position was, in effect, the creation of a straw man with whom the Commission could easily dispense (Townsend). In fact the Commission's failure to consider the claims of economic effectiveness for either of its alternative positions, or to consider the ineffectiveness of current British state provision and institutions, meant that the economic superiority of the Commission's approach, and of traditional British state-based approaches, was assumed from the outset.

Whilst much greater detail of the Commission's general proscriptive strategy was provided in the remainder of the chapter, alongside reiterations of their dismissal of the two alternatives considered, the general argument added little to the 'pen portraits'. The Commission argued that only the Investors' approach recognised the link between social and economic policy (CSJ, 1994, 97–8). This is simply untrue and merely evaded the potential criticism of Investor strategies from Deregulator or Leveller perspectives.

The Policy Options

The Commission's policy recommendations for a future government constitute the greater part of the report. Five chapters set out the Commission's policy preferences on education, employment, welfare, social policy and taxation. What is important here is to trace the way in which the principles set out by the Commission are reflected in policy proposals. Three policy areas will be considered to outline the Commission's approach: education, which the Commission itself identified as a crucial area; family policy, on which the principles set out by the Commission appeared contradictory; and employment, which is central to the creation of opportunity and the economic ability to meet other policy options.

Two general points should also be made about the policy proposals put forward by the Commission. Firstly, the policies proposed were designed to be applied largely within existing institutional frameworks and political and economic structures. As such broader questions of accountability and autonomy in policy design and implementation were largely ignored by the Commission.

Secondly, in this section of the report the Commission advanced the policies of the investors's strategy outlined above, but also felt it advisable to contrast their approaches with some alternatives. On these occasions it was with the deregulators' approach that the investors' strategy was compared (CSJ, 1994, 158–62 and 228–9). The levellers' approach was dismissed from consideration as a basis for policy. This might be defended on the grounds that the deregulators' policies are those currently being pursued by government, and therefore those against which the investors have most clearly to contrast themselves. Whilst this is true, the Commission's criticism of leveller preferences, rather inadequately promoted in its proscriptive section, might have carried greater weight had the Commission actually outlined the ineffective policy options levellers were deemed to favour.

Education was identified by the Commission as the key policy area, and in many ways its education policies, outlined in the first of the policy chapters, were the jewel in the crown of the Commission's policy proposals. This was highlighted by the fact that in this investors' strategy the education chapter was given the title of 'investment'. Its predominantly economic justification was emphasised by the chapter's subtitle: 'adding value through lifelong learning' (CSJ, 1994, 119). Here, as elsewhere in its report, the Commission saw individuals predominantly as contributing to economic improvement, itself measured through conventional economic measures such as growth. Policies were therefore considered as adding to individual's ability to contribute to economic performance; individual development for its own sake was, at best, secondary.

The chapter was structured into sections setting out six goals. These were: universal nursery education and investment in childcare; basic skills for every child; high achievement for every young person; training for every employee; expansion of higher education through a fair funding system; and a Learning Bank for lifelong learning. These goals might be accepted by most deregulators and levellers, though means of achieving these ends would differ. So did the Commission suggest that its approach was more effective in achieving these goals?

The clearest problem the Commission faced in its aspirations to improve educational provision was funding. This was exemplified in its proposals for nursery education which it estimated would require approximately an extra £1 billion (CSJ, 1994, 126). Because of this it argued that: 'it will take several years to achieve universal provision' (ibid.). This detracted from the Commission's commitment to this policy area. A clearer statement of priorities here would have been useful. Should nursery education be pursued if it is at the expense of spending in other areas of public service? Should it require greater levels of taxation? Should government pursue such policies at the expense of short-term economic goals? Or, indeed, should these policies be pursued for the sake of individual development irrespective of their economic benefits? A link was made between funding nursery education and phasing out the Married Couples Tax Allowance (CSJ, 1994, 315–16), but this was tentative, and once again focused on a specific policy change rather than a commitment to principle.

The Commission's most imaginative response to funding dilemmas emerged with its proposals in adult education for a 'Learning Bank'. These sections of the report were amongst the last to be drafted, but presented an intelligent attempt to tackle problems of access and expenditure in continuing adult education. The expansion of higher education was linked to the creation of a 'fair' funding system. Funding was seen as the key to expanding higher education places, and the raising of additional funds was proposed from graduates in employment. Three schemes for obtaining these funds were considered: a monthly repayment once a certain income had been reached; a universal surcharge on National Insurance; or a rising surcharge on National Insurance once a certain income had been reached (CSJ, 1994, 140). The Commission made no judgment between these options, which is surprising given their differing effects on equity and implications for social justice.

The decision to raise funds through a graduate employment tax or surcharge also affects the principles the Commission set for the application of policy. Firstly, the Commission argued that education is important because it will *educate* (handwritten margin note)

raise the productiveness and economic efficiency of society as a whole, bringing benefits to the whole community. If this is the case why should a proportion of the costs be borne only by a section of society? In the name of social justice and fairness should not a proposal benefiting the whole of society be paid for by the whole of society? This can be contested by the assertion that some individuals, in this case the graduates themselves, benefit disproportionately from this form of education. The benefit is incurred through increased earning power, and this should then be taxed. The problem here is that this seems to contradict the Commission's principle that inequality should be restricted. If graduates are taxed on an improved earning power which is the product of inequality, what are the implications for the promotion of equality, and thus social justice? Does the taxation of inequality created through the education system not only legitimise but encourage these inequalities? Can social justice be realised under these circumstances? These questions the Commission failed to address.

The Commission sought to develop adult education generally through the creation of a 'Learning Bank'. The intention was 'the creation of a learning society' (CSJ, 1994, 141). Again the main purpose of the Learning Bank was to provide funds for a more flexible approach to education and training. The creation of the Bank would encourage private funding, gather funding from employers, accept repayments of 'credits' from individual students and trainees in employment, and finally be funded by government.

Having proposed a genuinely interesting idea intended to extend access to education and training, and develop the kind of trained workforce Britain needs to compete effectively on a skills basis in the modern global economy, the Commission said nothing about control over and accountability of the Bank and its lending policies. In addition the balance of funding was not discussed despite the fact that it has similar implications for equality and social justice to graduate employment taxes.

In education the Commission's weakness in setting out its basic principles was reflected in its final policy proposals. The policies reflected a failure to consider the criteria for justifiable inequalities, and the implications of using inequality as a basis of funding. Similarly, they failed to take into account wider institutional, cultural and economic obstacles to education in Britain. For example, no mention was made of the implications for social justice of a continuing public school system and the concept of an exclusive 'excellence' which they embody.

The Commission's family policy was dispersed widely over the report, with policies with implications for family structure occurring in most of the policy chapters. Here attention will be given to the 'family-friendly employment' section in the report's chapter 5, and the 'children and their families' section in chapter 7 (CSJ, 1994, 188–91 and 310–23). These sections dealt most directly with the needs of children and represent one important strand of family policy. As with education policy, they also demonstrated the contradictions of the Commission's approach.

The Commission's proposals on employment made the assumptions on which the Commission operated clear:

> Crudely put, the time men spend at work determines how much time they have left over for their families; but the time women spend caring for their families determines how much time they have available for employment. (CSJ, 1994, 188)

Despite the fact that the report went on to say that: 'it is not for government to dictate employment or family patterns' (ibid.), the Commission's policy proposals were based on the assumption of a family norm, and their policies on parental responsibility positively encourage this 'norm'. The potential for choice for alternative family structures, particularly for women to choose to bring up children as lone parents, was simply ignored by the Commission.

The Commission's discussion of 'family-friendly employment' contained a number of proposals to increase parental contact with their children. These included improvements in paternity and maternity leave, and rights to 'emergency leave' for family reasons. However, these rights were conditional:

> The state of the British economy ... means that it will take time before we can expect all employers to reach the standards of the best. (CSJ, 1994, 190)

In this area, as in education, inequalities were recognised but not tackled:

> Professionals who control their own time are in a position to take a morning or day off as necessary, and make it up later; other workers may face the sack if they put their children first. (Ibid.)

The Commission's attempt to redress this imbalance took the form of enlightened employment practice and, eventually, statutory rights. Given the Commission's interest in promoting equality it might have been expected that the report would at least discuss the possibility of other workers having greater control over their hours of employment. With technological developments encouraging greater flexibility and mass unemployment surely the opportunity exists to provide greater equality with professionals in the area of autonomy over working hours amongst other occupations. The Commission's failure to consider such options again demonstrated that their commitment to equality only stretched to the confines of existing economic, political and social structures. Changing the balance of authority, control and autonomy within organisations was beyond their remit.

The Commission's approach to children and child welfare reinforced this conservative approach to social institutions. Whilst the report talked of social support for families, the major responsibility for children was firmly placed with families, or more particularly with parents. Once again the Commission identified the benefits of reform in this area as social:

> Children are 100 per cent of the future. Investment in their life-chances is the best social and economic investment we can make. (CSJ, 1994, 320)

Given the importance of this area it might be argued that children are too important to leave solely to the care of parents. Certainly the Commission raised the issue of social support, but finance for children was seen as the prerogative and responsibility of parents.

The report's defence of Child Benefit was argued on the grounds that the objective of Child Benefit is to create 'horizontal equity' rather than 'vertical equity'. That is to say that Child Benefit is intended to prevent childcare costs distorting the economic choices of individuals on similar income levels, not to provide a form of redistribution to those with children in lower income brackets (CSJ, 1994, 314). Despite this the benefit's 'horizontal equity' was eroded by the Commission's support for taxation of Child Benefit paid to those in higher tax brackets.

Equally interesting was the Commission's proposals for the reform of child maintenance. The Commission defended the principle of the introduction of the Child Support Agency, seeing its problems as largely the result of bad public relations and management. It contrasted this with the Australian Agency which: 'was clearly perceived by the public to be part of a broader strategy to improve children's well-being' (CSJ, 1994, 318). The belief that this was a failure of management rather than design was made clear by the Commission:

> The principle of the (Child Support) Act – that absent parents should accept and share financial responsibility for their children – is clearly right. (CSJ, 1994, 317)

The basis of this statement was far from clear. As with education, why should individuals be forced to shoulder the burden of payment for developments which will later benefit the whole of society? Surely if the development of children is the future of society then the maintenance of children is a social responsibility, not one to be restricted to parents.

The Commission also evaded any analysis of the failures of the Child Support Agency. Whilst a full analysis of this approach to child maintenance is beyond the scope of the argument here, two examples may serve to illustrate areas which the Commission might have considered as important to their concept of social justice. Firstly, the creation of an Agency to deal with child maintenance for separated and divorced parents introduces a bureaucratic and legalistic arrangement in an area of people's lives which might be best dealt with through informal arrangements amongst the individuals concerned. The need to agree financial arrangements for child support at a time of emotional crisis may add to the bitterness and sense of grievance in separation and itself make future reconciliation of families more difficult. Informal arrangements may also, at least potentially, be more effective means of providing financially for children by evading tax, legal and other costs which might arise otherwise.

Secondly, the biggest net beneficiary of Child Support Agency operations is not children at all but the state. A proportion of separated parents will have second families with children who will be denied a proportion of their former income. The income taken from these children, if paid to a lone parent or family receiving state benefit, will not fully benefit the children from whom the parent is separated. Their income will be reduced in proportion to the income extracted from the absent parent. As a result any informal payments made by absent parents, for holidays or family visits for example, are likely to become a matter of contention and the net income of both sets of children may be reduced, to the benefit of the state. This is a system which hardly seems designed to benefit the children involved, all of whom may end up in a more hostile and emotionally soured environment with a lower level of income. The Commission's failure to discuss such issues and to demonstrate how they might be resolved does little to advance their proposed concept of social justice.

One interesting aspect of the Commission's approach to child welfare is its demand that government publish 'an annual index of child well-being' (CSJ, 1994, 311). The assertion here was that general aggregate economic indicators are not adequate measures of child welfare and that other factors, such as the availability of pre-school education, should be included. To this might be added measures of literacy or infant mortality (Anderson), but if economic indicators are not adequate measures of child welfare are they adequate for the rest of the population? Why not a measure of well-being for the elderly, for parents, or for society as a whole? It is curious that the Commission should appear to endorse arguments suggesting the ineffectiveness of aggregate economic measures of welfare with regard to children without considering further implications, particularly for their concepts of social justice.

Finally with regard to family policy, the Commission's report suggested the need for a stronger awareness of parental responsibilities. The Commission argued for a statutory statement of parental responsibilities to cover all children (CSJ, 1994, 320–2). Whilst professing their lack of interest in dictating family structure this approach seems to assume a norm of parenthood involving two parents over the period of 'childhood'. Nor does the Commission say anything about how such a statutory statement should be enforced or interpreted. Without a clearly accountable process of adjudication, which is not readily apparent in Britain's existing structures of political and legal enforcement, there is at the least the potential here for a highly authoritarian approach to the family and moral behaviour. It must also be asked whether this really is delivering the best possible care to children. Is a parent forced to assume parental responsibilities going to provide the same kind of stable, caring environment as those who readily commit themselves to parental care? What if parents can afford to pay others to provide 'parenting services' on their behalf? Should this be allowed or must the responsibilities be carried out by the biological parent?

Here, as elsewhere, the Commission's professed commitment to opportunity and equality is difficult to discern. Benefits which accrue to society are paid for by the individual, and if the individual is incapable or unwilling to shoulder this burden then the implications are by no means clear. In addition individuals do not have control over their own situations, but instead are provided with parenting 'rights' by enlightened employers or the state.

The last policy proposals to be considered here are those regarding employment. In the light of the Commission's concern about the government's ability to afford some of the reforms they propose, employment is obviously a key area. If mass unemployment remains then this will greatly curtail a Labour, or any other, administration's ability to undertake expensive reform without increasing tax levels. There are two criteria which must be considered with regard to the Commission's strategy for employment. Firstly, is it convincing as an effective strategy to ensure increased employment? Secondly does it comply with the Commission's stated objectives and values?

The Commission's objective was not just to alleviate the problems of employment or to increase employment generally but to achieve full employment, defined as: 'a situation in which the number of job vacancies is at least equal to the number of unemployed' (CSJ, 1994, 155). The Commission claimed that to meet this objective seven conditions must be fulfilled:

1. A high and sustainable growth rate in overall demand, requiring action at international, European and national level.
2. The maintenance of low inflation and, in particular, an understanding by government, company directors, employers and unions that average money earnings should rise in line with productivity increases across the whole economy.

3. A tradeable sector which is sufficiently large and competitive, to ensure that a full employment level of demand can be sustained in the UK.
4. That we achieve great intensity of employment (so that increases in output are effectively translated into higher employment). This will require:

   Expansion of non-tradeable, labour-intensive sectors such as personal services.

   Matching total hours of employment as far as possible to the hours which individuals want to work at different stages in their lives.
5. A reintegration of the long-term unemployed into the labour market. This will require:

   High quality help with education, training, and personal development through a reemployment service;

   Wage subsidies, to reconnect the long-term unemployed to the labour market;

   Help with childcare (especially for lone parents);

   Development of intermediate labour markets designed to provide training and employment for the long-term unemployed, as well as subsequent access to regular employment;

   Sponsorship of small-scale entrepreneurs;

   Sustainable economic and social regeneration in the most disadvantaged areas.
6. The development of tax and benefits systems which provide incentives, not disincentives, to employment. This will require:

   A flexible benefits system to match the increasingly flexible labour market;

   A reduction in reliance on means-tested benefits, which have inevitable disincentive effects on both claimant and partner;

   Help for low-income owner-occupiers (to parallel help for low-income tenants);

   Gradual reduction in taxes on employment, particularly for less-skilled and lower-paid jobs.
7. A new balance between employment and family across people's life-cycles, in ways which promote greater individual choice and improve the quality of social and economic life. This will require:

   Opportunities for employment breaks to meet family needs, for both men and women;

   Opportunities for employment breaks to permit further education and training;

   Flexible retirement patterns, with appropriate pension structures. (CSJ, 1994, 155–7)

These conditions presented an interesting and important link between economic and social factors. For the Commission it was not just the aggregate level of employment which was important but the nature of employment, its distribution and the social conditions under which it was undertaken. These were seen as contributing conditions to full employment. This provided an ambitious strategy to tackle unemployment and usefully linked the Commission's economic and social objectives. However, this was also a strategy which covered many areas of government policy, and all of the policy chapters of the report. The Commission provided no idea of the proper balance between these different conditions and their relative importance.

There again appeared to be a problem for the Commission with regard to its aspirations for equality. In particular its insistence on low inflation, and that the main mechanism to ensure this should be the control of wage levels, needed to be put in the context of the Commission's wider aspirations. Whilst the Commission argued that the creation of employment opportunities would provide relief from the degree of inequality present in Britain today, restrictions on wage demands might be taken as an excuse to enshrine inequalities between those in work. Inequalities of income from work are as significant as the inequalities between those in work and those without work. Moreover, a restriction of union or workers' power over collective bargaining would change the balance of power in working relationships in favour of employers and government. The Commission could have made its intentions in this area clearer, and the implications for social justice of its low inflation strategy.

The Commission's approach to growth is also interesting. Whilst the promotion of growth through international coordination clearly makes sense given the global nature of economic activity, the Commission did not consider what can be done if such a strategy is not agreed. What can a national government do without international cooperation, and should an agreement on coordinated reflation be a condition of, for example, Britain's membership of a single currency? In addition the Commission was clearly concerned with the quality of growth (CSJ, 1994, 166–9). Here, as elsewhere, the Commission acknowledged the arguments of critics of growth as a measure of social and economic well-being, yet did not consider potential alternatives. It is difficult to see why the Commission failed to consider a wider measure of social and economic well-being such as the one it proposed to monitor child welfare.

Part of the reason for this failure was that the Commission really concerned itself with the quality of growth not predominantly from the point of welfare but of economic sustainability, not here demonstrating any environmental aspects to that term. The Commission argued that concentration must be given to growth in the tradeable sector of the economy partly because this was a good in itself, which was not necessarily the case with regard to other areas of economic activity, and partly because this sector was the basis of growth in other sectors. This reflected the approach of the Policy Review and its intention to develop the Department of Trade and Industry to stimulate this sector of the economy. This needs to be seen alongside the Commission's desire to expand 'personal services' as a sector of employment. Again this provided an interesting area of potential development, but the Commission did not discuss the nature of these services or whether existing social and institutional structures are effective as a means of encouraging this sector.

Despite a more imaginative set of objectives, and a stronger link between economic and social objectives, the Commission's proposals did not match up to the employment proposals of the initial stages of the Policy Review. This was centrally because the Commission did not consider the institutional frameworks within which their policies would need to operate. Whereas the Policy Review proposed a range of new institutions, a developed Department of Trade and Industry, British Technology Enterprise, a British Investment Bank, and a Skills UK network (Labour Party, n.d.b), the institutional framework of the Commission's proposed provisions was not considered. In essence the initial documents of the Policy Review represent a far more developed and cohesive programme in this area than that provided by the Commission. Whilst the link between economic and social objectives is important, the Commission needed to develop this and to show the importance of social factors to economic factors; to argue for the interconnections between these two sets of objectives, not merely to reiterate the need to create the economic wealth to afford social welfare; and to outline the balance between these objectives, in particular with regard to concepts of social justice.

Overall the Commission's consideration of policy options was restricted by its lack of consideration of wider political questions, notably the effectiveness of Britain's political and economic institutions as delivery mechanisms for social and economic welfare programmes; its failure to demonstrate clear links between its favoured policy proposals and its concept of social justice, particularly with regard to the relationship between the individual and the state; and its failure to adequately determine the nature of acceptable inequalities, especially where policy proposals seemed to legitimise and even promote inequality. In many ways, particularly in economic policy, the earlier Policy Review documents provided a more convincing policy programme. However, both the Review and the Commission's report shared similarities of approach, both failed to consider the nature of the British state as a potential barrier to achieving their objectives, both worked within existing frameworks of economic and political behaviour, and both followed a broadly liberal democratic ideological approach.

Conclusion: The Impact of the Commission

The impact of the Commission's report on the Labour Party is difficult to judge. Firstly, the Commission's instigator and advocate as Labour Leader, John Smith, died during the concluding phases of the Commission. Secondly, under new Leader Tony Blair the Labour Party was very quickly diverted by a re-examination of its basic ideology, to be considered in depth in the next chapter, which kept it absorbed for a year. Thirdly, many of the Commission's proposals, for example support for a reformed Child Support Agency, were already Party policy and the Commission's general approach was similar to that of the Policy Review. The combination of these factors means that the Commission's impact has, as yet, been marginal, but some assessment of the likely long-term effects can still be made.

The death of John Smith certainly made an impact on the Commission's members, who acknowledged Smith's contribution in their opening remarks (CSJ, 1994, ix). Whether Smith's death, and his replacement as Leader by Tony Blair, will affect the adoption of the Commission's recommendation is more difficult to assess. Undoubtedly Smith felt personally identified with the Commission. It was his attempt to broaden Labour's agenda away from the perceived failings of the 1992 election campaign, and therefore of the product of the Policy Review. This does not imply that if Smith had lived he would have uncritically accepted the Commission's report and adopted the proposed policy options. Nonetheless, the fact that Smith was closely involved with the drawing of the Commission's terms of reference and had fairly close contact with Patricia Hewitt and Gordon Borrie, particularly in the initial stages, suggests that the Commission probably reflected Smith's approach to these areas more closely then it did Blair's approach. Nonetheless some of the restrictions which face Blair's policy formulation would also have been faced by Smith.

One definite interruption to the consideration of the Commission's report by the Party which was clearly a result of Blair's accession to the Party leadership was the debate over Clause IV. This distracted the Party from policy consideration for a year or more whilst it was engaged in internal debate over its ideological base and constitution. Only quite recently has the Party returned to consideration of a policy programme and the Commission's contribution to that. One of the most encouraging signs for the Commission was the appointment of Donald Dewar as Shadow Social Security Secretary. Dewar was an enthusiastic advocate and supporter of the Commission and sympathetic to its general approach (CSJ, 1994, xvii). Another encouraging aspect was its favourable reception by some key Party figures. Perhaps most important amongst these was Clare Short, who responded positively to the prominent discussion of women's role in society which she perceived as an improvement in Labour's approach to women's issues.

In addition members of the Party leadership have been broadly supportive of the general approach of the Commission. Blair in a speech marking the fiftieth anniversary of the 1945 Labour Government, spoke enthusiastically of the 'radical left-of-centre tradition outside our own Party' and of the Party's commitment to 'social justice' (Blair, 5). Presumably this referred to initiatives such as the independent Commission rather than the activities of trotskyite or communist groups. As such Blair has identified himself as broadly sympathetic to the liberal democratic approaches enshrined in both the Policy Review and the Commission's report. Against this the Party has also been prepared to adopt policy positions which seem to conflict with the Commission's desire to improve equality, for example by accepting league tables and grant aided schools, and no support has been given, so far, to some of the major policy proposals the Commission made, for instance to the Learning Bank.

Equally important are the reasons why the policy proposals of the Policy Review were so rapidly abandoned and whether the Commission's proposals are likely to fair any better. As was made clear in chapter 4, the more ambitious proposals of the Review had been abandoned well before the drafting of the 1992 manifesto. In that chapter it was argued that this was the result of Labour's calculation of the effects of the more radical of these policies on public opinion. The Commission's approach is similar in its principles to the Review, and contains elements which are more radical than those accepted in Labour's 1992 campaign, though it is considerably less radical than the initial phases of the Review, particularly with regard to institutional reform. This suggests that even if a more anodyne agenda for Party policy was the objective of the Kinnock leadership it was not necessarily the objective of John Smith.

The Review was abandoned as a source of policy because it failed to achieve its core objective: a Labour victory at the 1992 General Election. It is argued here that this was the result of three central failings of the Review which themselves reflected Labour's traditional approaches to British politics. Firstly, the Review did not provide a clear ideological basis for the Party; secondly, it did not provide a critique of the British state as a mechanism for achieving Party objectives; and thirdly, it failed to provide an adequate mechanism for the Party to reach out to and engage with its core support. The Commission on Social Justice shares all of these failings.

The principles of social justice outlined in the report do not provide a consistent ideological basis for the Party and its activities, though it might provide a useful slogan for public relations purposes. I have argued here that the principles of social justice outlined by the Commission do not resolve the problems of accountability and power implicit in the relationship between the individual and the state, and more particularly the British state. These were precisely the areas which the Review also failed to resolve.

Both the Review and the Commission took the political structures and approaches of the British state as given. Neither effectively questioned the accountability of the state to ordinary people. As a consequence neither considered whether the structure of the British state biased attempts by government to use the state as a means to obtain greater equality. In their political discussions the Commission, like the Review, saw political leadership, not power and accountability, as the key factor. For both, it was who populates the government, not the nature of governance, which was the problem.

Finally, the Commission's collection of data and evidence followed a similar pattern to the Review's. However, there were real and significant differences. The Commission was not burdened with the need to use public meetings for propaganda as well as consultation purposes – the fate which befell the *Labour Listens* campaign. Conversely the Commission was not able to advertise its public meetings in quite the same way as the Review. Crucially, both Commission panels and policy review groups interpreted the data with which they were presented with respect to a similar intellectual framework. I argued in chapter 3 that the lack of controversy over policy-making in the Review was due to a broad consensus of opinion within the Party leadership with regard to the desired approach, though not necessarily the desirable outcomes. The same is, I would argue, true of the Commission. Both reflect a general view on what Blair calls the 'left-of-centre' approach to government needed in the face of 16 years of Conservative rule. They also reflect the 'lust for power' which the 'left-of-centre' has developed (Seyd, 1992, 96).

The reason why the Review's policy proposals were heavily moderated before the 1992 election campaign was because their more radical manifestations were perceived as vote losers. They were measured against the Party's private polling and ditched if the results were not satisfactory. This is an essentially short-term approach. The failure of the Party to persuade the public toward a long-term strategy served the proposals of the Review poorly. The same may well be true of the Commission. The results are likely to be equally anodyne, unadventurous and fundamentally conservative.

As with the Policy Review, the real achievement of the Commission was in providing an interesting set of policy proposals, with concrete programmes for improving nursery education, cutting long-term unemployment, and tackling pension provision. The fundamental problem is that these were neither based on, nor tied to, the Commission's stated principles. In fact the

Commission was at its most radical where it came closer in practice to a 'leveller's' approach than an 'investor's' approach. This has left the door open for a Labour leadership to adopt the Commission's concept of 'social justice' and reinterpret them to its own ends.

The Review's proposals were watered down to win an election which they failed to do, to the extent that the Commission's policy options are taken up by the Party they are likely to face the same fate. Whether the anodyne impact which may remain by the time of the next election informs Party policy in the future may depend on whether Labour become the next government or not. If Labour does form a new administration then a more radical edge may emerge, certainly if it is serious about a long-term strategy for renewal. However, the lesson of the Policy Review was that Labour's determination to achieve office outweighed its determination to pursue a radical agenda.

7 New Clause IV: From Renewal to Modernisation

Introduction

Tony Blair's biographer, Jon Sopel, talks of the 1992 General Election as being a turning point in Blair's life. His determination to make the party electable after 1992 made him appear 'like a different man' (Sopel, 128). Sopel sees this as the birth of the 'modernisers' led by Blair, ranged against the 'traditionalists' opposed to change. This division has been exemplified, if not necessarily resolved, by Blair's dramatic reform of the Party's constitution, and in particular its Clause IV.

The historic importance of Clause IV to the Labour Party was examined in chapter 1, and the ideological aspects of the Policy Review considered in chapter 2. The reform of Clause IV went far beyond anything attempted in the Policy Review, and to some extent this was the point. It was intended, amongst other things, to illustrate a determination on behalf of the Blair leadership to move the 'modernisation' project beyond what were perceived as Neil Kinnock's achievements (Blair, 1993, 9). This was so important to Blair that, in almost a parody of Mrs Thatcher's 'them and us' mentality, he began to identify individuals as for and against 'the project' (Sopel, 259). Nonetheless, this division also fits easily into the longer historical perspective identified in chapter 1.

In chapter 1 it was argued that Labour's Clause IV was important not as a guide to action, but as a statement of faith – a dividing line between Labour and the Conservatives which Conservatives could never endorse or adopt. Interestingly the defection of Alan Howarth, the first MP ever to defect directly from Conservative to Labour, occurred a few months after the replacement of Labour's Clause IV with the modernisers' rewritten version.

Labour's ideological identity, far from being a reflection of Labour's constitution, is linked with the actual programme of Attlee's 1945 government, which was essentially a liberal and statist approach. It was Thatcherism's attack of the postwar settlement which created 'ideological' problems for a fundamentally pragmatic Labour Party. All of these elements are reflected in the 'modernisation' of Labour's constitution pursued by Blair.

It was suggested in chapter 1 that ideological divisions within the Party were really about a division over the relative importance of power and principles. In the analysis of the Policy Review's ideological statement

Democratic Socialist Aims and Values, it was argued that this division was reflected in the 'renewal' of the Policy Review. The same themes are present in the fight between 'modernisers' and 'traditionalists'. As one moderniser observed about the challenge to Clause IV:

> The challenge represents an alternative form of symbolism, with its object clearly the electorate. (Thompson, 1995a, 3)

As this quote demonstrates, there were two aspects to the challenge of Clause IV. There was the challenge to what was perceived as an outdated ideological commitment enshrined in Clause IV, but there was also the symbolic element demonstrating Blair's control over the Party and his intent to stand up to 'old' Labour. This, too, paralleled the intent of the Policy Review to demonstrate Kinnock's leadership and visionary qualities.

Did the modernisers succeed in achieving their deeper ends through the reform of Clause IV? This chapter will consider the conduct and nature of the debate initiated by the proposed reform of Clause IV, the consultation undertaken to justify the change, and the content of the reformed Clause IV.

The Debate

The handling of the debate and consultation over the reform of Clause IV suggests that the Blair leadership felt that it was embarked on a significant gamble. In fact, during the campaign for the Party leadership Blair had ruled out changing Clause IV to avoid alienating significant sectors of his potential support. According to Sopel this was no more than a ruse to win the leadership as Blair was already sketching the outlines of change to Clause IV (263).

The announcement of Blair's 'change of heart' concerning the need to pursue the reform of Clause IV was itself disguised, presumably to head off potential opposition. The announcement came in Blair's first Leader's speech to the Party Conference in October, 1994, and when it came it contained no direct reference to Clause IV, only the aim to create 'a clear up-to-date statement of the objects and objectives of our Party' (Sopel, 270). In fact the desire to replace Clause IV had been clearly signalled by Party modernisers and had prompted resolutions to the 1994 Conference supporting the retention of Clause IV. These were duly passed two days after the Leader's speech (Sopel, 271).

The intention of modernisers to attack Clause IV was signalled in many ways. The Archer Committee Report for the Fabian Society proposed a new constitution for the Party which contained a new statement of aims and objects as Clause II replacing the old Clause IV (Archer Committee, 5). Labour front bench speaker, Jack Straw, published a pamphlet calling for a new Clause IV (Jones), and Will Hutton summed up the wider views of modernisers when he wrote:

If Autumn's Labour Party Conference can agree a new constitution enshrining the policy of one member one vote; and if subsequently it can amend Clause IV to express the aims and values of a modern socialist party, then Labour will have positioned itself to contest the Conservative legacy. (Hutton, 1993b, 50)

Once the initial move to one member one vote had been secured at that year's conference, the next target was reform of Clause IV. It was in this context that Blair's Conference speech on constitutional change was made, and very quickly the debate focused on Clause IV of the constitution. This, after all, was the Party's statement of its aims and objectives which was highlighted in Blair's speech. This raises the question of what was wrong with Clause IV, and why modernisers felt it to be in need of reform. To make a comparison the two clauses are presented below.

Labour Party Constitution Clause IV

Original

1918 Clause (as amended)

National

1. To organize and maintain in parliament and in the country a political Labour Party.

2. To cooperate with the General Council of the Trades Union Congress, or other kindred organisations, in joint political or other action in harmony with the party constitution and standing orders.

3. To give effect as far as may be practicable to the principles from time to time approved by the party conference.

4. To secure for the workers by hand or by brain the full fruits of their industry and the most equitable distribution thereof that may be possible upon the basis of the common ownership of the means of production, distribution, and exchange, and the best obtainable system of popular administration and control of each industry or service.

5. Generally to promote the political, social and economic emancipation of the people, and more particularly of those who depend directly upon their own exertions by hand or by brain for the means of life.

Inter-Commonwealth

6. To cooperate with the labour and socialist organisations in the Commonwealth and overseas with a view to promoting the purposes of the party, and to take common action for the promotion of a higher standard of social and economic life for the working population of the respective countries.

International

7. To cooperate with the labour and socialist organisations in other countries and to support the United Nations Organization and its various

agencies and other international organisations for the promotion of peace, the adjustment and settlement of international disputes by conciliation or judicial arbitration, the establishment and defence of human rights, and the improvement of the social and economic standards and conditions of work of the people of the world.

Source: Labour Party, 1994, 4

1995 Clause

1. The Labour Party is a democratic socialist party. It believes that by the strength of our common endeavour we achieve more than we achieve alone, so as to create for each of us the means to realize our true potential and for all of us a community in which power, wealth and opportunity are in the hands of the many not the few; where the rights we enjoy reflect the duties we owe and where we live together freely, in a spirit of solidarity, tolerance and respect.

2. To these ends we work for:

(a) **a dynamic economy**, serving the public interest, in which the enterprise of the market and the rigour of competition are joined with the forces of partnership and cooperation to produce the wealth the nation needs and the opportunity for all to work and prosper with a thriving private sector and high quality public services where those undertakings essential to the common good are either owned by the public or accountable to them;

(b) **a just society**, which judges its strength by the condition of the weak as much as the strong, provides security against fear and justice at work; which nurtures families, promotes equality of opportunity and delivers people from tyranny of poverty, prejudice and the abuse of power;

(c) **an open democracy**, in which government is held to account by the people, decisions are taken as far as practicable by the communities they affect and where fundamental human rights are guaranteed;

(d) **a healthy environment**, which we protect, enhance and hold in trust for future generations.

3. Labour is committed to the defence and security of the British people and to cooperating in European institutions, the United Nations, the Commonwealth and other international bodies to secure peace, freedom, democracy, economic security and environmental protection for all.

4. Labour will work in pursuit of these aims with trade unions and cooperative societies and also with voluntary organisations, consumer groups and other representative bodies.

5. On the basis of these principles, Labour seeks the trust of the people to govern.

Source: Labour Party, 1996, 4

A detailed comparison will be made later. First, the achievement of change needs to be measured against the reasons put forward for, and against, the reform of Clause IV.

Straw provided a good starting point to consider the criticisms of modernisers. He outlined five objections to Clause IV:

(i)   written in 1918, the Clause was a product of an age of class polarisation which was characterised by a notable consensus on the apparent superiority of state-run enterprises;
(ii) its was an ambiguous compromise between different conceptions of collectivism;
(iii) it confused ends and means;
(iv) its statist connotations have been contradicted by subsequent events;
(v)   other European socialist parties which have evaded any commitment to common ownership have been more popular. (Jones, 55–6)

These five points reasonably cover the various arguments put forward for change by the modernisers. The Archer Committee concluded:

> We are of one mind that the existing Clause IV (4) should be replaced, both to separate principles from policies and to reflect contemporary thinking. (Archer Committee, 5)

Hutton argued that:

> The establishment of a congruence between the Party's constitution and its political aims is the essential precondition for the political integrity that the electorate demands. (Hutton, 1993b, 53)

Thompson provided a more positive case for a new Clause IV:

> In the 1980s Labour rushed around trying to *appear* modern, but did this by dropping the burden of past policies, rather than finding a vision of the future. (Thompson, 1993a, 2)

It is certainly possible to question the historical and political assumptions on which the case against Clause IV rested (Jones; Coates, 1995a), but that is not the point here. In order to assess the argument and to consider the effectiveness of the change made it is necessary to determine the coherence of this case and its relevance with regard to Labour's original Clause IV.

The first thing to note is that Straw's five objections are, to some extent, contradictory. On the one hand Straw wishes to assert that Clause IV was limiting because of its 'statist connotations', on the other that it was open to interpretation as a compromise between different conceptions of collectivism. Straw identifies some of these conceptions as: 'municipal socialists, state socialists and nationalisers, guild socialists and cooperators' (Jones, 56). Only one of these four is, in fact, statist. Nonetheless, Straw is exceptional amongst modernisers in admitting that Clause IV is open to interpretation.

Hutton is more typical with his assertion that Clause IV makes Labour:

A Party formally wedded to wholesale nationalization in its constitution (and therefore) potentially a party of high taxation and inefficient statism. (Hutton, 1993b, 50)

Thompson is even more damning:

Even less convincing (in the arguments to retain Clause IV) is the resounding silence about the collapse of state socialism. ... But this system did implement Clause IV, at least to the extent that these were societies in which the market and private ownership were abolished. (Thompson, 1995a, 2)

This identification of Labour's former Clause IV with nationalisation and state socialism is, on the face of it, curious. Firstly, it is difficult to read Labour's former Clause IV, part 4 as sanctioning the state socialism of countries like the Soviet Union. Clause IV (4) argues for 'the best obtainable system of popular administration and control of each industry or service' (Labour Party, 1994, 4). Whilst the judgment that state socialism does not represent the 'best obtainable' system may be easier to make in retrospect than it was at the time, it was always a problem passing off events such as the collectivisation of agriculture as popular. In fact Thompson is wrong in his assertion that the market was abolished in such societies. Black markets were a significant and important attribute in the Soviet Union (Lane, 64–7).

The same point can be made about the association of Clause IV (4) with nationalisation in Britain. Nationalised industries have rarely been regarded as models of popularity. In addition the 'common ownership' stipulation of Clause IV can only be accommodated with nationalisation in Britain in a strictly legal and constitutional sense. Nationalisation provided little in the way of improved democratic control, greater openness or more public involvement in the industries concerned. What is notable about Labour's attachment to nationalisation is that, given its lack of popularity and perceived economic weaknesses, so little energy was expended in exploring other avenues of 'common ownership' which might have afforded a better and more popular system of administration and control.

In chapter 1 it was argued that Labour's Clause IV had had little effect on the Party's activities and actions. As Thompson puts it:

The leadership, the true believers and the electorate all know that no-one had any intention of doing anything about it and that suited everyone all round. (Thompson, 1995a, 3)

The ideological vacuum left by the failure to implement Labour's core statement was filled by Labour's pragmatic approach. In particular this led to Labour's association with the values of their greatest hour: the 1945–51 Government. Labour became identified with the Keynesian–Beveridge postwar settlement, and with Morrisonian nationalisation, the form of 'common ownership' adopted by the government. It is notable that this form of 'common ownership' is one which fits in easily and comfortably with the structure of the British state. It is also worth noting that in his speech marking the anniversary of Attlee's 1945 Government Blair made little mention of its nationalisation programme (Blair, 1995a).

It is this ideological identification of Labour with nationalisation that modernisers reacted against, Clause IV had merely acted as a justification for the actions of Labour in office. Straw's other points are also open to criticism. The mere fact that Clause IV had been drafted in 1918 was not a reason, on its own, to be rid of it. It could, after all, be argued that its longevity was a sign of its continuing relevance in very different social and political circumstances. The argument that Clause IV was an electoral liability, in Straw's version that it made Labour less popular than other European socialist parties, was difficult to establish. Why had Clause IV become an electoral liability since the 1970s? It might be argued that nationalisation had been tainted by its association with the dominant left in the early 1980s. The experience of Thatcherism could also be seen as undermining support for nationalisation as an economic strategy, but this threw opposition to Clause IV back on to the narrow interpretation which the modernisers favoured. One interesting variation on this theme, alluded to by Thompson's concern over the lack of vision, was that Clause IV, as a Party sacred cow, was actively hampering debate on ownership in which the Party needed to engage. This is an interesting point, and it must be judged in the light of the conduct of the debate over reforming Clause IV and the quality of its replacement.

Another aspect of the moderniser's positive appeal reflected the ideas behind the Policy Review. As a new and untried Leader Tony Blair may have felt that he needed to stamp his identity on the Party, and to demonstrate his leadership credentials to a wider public. As such, a frontal attack on Clause IV, whilst a gamble, would be taken by the media as a sign of political courage. As the third Party Leader in two years, and leading a Party desperate for electoral success, the gamble may not have been as great as it was portrayed. As Thompson noted:

> No-one should be under any illusion that if Blair is defeated (over Clause IV), Labour will be dead in the water as far as the next election goes. (1995a, 3)

From this perspective the attack on Clause IV was an electoral strategy designed to create the perception of a party with a set of principles providing a wide appeal, and a strong Leader willing to stand up to the Party's left. In essence this was no different from the approach of the Policy Review.

The final criticism of the modernisers was that Clause IV confused ends and means, that what it was really about was the means to create socialism rather than the principles of socialism. There are two problems with this criticism. Firstly it ignores the possibility that a commitment to specific means can itself reflect a matter of principle. Secondly, the choice of means can determine which ends are capable of being reached. This is well reflected in Labour's original Clause IV.

Take, for instance, parts 1 and 3 of the 1918 Clause IV. These commit Labour to maintaining a Party in Parliament and in the country, and commit the Party to expressing the principles approved by Party Conference (Labour Party, 1994, 4). These are prime examples of a commitment to means. At first glance they appear concerned with the technical administration of the Party and their presence in a Clause concerning the Party's aims and objects, its principles, is puzzling. However, there are good reasons for including these commitments here. In effect they act as the Party's commitment to democracy.

In part 1 the Party commits itself to electoral democracy, whilst part 3 provides a commitment to internal Party democracy. The nature of this commitment must have been even more readily apparent in 1918, the year after the Russian revolution. In effect, in this commitment to means rather than ends, the Party was separating itself from communism. The same point can be made about part 4, the commitment to common ownership. This can also be seen as a means rather than an end, but the real point of the commitment is the link it makes between democracy, power and claims over and control of economic resources. This might be considered an important statement of principle for a party faced with market-based capitalism.

Of the five criticisms made of Clause IV only the desire for a more positive statement of wider electoral appeal really holds water. It might be added that this argument has been afforded credibility by the failure of Labour in power to seek to apply what the 1918 Clause IV actually required. Whether the new Clause fits the role more effectively than its predecessor will be considered later, but the desire to project a strong leadership image had as much to do with the debate itself as with its final outcome. How was the debate conducted and what does its conduct tell us of Blair's leadership style?

The debate prompted four responses: the modernisers supported change along the lines Blair proposed; a second group was supportive of the idea of change but wished to see an open and wide ranging debate on what should replace Clause IV, without ruling out the possibility of retaining a commitment to common ownership; a third wished to see the retention of Clause IV, but was willing to cooperate in the creation of a complimentary statement of aims and values similar to that agreed when Gaitskell's attempt to replace Clause IV was defeated (Coates, 1995a); finally there were those who wanted to retain Clause IV at all costs, unchanged and pure, these were grouped around the *Defend Clause IV* campaign (Defend Clause IV, 1995a, 1995b). These different foci of opposition were dealt with differently in the leadership strategy followed by Blair. Whilst those sympathetic to some form of altered Clause had cause to complain that: 'Blair ... has failed to supply a proposition around which the debate can take place' (Aitken, 14), they were prepared to accept the proposed changes based on the consultation undertaken.

Those wishing to retain Clause IV, even with some form of amendment, found themselves more at odds with Labour's new Leader. This was illustrated by two events during the campaign: the MEPs' statement in support of Clause IV, and the treatment of Ken Loach. These will be considered below, but first we must consider how the case for modernisation was presented.

Whilst formally endorsing a consultation process to formulate a new Clause IV, Blair was able to use his position as Party Leader to mobilise the resources of the Party in support of his favoured outcome (Sopel, 288). Despite mostly being excluded from Blair's decision to institute constitutional reform (Sopel, 269) the Party leadership was prepared to endorse a timetable which would see a new Clause IV agreed at a special conference the following April. This allowed seven months from the first indication of potential change till the finalised agreement. Whilst *Defend Clause IV* had a very straightforward objective, to oppose change, their campaign was dependent on mobilising support in the constituencies, an impossibly difficult task given the tight deadlines. In addition the wording of the proposed new Clause would not be known until March, the month before the decision was to be made, allowing the modernisers to tempt those who might be willing to see limited change to support the process until the last minute.

More importantly than this, the Party machinery was utilised in a number of ways. The consultation process was conducted on the assumption of change, rather than its discussion (see below). A Party video was filmed promoting change to Clause IV, and a speaking tour organised to enable Blair to provide his case for change (Sopel, 291). In addition to this Blair could also call on the support of a Party Leader's media access and press staff to promote his perspective and defuse opposition.

Blair and the modernisers had been given notable advantages in this contest, irrespective of the fact that as a newly elected Leader in a party desperate for power he was likely to be given a generous hearing. With these advantages it is hardly surprising that Blair's camp found the opposition, at Party meetings at least, predictable (Sopel, 291). Nonetheless, it may be indicative of the fragility of Blair's leadership at this time that even in this situation the opposition aroused promoted in January 'a real feel of panic' amongst the modernisers (Sopel, 284).

This may account for the nature of the reactions to two events during the campaign. The first of these, a confrontation with Labour's Members of the European Parliament, came in Brussels – also in January. The basic events which led up to confrontation were simple enough. Blair had planned a high profile visit to Brussels for some time, during which he would meet with Labour's MEPs and with European business representatives. The day before Blair had held a press conference in London at which he had outlined Labour's campaigning themes for the coming year. These two events were intended to dominate the news coverage, but Blair found himself upstaged by a statement, advertised on the front page of the *Guardian*, signed by about half of those MEPs Blair was due to address.

The statement declared:

> The object of the debate should not be to change Clause IV but to build upon it. What is called for is a separate statement to express the Party's aims today. (Coates, 1995a)

The meaning of the timing and content of this statement seemed clear to Blair:

> It was calculated to do maximum damage to the leadership. It completely overshadowed Blair's Brussels speech that was coming up, and buried reports about Labour's campaigning aims for the year ahead. (Sopel, 285)

Blair's subsequent meeting with Labour's MEPs was apparently used by Blair and his Press Secretary, Alistair Campbell, to demonstrate Blair's strong leadership. Sopel paints a rather farcical picture of Campbell standing at the back of the hall and popping out to the waiting press occasionally to keep them informed of Blair's dressing down of the MEPs (285). However, the MEPs involved in the statement remember events rather differently.

In fact the MEPs' statement had been originally signed toward the end of 1994 and published at that time in the *Morning Star* and *Tribune*. When this failed to elicit the publicity the organisers had originally hoped for, a meeting of some of the signatories decided to publish the statement in the *Guardian* at the earliest possible opportunity after the Christmas break. From this perspective the coincidence of the publication with Blair's visit was more by accident than design, and the publicity it received a matter of surprise, though the failure to realise how this might be presented suggests a lack of acumen on the part of the statement's sponsors.

It could be argued that Blair's handling of this affair actually increased the publicity for significant and important opposition to the dumping of Clause IV than had been clear before. On the other hand this might be the very reason why Blair felt it necessary to regard this meeting as a demonstration of his leadership capabilities. Whatever the attitude to these events, it is clear that Blair's commitment to debate over Clause IV did not stretch as far as allowing real opposition to the removal and replacement of Labour's Clause IV from its constitution, and that Blair's view of leadership was, in line with past Labour Leaders, to demonstrate his domination over his own party.

Another illustrative event was the treatment of the video produced for the *Defend Clause IV* campaign by Ken Loach. The video was intended as a response to the Party video putting the case for change. Loach's involvement as an internationally renowned director drew considerable media attention. Journalists approaching Loach for interviews also found themselves approached with a story that Loach had allowed his Party membership to lapse. The truth was that Loach had refused to allow his membership subscription to be transferred to Labour's direct debit system when the Party had introduced central membership. He had objected to this on the grounds that it took power away from the constituency parties and gave too much to the central Party (Loach, 20).

What is interesting about this is that the Party machinery was used to undermine opposition to the replacement of Clause IV. As Loach complained, there was no commitment to allow real debate within the Party (ibid.). The fact that these two events were largely isolated examples of interference with opposition to the modernisers' intentions reflected the lack of serious opposition to the changes which were pushed through. Whether this opposition would have been greater with a more open or protracted debate is impossible to determine. Nonetheless, particularly given the restricted and predictable nature of the opposition, the use of the Party to undermine opponents and to demonstrate Blair's 'leadership qualities' is illustrative of the nature of Blair's leadership in its early stages at least. Of real importance to the modernisers was the impact of all this on Party consultations. It is this consultation process and its results which must now be assessed.

The Consultation Process

The consultation process initiated for the reform of Clause IV was dictated by the timetable for change. The Party's National Executive Committee decided to meet to agree a wording for a revised Clause IV in March, and to call a special conference to agree the new Clause in April. This meant that a new Clause had to be drafted by the first of these dates. Consultation on the formation of a new Clause had thus to be completed by March. In addition the Party leadership wished to consolidate the perceived gains of one-member-one-vote by encouraging constituencies to ballot their membership over the final decision to change Clause IV to be made at the special conference.

The consultation was conducted through the publication of the document *Labour's Objects: Socialist Values in the Modern World* (Labour Party, 1994), and its results published in *Labour's Aims and Values: The Consultation Report* (Labour Party, 1995). The first of these was a 12-page document setting out the rationale for change and suggesting topics for discussion and debate at Party meetings. It contained a questionnaire intended to form the basis of responses to the document.

This document was distributed to the Party's affiliated trade unions, socialist societies, constituencies and branches. In addition a special issue of *Labour Party News*, the Party's membership magazine distributed to all individual members, was published which contained the arguments of *Labour's Objects* as well as statements from a number of leading Party figures, and reproduced the questionnaire. In this fashion all of the Party's members and affiliates were given the opportunity to respond. In many ways this represented an unprecedented attempt at consultation within the Party.

The consultation document itself formed part of the debate around the replacement of Clause IV. This was underlined by the special edition of *Labour Party News* which contained contributions from a number of individuals in the Party's higher echelons, or amongst affiliated groups. In all twelve contributions to the debate were published, of which eight were MPs, two MEPs, one a trade union General Secretary, and the last the General Secretary of the Fabian Society Labour's biggest internal think-tank. This excluded contributions from the Party's grassroots. Of course the consultation was intended to elicit grassroots contributions, but once again the problem of different levels of articulation was clear. As one moderniser observed:

Having participated at a number of branch meetings round the country, my feeling is that no-one should be deceived that the high vote for the change to Clause IV means that the bulk of the membership has been wholly persuaded by the shift to New Labour. (Thompson, 1995b, 7)

Whilst biased toward the Party's elite, and particularly its Parliamentary elite, there was some attempt to provide a balanced contribution with regard to support for the various positions within the debate. The contributors can be placed in the four positions in the debate outlined above. Of the twelve, five – Hilary Armstrong, Harriet Harman, Bridget Prentice, Alan Johnson, and Simon Crine – can be seen as broadly supporting modernising positions; four – John Prescott, Robin Cook, Clare Short, and Derek Fatchett – as supporting a new Clause IV which embodied the economic principles of the old Clause; the two MEPs, Wayne David and Stan Newens, were both in support of retaining all or part of Clause IV alongside a new statement of aims and objectives; whilst only Tony Benn, on behalf of the Campaign Group of MPs, called for no change. So three-quarters of the contributors were in favour of a new Clause IV in some form. In addition eight of the contributors felt it necessary to justify or support Tony Blair's call for a debate, with only Clare Short offering direct criticism of the timing and nature of the debate (Labour Party News, 1995a, 7–14). It is probably no accident that the defenders of Clause IV were either MEPs associated with a statement Blair himself had been reported as ridiculing, and Tony Benn, the standard-bearer of 'old Labour'.

Perhaps even more illustrative of the use of consultation processes to lead the Party in the direction of change was the questionnaire respondents were asked to complete. The questionnaire was grouped around four discussion areas. These were subdivided into a series of questions. On 'Labour's objects' two questions were asked; on 'values' six; on 'the economy' one; and on 'Labour and the people' two. This weighting itself was important, with economic issues providing only one of the questions asked, whilst value concepts proposed in the document provided more than half the questionnaire. Whilst respondents were given the opportunity to provide open-ended responses to these questions, the wording of the questions themselves led the respondent to particular conclusions. Central to the strategy of this document was the first discussion which dealt with the existing Clause IV. The first question in this section asked:

> Thinking about an updated statement of Labour's aims and values do you agree with the argument in the booklet that the current Clause IV does not set out Labour's actual *values* in a clear and concise manner? (Labour Party, 1994, *Response Sheet*)

Not only did this question presume the change to Clause IV which the document was supposed to be consulting over, but it started the exercise by inviting criticism of the existing Clause. It is unlikely that many broad statements of faith would avoid extensive criticism under such circumstances, and this criticism can then be used to justify the desired change. To some extent it can be argued that discovering the limitations of current practice was a necessary first step in discussing the idea of change. Nonetheless the questionnaire provided no opportunity for those who might have wished to opt to retain the status quo, except to reject the option proposed by the official Party document.

The second discussion area then asked for responses to the six value concepts raised by the document itself. These were: social justice, freedom, opportunity, equality, democracy, and solidarity and responsibility at home and abroad. In this way responses considering what should replace Clause IV were directed to the areas the advocates of change supported. This was even clearer in the one question in the economy discussion. This asked:

> Thinking about our new statement – how do you believe that Labour should express its commitment to an economy in which there is an efficient, accountable and socially responsive private sector, with effective public ownership, control and regulation of key public services and utilities? (Labour Party, 1994, *Response Sheet*)

This was a move away from the 'common ownership' of the existing Clause IV, and intended to lead respondents into considering the enshrinement of the mixed economy approaches Labour Governments in practice favoured. The final section rounded this up with a direction to consider the electoral implications of the new Clause. The two questions in this section asked:

> How should the Party communicate its new statement of objects to the public?
>
> [and] How can a clear statement of objects be used to build Party membership? (Labour Party, 1994, *Response Sheet*)

This had the dual benefit of highlighting the electoral and membership effects of a new statement, and the perceived electoral liability of the existing Clause. Finally respondents were asked for any further comments, but by the end of the response sheet the tenor and wording of the questions must have left few respondents in much doubt about what was required.

Responses were invited to arrive before 3 March to enable analysis for the drafting of a new Clause to be presented at that month's National Executive Committee meeting. This analysis was presented in the extensive document *Labour's Aims and Values: The Consultation Report* (Labour

Party, 1995). This provided a wealth of analysis on the responses received. In all 8000 questionnaires were returned. Of these 6600 were from individual members, 1400 from branches and 210 from constituency parties. As the response sheets had asked respondents to detail the numbers at branch and constituency meetings it was also possible to report that 18 000 attended the branch meetings and 5500 the constituency meetings (Labour Party, 1995, 2). In total, then, some 30 000 members had been involved in consultation, a figure which presumably double counts individuals who responded and attended branch and constituency meetings. All the attempts to involve Labour's grass roots had encouraged, at best, only one-tenth of the Party's 300 000 members to participate. This, incidentally, was almost exactly the same number that Blair claimed to have attended his tour of meetings promoting constitutional reform (Sopel, 289). Whilst it may be argued that 10 per cent is a good response level for a mail shot survey, it hardly seems an enthusiastic endorsement of such a fundamental change in Labour's constitution. Nonetheless, the widespread responses from branches and constituencies in a relatively short period of time does suggest a considerable debate at the activist level, which must have been reinforced by discussion over the new Clause draft when that was published. In addition 18 affiliated trade unions and 3 affiliated societies also responded.

The open-ended responses were analysed on the basis of common themes. A random sample of 200 was assessed to determine themes, and the whole sample was analysed on the basis of 130 criteria established from this selection (Labour Party, 1995, 4). The results were provided in some detail, but narrowed down to a few key themes in each area. In the first discussion area on Labour's objects, the question, predictably, found a majority in all areas agreeing that the existing Clause IV was not a clear statement of Labour's values. Amongst individual members and branch responses 69 per cent agreed with this perspective, whilst 58 per cent of constituency party responses agreed and 56 per cent of affiliated trade unions, but perhaps considering the wording of the question, and the debate, it was surprising that nearly a third of responses felt the existing Clause was a clear statement. Of course agreement that the existing Clause was not clear and concise does not necessarily presume support for its abandonment, but this point was not raised in the analysis.

The majority of the analysis focused on the shape of a new clause. The questions on value concepts and on what the existing Clause left out were considered to provide themes for a new draft. The themes identified were narrowed to the two or three regarded as most significant. The themes left out of the existing Clause were identified as equality and social justice, with democracy, opportunity and the environment also seen as important (Labour

Party, 1995, 8). Interestingly, of these themes only the environment is missing from the section on value concepts in the response sheet. This may be taken to indicate either the extent to which the values identified in the questionnaire were in tune with those of the grass roots of the Party, or the extent to which the respondents were taking their cues from the response sheet itself.

In each of the value concept responses, key themes were adduced. Under social justice, the three most important themes identified were reducing inequality, meeting basic needs, and access to justice, with socialist societies identifying common ownership (Labour Party, 1994, 11). Under freedom, the balance with responsibility clearly stood out as an important theme, with freedom from poverty also important (ibid., 12). Education was highlighted as a key theme under opportunity, with personal fulfilment also highlighted (ibid., 13). For equality, the themes were a fair distribution of wealth and equal opportunity (ibid., 14), the extension of democracy and the accountability of quangos was seen as important under democracy (ibid., 16), and international cooperation was a clear winner under solidarity and responsibility at home and abroad (ibid., 17).

These responses presented a bit of a problem in contributing to a new Clause IV. One problem was that they were very wide-ranging, and in particular some of the themes, education for example, seemed to present the same confusion of ends and means which modernisers had criticised the original Clause for containing. One clearly important theme was redistribution. This had appeared amongst the top themes in relation to social justice, reducing inequality and redistribution; freedom, freedom from poverty; and equality, fair distribution of wealth. Despite this consistency the links here were not raised, and the general themes from this section of the analysis were not taken forward into the conclusion.

The section on the economy also provided three themes: regulation in the public interest, public ownership of essential services, and a mixed economy (ibid., 18). In effect these were the themes which had been identified in the question asked in this section. These were added to the themes identified as missing from the original Clause, that is to say the themes identified by the response sheet itself, as the conclusion from the consultation document (Ibid., 21). In other words the analysis concluded that what members 'would like to see a new Clause IV reflect' were, with the exception of the environment, the themes which had been identified for members in the response sheet itself. The original themes raised by respondents in the section on value concepts, in particular the marked commitment to some form of redistribution, was ignored.

Following this consultation a new Clause was drafted and agreed by the Party's NEC by a margin of 21 to 3 (Economist, 1995b, 31). The extent to which the finally agreed Clause reflected the principles emerging from the consultation process will be considered below. However, it has been claimed that the draft Clause emerging from consultation was 'shredded' because it went further than the modernisers intended (Sopel, 293). It is impossible to judge the accuracy of this claim, apart from seeking to assess the eventual content of the new Clause, but two things do emerge from this consultation. Firstly, the consultation involved no more than 10 per cent of the Party's membership, and probably a good deal less. Secondly, the key themes emerging from the consultation process were clearly the major themes identified on the response sheet itself.

If participation in consultation over the content of the new Clause was disappointing, the second phase, obtaining agreement for the replacement of the existing Clause with the new draft, offered the opportunity to push for wider involvement. In line with the intention to develop one-member-one-vote, constituencies were encouraged to ballot their membership over the simple question of whether to retain or replace the existing Clause IV in the month between the agreement of the new draft and the Party's special conference. This proved far more successful as an exercise in participation.

Table 7.1: Regional Constituency Responses to Clause IV Balloting 1995

Region	No.	Papers Issued	Turnout %	Yes	%	No	%
Scotland	38	12592	41.41	4466	85.65	748	14.35
Wales	33	16823	50.75	7606	89.09	931	10.91
Northern & Yorks.	60	32010	46.87	12899	85.97	2105	14.03
North West	44	21254	45.74	8143	83.76	1579	16.24
Central	49	23716	45.27	9153	85.25	1584	14.75
West Midlands	46	18874	46.11	7497	86.14	1206	13.86
Greater London	59	46382	41.55	15662	81.27	3610	18.73
South East	59	25701	52.81	11706	86.25	1866	13.75
South & West	53	19364	51.64	8678	86.78	1322	13.22
Total	441*	216716	46.49	85810	85.16	14951	14.84

Source: The Labour Party, 1995. Note: *Analysis based on preliminary results with 63 constituencies still to declare.

The results of balloting were perceived by the Party leadership as a vindication of the modernisers' project (Sopel, 297). Over 500 Constituency Labour Parties opted to ballot their members over acceptance of the new Clause. Preliminary regional results are presented in Table 7.1.

These results represent a distinctly mixed bag for both modernisers and supporters of one-member-one-vote. On the one hand the support for the new Clause amongst those balloted and returning their forms is overwhelming, consistently over 80 per cent. On the other hand turnouts are distinctly average, reaching over 50 per cent in only three regions. This means less than 40 per cent of Labour's members who were given an opportunity to do so were prepared to fill in and return a simple ballot form in support of an issue of fundamental importance to the Party and the leadership which was widely publicised. Unless the Party is able to inculcate a culture of participation, something which has been noticeable by its absence up until now, the outlook must be for participation rates on one-member-one-vote ballots to decline from this level.

Nonetheless the immediate result at Labour's Special Conference in April was a clear victory for the new Clause IV. This was made even sweeter for the leadership by the support amongst those constituencies which balloted their membership, with all but three of these voting in favour. As a result common ownership as a statement of faith in Labour's constitution became a part of its history, but did the new Clause IV fulfil the expectations of the modernisers and its other supporters?

The New Clause

One problem in considering the replacement Clause IV, which was adopted as part of Labour's constitution at the April Special Conference, is what criteria to use for its assessment. For the modernisers in the Party achieving victory at the Special Conference was itself a success, whilst for those defending the old Clause it was a failure. This is clearly not an adequate basis for assessment, but what might be?

Here the new Clause will be examined in the light of three criteria, firstly with regard to the criticisms made of the old Clause by the modernisers, and in particular the five points raised by Shaw mentioned above. Secondly an assessment will be made as to how well the new Clause fits the themes raised by the consultation process, outlined above. Finally the Clause will be considered as a consistent ideological statement. These criteria seem the most obvious to apply as they are both directly related to the intentions of those who pursued this change, and they provide some guidance as to the improvement, if any, the new Clause represents. The full text of the new and old Clause is included earlier in this chapter, and a comparison between the two will help to bring out salient changes.

A number of aspects of difference between the two Clauses is striking. Firstly the new Clause states unequivocally that the Party is a democratic socialist party. Whether this claim is justified by the Clause's content will be considered later. Secondly the new Clause, while seeking the trust of the people to govern, contains no commitment to maintaining a democratic structure in the country or to internal party democracy. There are statements regarding the commitment to maintaining a party in the country in Clause I of the new constitution (Labour Party, 1996, 3), and the role of Party Conference is outlined in Clause VI (Labour Party, 1996, 4–5), but these are no longer seen as statements of ideological faith. Instead the Party is committed to 'an open democracy' reforming government structure. Whilst not necessarily undermining the parliamentary nature of the Party, this clearly does relegate internal democratic control over the Party leadership, in particular the role of Conference.

Three other aspects are also worth noting at this point: that the central commitment to common ownership and to redress inequalities in political, social and economic power enshrined in parts 4 and 5 of the 1918 Clause are replaced with four general commitments in part 2 of the new Clause; the internationalist commitments of the 1918 Clause are replaced with a commitment to 'the defence and security of the British people' in an international setting; and that the trade unions are removed from their place as the main group with which Labour identifies itself, in part 2 of the 1918 Clause, to one of many different groups, in part 4 of the new Clause.

The question is, do these changes represent a merely superficial tampering with the old Clause, or are they representative of a change in Labour's attitude or approach which will prove of fundamental significance in the future? In order to answer this question we must consider the changes in the light of the criteria described earlier. Firstly, what of the criticism of the 1918 Clause by the modernisers? To what extent has the replacement improved on what went before in this regard?

Straw's five complaints were that: the old Clause enshrined a mistaken belief in the superiority of state-run enterprises; it was an ambiguous compromise; it confused ends and means; its statist connotations had been contradicted by history; and it was an apparent electoral liability (Jones, 55–6). The accuracy of this description of the old Clause has already been questioned above, but to what extent does the new Clause improve in these areas?

Firstly, what does the new Clause say about state-run enterprises? It replaces the blanket commitment to 'common ownership' with a statement that 'those undertakings essential to the common good are either owned by the public or accountable to them'. Whilst this does not specifically commit Labour to state-run enterprise, any more than common ownership does, it is a wording which seems more in line with British state practice. The notion that nationalised industries were accountable to the people through Parliament was its justifying feature, not that it formed a popular structure of common ownership. In terms of the modernisers critique, the question here must be why is this necessary? If state-run services are not superior, in some sense, to the private sector then why is there a need for any, even the most essential, to be in public hands?

What, then, about the clarity of Clause IV? Does the new formulation overcome the ambiguity modernisers complained about? In fact the new Clause seems to contain a variety of different ideas, not only from different conceptions of a particular perspective, but from different ideological perspectives entirely. The Clause's use of communities has been linked with conservatism (Giddens), whilst commitments to 'family values' were a central plank of Thatcherism (Letwin); on the other hand the section on 'a just society' seems to embody the ideas of liberal philosopher John Rawls (Rawls). This seems a more strained and diverse compromise of different ideas than was true of the 1918 Clause.

The third criticism was of a confusion of ends and means. How does the new Clause resolve this? Clearly there has been a concerted effort to concentrate on ends within the new Clause. Nonetheless, parts 3 and 4 clearly identify particular institutions and organisations which Labour will involve itself with in pursuit of its ends. As was stated earlier, this may be perfectly justifiable as a commitment to the use of specific means may reflect the desired ends. However, some of the particular organisations included are interesting. Notably, the inclusion of European institutions commits the Party to some sort of involvement in Europe. It is difficult to see this as related to anything other than the European Union, though more oblique interpretations may be possible. This is a surprising statement of faith from a British political party in the future of Europe and of Britain's role in this future. Whilst reflecting the views of the current Party leadership, it seems at least conceivable that this statement could become a hostage to fortune.

What about the statist connotations perceived by Straw in the old Clause? What does the new Clause say about the role of the state? In fact neither Clause directly mentions the state, and it is conceivable that both sets of principles, with the arguable exception of the international aspects, could operate equally well without a state. The only real alteration in the new Clause is the mention of 'high quality public services' which does suggest some system of public, state-based provision. It should also be noted that the use of terms such as 'the public interest', 'partnership', the idea of accountability, and the

international stress on 'defence and security' do seem to bring the new
Clause more in line with the operation of the British state than the old
Clause.

Finally, what of the Party's electoral aspirations? Does the new Clause
help electorally? The new Clause does not obviously lend itself to campaigning.
It does not present a central theme similar to the common ownership it
replaced, and the applications of its principles are open to interpretation just
as much as, if not more than, the 1918 Clause. Indeed, since its adoption the
new Clause has hardly been mentioned in public by the Party, let alone formed
the centre of its campaigning strategy, though this may change closer to a
General Election. The *Economist* called the new Clause: 'a waggonload of
waffle designed to appeal to as many voters as possible' (1995c, 20). As Labour
might regard itself as seeking to win over those very educated middle-class
readers attracted to such journals this judgment is hardly reassuring.

Indeed even the modernisers themselves seemed less than convinced that
the achievements were worth the risk:

> The conflict over Clause IV could have been a disastrous internal battle.
> While the campaign and final settlement were far from perfect, the dominant
> message was directed towards the electorate. (Thompson, 1995, 4)

Whilst the message may have been directed towards the electorate, if it was
not included in the final statement, where was the message? The message
the electorate was intended to hear was that the victory over Clause IV
demonstrated Tony Blair's control over his own Party, and ended the spectre
of the 'left' which proved so unpopular in the early 1980s. This achievement
was regarded as significant by the *Economist* which argued that Blair had
brought about two important changes: he had destroyed the myth of Party
activist power; and he had reversed the polarity of radicalism within the Party
by establishing the right of the Party as the innovators, and the left as the
defenders of a historical tradition (1995c, 20). To what extent these
achievements can be sustained, and what their electoral impact will be, it is
far too early to tell. Whether this represents a truly innovative change in
Labour's approach is open to question.

From the perspective of the modernisers' critique the real achievement
has been to project the Party Leader, and possibly to re-establish the Party
elite, as the dominant force in the Party. Following these comments did the
new Clause reflect the principles emerging from the consultation process?
As was shown above, the principles perceived as emerging through the
consultation process were prompted by the consultation questionnaire. One
principle to emerge strongly independently of the questionnaire was a call
for a commitment to some form of redistribution, but this was ignored by

the consultation report and did not feature in the new Clause. Five recommendations were made by the consultation report, three of them aimed at the economy. How were these reflected in the new Clause?

The first called for 'a strong commitment to equality and social justice' (Labour Party, 1995, 21). The concept of social justice was embodied in one of the subsections of part 2 of the new Clause: 'a just society'. This included a commitment to 'equality of opportunity' but also argued that a just society: 'judges its strength by the condition of the weak as well as the strong', which implies continuing inequality of outcome. This is perhaps surprising given the fact that opportunity was identified separately from equality in the consultation process.

In fact opportunity was part of the second set of objectives identified by the consultation report: 'commitments to democracy, opportunity and protection of the environment' (ibid.). These were all included in the new Clause, though the commitments to democracy and the environment, contained in subsections c and d of part 2 of the Clause were unspecific and said little which could not be endorsed by a 'one nation' conservative.

The three economic objectives identified: 'regulation in the public interest; public ownership of essential services; and support for a mixed economy' (ibid.), again all featured, but all were adapted to somewhat different forms. There was no specific mention of regulation, though the 'dynamic economy' would be 'serving the public interest'; the essential services would be 'owned by the public or accountable to them'; and the mixed economy was a mixture of 'the market and the rigour of competition' and 'the forces of partnership and cooperation', though what the latter amounted to was by no means clear.

It seems that the principles identified in the consultation process were only adopted to the extent that they supported the intentions of the drafters of the new Clause. This was the case even though the principles identified were prompted by the consultation process itself. It is difficult to see this consultation as being an effective constraint on the drafting of the new Clause, and it seems likely that the final appearance in the new Clause of the principles identified was in a very different context from that envisaged by the respondents to the consultation.

Finally, it should also be said that the overall coherence of the new Clause is also problematic. The new Clause sought to solidify the concepts raised in both the Policy Review and by the Commission for Social Justice into a new ideological statement for the Party. Themes of social justice, partnership, equality of opportunity, and a move away from the perceived ideological baggage of the postwar Labour Government were central, but the new Clause also suffers from the same problems as both the Review and the Commission: it fails to resolve questions of priority.

Values not given priority

The new Clause presents four areas of concern for the Party: the economy, social justice, democracy, and the environment, but it fails to suggest which of these is most significant, or to provide a mechanism for resolving clashes in priorities. In short it provides a ragbag of different principles and ideas but without an underlying reason why they are associated and what should be regarded as their importance. Unlike the 1918 Clause, which provided a central theme of common ownership embodying concepts of democracy and equality, the new Clause refers to these concepts in the abstract, as principles in themselves. As such it provides no mechanism for applying these principles.

What, for example, should the reaction of a Labour government be if the need for economic action to 'produce the wealth the nation needs' clashes with the need to 'protect, enhance and hold in trust' the environment? What if environmental action cuts across the need to provide 'security against fear and justice at work'? Or this requirement interferes with decisions being taken 'by the communities they affect'? Whilst there are a number of ways that a set of priorities might be deduced from the Clause, by considering the ordering of these four areas of concern for instance, there are no underlying principles linking the concerns of the Clause together. This means that the principles just appear as a more or less random assortment of desires and intentions.

The practical offshoot of this is that actual decisions over priorities and applications will be left to Labour's leadership and particularly its parliamentary leadership. This, perhaps more than anything else in the new Clause IV, thoroughly reflects the traditional behaviour of the Labour Party.

Conclusion

The adoption of Labour's new Clause IV has been portrayed as a victory for Labour's modernisers in the face of conservative intransigence from a diehard old left (Blair, 1995, 4). In fact there is little in this change which marks Labour as a 'new' Party, separate from its history and traditions. Whilst it is true that the Party's stated aims and objectives are radically different from what they were, the change is one which serves to bring them more in line with the practice of Labour government. As such this represents neither a radical innovation nor a modernisation but the ultimate victory of Labour's pragmatic tradition.

In addition the modernisers, just like the Commission on Social Justice, have failed to address the three key problems identified in the analysis of the Policy Review. Far from providing a new Clause which might be the base for a radical challenge to, or at least a re-evaluation of, the British state, the modernisers' new Clause IV adopts the language and the style which has exemplified Labour administrators of that state.

Despite the consultation process and the challenge to activist power it is clear that the results of the consultation had little impact on the final form of the Clause, except where they could be moulded to the intentions of the drafters. In addition it seems that the debate did not persuade all Party activists of the benefits of modernisation. Instead the prospect of potential electoral defeat encouraged support for the new Clause. Even so this support was far from enthusiastically given. The proportion of members who involved themselves in consultation and balloting, whilst reasonable for mail shot surveys, hardly represented overwhelming endorsements of the proposed change. This does not suggest a party in touch with its grass roots, contrary to Blair's claims for modernisation (Blair, 1995, 15). Indeed the belief that activist power has been defeated may also prove premature if activists have subsumed their true beliefs to ensure short-term electoral victory. Far from resolving the issues of difference between the Party leadership and its grass roots, these events may have stored up trouble for a future Labour government. Perhaps crucial in all this will be the make up, political attitudes, and subservience of the new membership who have joined the Party since Blair became Leader. No new ideology

Finally the new Clause, despite its stated intentions, does not provide a new ideological base for the Party. Instead it places the Party firmly on the pragmatic ground traditionally favoured by the leadership. The modernisers were not objecting to, or indeed arguing against, the content of Clause IV itself, which made defence of Clause IV based on what it said rather redundant. In fact they were objecting to the practice of postwar Labour government. This had been justified by reference to Clause IV, but had far more to do with the pragmatic necessities of government than a great commitment to the ideological principles of public ownership. However the new Clause IV has merely served to legitimise the practice of Labour Governments.

The achievement of Blair has been to stamp his authority, albeit perhaps temporarily, on the Party he leads, and to trim Labour's sails to head in a new direction based on the perceived immediate political need of electoral victory and a tacit acceptance of the status quo. Far from a radical and innovative challenge in British politics and a moderniser of Labour's traditions, Blair's leadership continues the pragmatic heritage of British labourism, and its support for British political practice.

8 Conclusion

[handwritten margin note: great statement of difficulty of, & need for modernisation]

By the time of the next General Election Labour will have gone through three major policy reviews in ten years; two major membership drives; a series of consultation exercises; an ideological statement, a re-examination of principles, and finally the reform of Clause IV; significant changes to its policy-making structures; and numerous launches and relaunches. They will also have failed to win a General Election for over 20 years; have failed to achieve 40 per cent of the popular vote in a General Election for 25 years; and needed to overturn a Conservative lead of 7 per cent on the popular vote. From this perspective Labour's renewal and subsequent modernisation hardly appears an unalloyed success. Nonetheless, Labour has been involved in a series of ambitious attempts to address the serious problems with which they have been faced. The ambitious elements of these reforms have been overshadowed, indeed intentionally overshadowed, by short-term electoralism. This domination of electoral concerns in fact reinforces, rather than addresses, Labour's core problems.

The Policy Review sought to affect four elements of the Party: its ideological basis, through the publication of a new statement of ideology; the Party's policy-making structure, by providing an alternative system and bringing together the various confederal elements of the Party's system; the Party's policy output, by providing a comprehensive reworking of the Party's policy options; and the Party's electoral appeal, by providing a four-year electoral strategy designed to galvanise the Party for the forthcoming General Election. These elements were also a focus for the reforms of John Smith and Tony Blair. The Commission on Social Justice provided a re-examination of Party principles; another separate policy-making system; another new set of policies; and an attempt to provide an electorally popular means of changing Party policy. The reforms to Clause IV did not provide a new policy base for the Party, though this has been addressed separately by the Party leadership, but it did focus on the Party's ideology, for electoral purposes, and did seek to reinforce changes to Labour's decision-making systems through consultation.

[handwritten margin note: 4 foci of refm.]

The Policy Review and its successors have reflected Labour's traditional, pragmatic considerations. It might be asked what, apart from a central concern with electoral pragmatism, the 'reformism' of Neil Kinnock and Tony Blair shares with that of Gaitskell and Crosland. The concerns of redistribution, economic growth, full employment, and social progress do not seem as central, or arguably as relevant, in the 1990s as they did in the 1950s and 1960s (Foote, 1985: 15).

The question must be asked: if these events were no more than a return to the fundamental pragmatic concerns of a party seeking government, why did the fierce internal divisions of the early 1980s disappear? Why have they not resurfaced, either in the review period, or since? Hughes and Winter claimed that the Party was 'tamed' by the success of the Review (Hughes and Wintour, 1990: 186). I have argued that the Review was associated with a wider realignment within the Party based around the Kinnock leadership. The Review did not make this realignment possible, but rather that the Review was made possible by the realignment.

In achieving this harmony, Labour may have lost more than just internal divisions. Labour's Conference lacks the vitality it once had, and internal divisions may be an important element in formulating a distinctive ideological base (Taylor, 1988: 27), which may itself be important in Labour's appeal and activities (Cole, 1977: 17; Bevan, 1978: 126). A loss of ideological identity is not the sole problem facing Labour. It has been argued that Labour is pursuing the same pragmatic perspectives that have dominated its history. So why have these proved electorally less successful in the 1980s and 1990s than in the 1960s and 1970s?

Of course it could be said that Labour were not as electorally healthy in the 1960s and 1970s as might be presumed from electoral victory. They were in decline even then. It could also be observed that the left appears to be more quiescent in the 1980s than at almost any other time in Labour's history. This is certainly true, but the electoral resurgence of the Conservatives, which has helped to put Labour's electoral failings in stark relief, and the loss of confidence of Labour's left are both related to the fundamental cause of Labour's loss of identity: the general crisis of socialist ideology, and particularly of the postwar approaches of social democracy, in the face of the New Right challenge, and in Britain of the challenge of Thatcherism.

Whilst it might be argued that it is a lot to ask one party to resolve the crisis of social democracy, it must be noted that Labour has never effectively been a socialist party – the point for Labour would be to provide a convincing pragmatic response to its problems. Not only has it failed to do so, it has failed even to acknowledge the importance of the challenge of the New Right to Labour's traditional concerns. It might be thought that for a pragmatic Party there would be no better forum for outlining a response to the challenge of the New Right than a comprehensive policy review. The failure of the Review on this score, illustrated by two further restatements of policy since 1992, is central to the problems of the Party and any possible resolution.

There are two interrelated aspects to this failure. Firstly, Labour has failed to provide a convincing outline of the legitimate relationship between the individual and the state in relation to Labour policies in government. Secondly, Labour is restricted by public perceptions, at least amongst its electoral constituency, of the Party's failures in office. Labour has traditionally regarded the nature of state power as unproblematic to the exercise of state power. Both the Commission on Social Justice and Labour's new Clause IV continue to accept the British state as a neutral instrument for the use of the correct political leadership. This fitted Labour's long-standing views of the British state and was not helped by the perception of Labour's failures in its past exercise of state power. This is, perhaps, surprising given the support of some modernisers for state reform and their criticism of past Labour governments on precisely these grounds (Hutton, 1993b, 53).

The problem here is not what Labour is promising, but the fact that nobody believes that it will carry out whatever promises it makes. Whether or not these perceptions of poor performance and broken promises are correct, the problem for Labour is that the perceptions exist. This is not helped by Labour's refusal to accept the perceived failings of former Labour governments, or to effectively criticise the state which it is seen to have run so badly. If Labour insists that it is not the state which causes problems but those who run the state, the voters' perceptions of Labour Governments will continue to hamper their attempts at re-election.

One final consideration which renewal raises relates to the structure of the Party and its ability to reach its electoral constituency. The intention of the Review was to build new links to its voters and, to a lesser extent, its grass-roots members. This attempt was continued with the consultation undertaken by both the Commission on Social Justice, and over the reform of Clause IV. To what extent have these attempts brought the Party closer to its members and supporters?

The Review clearly failed in its attempt to reach ordinary Party members, and to provide them with a meaningful input into the Review process. These experiences were used to inform later attempts at consultation. However, these were inevitably structured by those doing the consultation, and interpreted in the terms of the project instigated by the leadership. Moreover, under Blair and Kinnock consultation was conducted in the context of electoral pragmatism. Both leaders focused on the electoral importance of the reforms they promoted. This suggested that a failure to endorse change would mark the Party out as being either unfit for, or uninterested in, government office.

Another important reform has occurred in Party policy-making. Central themes have been retained, like the concept of social justice; a continuing link between the Shadow Cabinet and the NEC has been developed; the

National Policy Forum created; and the use of polling data as a source for policy-making and presentational information has become a central feature of Party organisation. It seems clear that Labour has not created a pluralist policy-making system which effectively reflects the perspectives of its members, or potential support.

The problem for Labour is not just that it is out of touch with its constituency, its potential support, but that its means of reaching this constituency are not equal to the task of persuading it towards Labour's perspective. The media, in Britain at least, does not appear to be the greatest means of persuading the electorate towards radical and critical perspectives; trade unions no longer seem as capable of disciplining and delivering their members to the Party as appeared the case in the past; and polling techniques discover what the electorate think – they do not persuade voters to alternative conclusions. This neglects an important function of Party activity, particularly of a Party of opposition and one with socialist pretensions: the Party's role in shaping the political environment in which it operates (Dunleavy, 1991: 125–8; Seyd and Whiteley, 1992: 208; Callaghan, 1990: 1–2). The problem for Labour is that without a membership, active in the local community, through which the Party feels comfortable reaching out to its constituents, Labour remains detached from its potential support. Its attempts to reach them through the organised labour force, through the media, and through polling techniques are passive rather than interactive, and are precisely the means which have failed over the past 30 years.

Conclusion

Labour's period of renewal, and now of modernisation, has emphasised themes which have been a part of Labour politics since its inception. Supporters have been able to portray these as a departure not because they were original, but because they were a reaction against the perceived victories of the Party's left in the early 1980s.

In the early 1980s Whiteley demonstrated three crises within the Party: an ideological schism; a membership crisis; and an electoral crisis (Whiteley, 1983: 2–12). The nature of these crises have changed dramatically, notably with the reforms of Tony Blair. Whilst there is little evidence that Labour's 'ideological schism' has been resolved, the victory of Party 'modernisers' over the reform of Clause IV will alter the way in which this is articulated in future. On the other two fronts: Labour's membership is rising steadily; and Labour is well ahead in the opinion polls. Both the last two improvements also occurred, and were reversed, under Kinnock's leadership.

It has been argued above that there were three causes of these crises: a loss of ideological identity; a refusal, or inability, to criticise the nature of state power; and an inability to reach the Party's potential constituents in a way capable of persuading them towards Labour's objectives. Of course these three factors are interrelated and as such it is by no means easy to determine which is more important and fundamental.

Labour's loss of ideological identity has resulted from three other factors: the general crisis of socialist thought in the Western world; the marginalisation of the Party's left amongst the Party elite; and the identification of Labour with postwar state power. This may have led to the resolution of the division between the Party's leadership and those on the left who regarded themselves as representatives of Labour's grass roots, though it has not necessarily resolved Whiteley's observed schism between the elected representatives of the Party and Party members and activists.

Labour's inability to provide a convincing critique of state power has become a problem because of its failures as controller of state power, that is as a party of government. It is this lack of state critique which has led to Labour's inability to formulate a convincing policy agenda. Without a clear idea of what the state can and cannot achieve Labour has no effective way of judging the state's limitations in policy implementation.

Finally, Labour's inability to reach its constituents creates further problems for the Party. In the light of Thatcherism, Labour needs to persuade its supporters that it is either capable of being a better Thatcherite Party than the Conservatives, or that it has a viable alternative. The first is difficult given the association of Labour with postwar state power; the second equally difficult because of Labour's inability to reach its constituents directly. Labour's leadership is distanced from the Party's activists and unwilling to work through the Party to contact its supporters.

The problem for Labour is that it is too wedded to the state power of the past; that Labour's brand of socialism is too closely identified with the achievements of the Labour Government of the 1940s (Leach, 1991, 145). Whilst renewal and modernisation have been portrayed as separating 'new' Labour from the 'old' Labour of nationalisation and state intervention, the Party has failed to provide convincing alternatives, particularly with regard to the use of state power. Regulation may be different in form from nationalisation, but it still relies on the state to compensate for market failure. The problem Labour faced with nationalisation was that it was created to fit the British state; if unaccountable public ownership is replaced by unaccountable, quango based, administration in what sense can this be regarded as an improvement?

Labour remains firmly embedded in its past traditions. This, indeed, is Labour's main problem. If it is to regain its position as a party of government then it must find a practical alternative to the concerns of the New Right. This much has been recognised, but has not been related to the fundamental problems which the Party has failed to resolve. These problems of ideological identity, the exercise of state power, and of reaching its constituency may prove beyond the Party's ability to overcome. Some certainly have very deep roots which are inherent within the Party's structure.

If these problems do prove beyond Labour's scope this does not lead to the conclusion that Labour is condemned to the Opposition benches. What it does suggest is that Labour's future electoral success may be dependant on dissatisfaction with the Conservatives, and that future Labour Governments may struggle to implement policies for which they have not achieved popular support. This in turn may reinforce public perceptions of Labour's inadequacies as a party of government, and may fuel public dissatisfaction not only with Labour, or the Conservatives, but with the British political system as a whole. This leads to the obvious conclusion that the real test of potential Labour Leaders is not in Opposition, where their actions may, in any case, have limited effect on public opinion, but in Government.

In office Tony Blair's job will have only just begun. The fact that the Labour leadership prioritised consultation over Clause IV, and is also seeking Party consultation over policy proposals, demonstrates that Blair's advisers are well aware of this. Safe in the knowledge that the Party is almost certain to support a Leader who appears electorally popular at a time when Labour is desperate for office, Blair has sought to use this opportunity to tie the Party into agreeing a programme before the General Election in the hope that this will deflect criticism if Labour comes to office. The success of this strategy may have more to do with whether Labour actually can deliver anything in office for its core support.

If Blair does not satisfy Labour's core support, or create a new constituency for the Party, than another disappointing phase of Labour government may return Labour to its downward long-term electoral path. Renewal and modernisation have done nothing to help Labour achieve truly radical objectives in government. Indeed, Labour remains the deeply conservative party it has always been, and whilst its particular policies and approaches and statement of faith may have changed, they have changed to preserve Labour's statist nature, not to challenge it.

Bibliography

Aitken, Ian, 1995: 'Remember Who the Real Enemy Is' *New Statesman* 20 January.

Anderson, Perry, 1992: *English Questions* London: Verso.

Anderson, Victor, 1991: *Alternative Economic Indicators* London: Routledge.

Archer Committee, The, 1993: *A New Constitution for the Labour Party* London: Fabian Society.

Bacon, Robert and Walter Eltis, 1978: *Britain's Economic Problem: Too Few Producers* (2nd Edn) London: Macmillan.

Ball, Alan R., 1981: *British Political Parties. The Emergence of a Modern Party System* Basingstoke: Macmillan.

Ball, Michael, Fred Gray and Linda McDowell, 1989: *The Transformation of Britain: Contemporary Social and Economic Change* London: Fontana.

Balogh, Thomas, 1982: *The Irrelevance of Conventional Economics* London: George Weidenfeld & Nicolson.

Barnett, Anthony, Caroline Ellis and Paul Hirst (eds), 1993: *Debating the Constitution: New Perspectives on Constitutional Reform* Cambridge: Polity Press.

Barratt Brown, Michael, 1972: *From Labourism to Socialism: The Political Economy of Labour in the 1970s* Nottingham: Spokesman Books.

Barratt Brown, Michael, 1995: 'Whatever Happened to Capitalism' Coates *Common Ownership*.

Barratt Brown, Michael and Hugo Radice, 1995: *Democracy Versus Capitalism: A Response to Will Hutton with some Old Questions for New Labour* Nottingham: Spokesman/European Labour Forum Pamphlet no. 4.

Bayliss, Fred, 1991: *Making a Minimum Wage Work* Fabian pamphlet 545 London: Fabian Society.

Beecham, Jeremy, Donald Dewar, Martin Linton, Oonagh McDonald, Austin Mitchell, Tom Sawyer and Chris Smith, 1987: *Labour's Next Moves Forward* Fabian pamphlet 521 London: Fabian Society.

Beilharz, Peter, 1993: *Labour's Utopias: Bolshevism, Fabianism, Social Democracy* London: Routledge.

Beishon, John, 1989: 'Empowering Consumers' *New Socialist,* June/July.

Benn, Tony, 1980: *Arguments for Socialism* Edited by Chris Mullin. Harmondsworth: Penguin.

Benn, Tony 1982: *Arguments for Democracy* Edited by Chris Mullin. Harmondsworth: Penguin.

Benn, Tony, 1982: *Parliament, People and Power: Agenda for a Free Society. Interviews with New Left Review* London: Verso.

Benn, Tony, 1988: *Out of the Wilderness: Diaries 1963–67* London: Arrow.

Benn, Tony, 1989: *Office Without Power: Diaries 1968–72* London: Arrow.

Benn, Tony, 1990: *Against the Tide: Diaries 1973–76* London: Arrow.

Benn, Tony, 1991a: *Conflicts of Interest: Diaries 1977–80* London: Arrow.

Benn, Tony, 1991b: *A Future for Socialism* London: Fount.

Benn, Tony and Andrew Hood, 1993: 'Constitutional Reform and Radical Change' Barnett, Anthony, Caroline Ellis and Paul Hirst (ed.): *Debating the Constitution: New Perspectives on Constitutional Reform*.

Bevan, Aneurin, 1978: *In Place of Fear* London: Quartet.

Blair, Tony, 1993: 'Why Modernization Matters' *Renewal* vol.1, no. 4 October.

Blair, Tony, 1995a: *Let Us Face the Future: The 1945 Anniversary Lecture* London: The Fabian Society Fabian Pamphlet 571.

Blair, Tony, 1995b: 'Power for a Purpose' *Renewal* vol. 3, no. 4 October.

Bosanquet, Nick and Peter Townsend (eds), 1980: *Labour and Equality: A Fabian Study of Labour in Power, 1974–79* London: Heinemann Educational.

Bromley, Simon, 1992: 'The Labour Party and Energy Policy' Martin J Smith and Joanna Spear (eds): *The Changing Labour Party.*

Brown, C.V. and C.T. Sandford, 1990: *Taxes and Incentives: The Effects of the 1988 Cuts in the Higher Rates of Income Tax.* Economic study no. 7 London: IPPR.

Brown, George, 1972: *In My Way* Harmondsworth: Penguin.

Brown, Gordon, 1988: *Maxton* Glasgow: Fontana.

Brown, Gordon, 1989: *Where There is Greed... Margaret Thatcher and the Betrayal of Britain's Future* Edinburgh: Mainstream.

Brown, Henry Phelps, 1986: *The Origins of Trade Union Power* Oxford: Oxford University Press.

Brown, Phillip and Richard Sparks (ed.), 1989: *Beyond Thatcherism* Milton Keynes: Open University Press.

Brunskill, Irene, 1990: *The Regeneration Game: A Regional Approach to Regional Policy.* Industrial policy paper no. 1 London: IPPR.

Burden, Richard, 1995: 'Clause for Concern' *New Statesman* 20th January.

Butler, David, 1989: *British General Elections Since 1945* Oxford: Basil Blackwell.

Butler, David and Dennis Kavanagh, 1992: *The British General Election of 1992* Basingstoke: Macmillan.

Butler, Nick, Len Scott, David Ward and Jonathan Worthington, 1989: *Working for Common Security.* Fabian pamphlet 533 London: Fabian Society.

Cairncross, Alec, 1992: *The British Economy Since 1945: Economic Policy and Performance, 1945–1990* Oxford: Blackwell.

Callaghan, Bill, Anna Coote, Geoffrey Hulme and John Stewart, 1990: *Meeting Needs in the 1990s: The Future of Public Service and the Challenge for Trade Unions.* Social policy paper no.2 London: IPPR.

Callaghan, John, 1989: 'The Left: Ideology of the Labour Party' Leonard Tivey and Anthony Wright (eds): *Party Ideology in Britain.*

Callaghan, John, 1990: *Socialism in Britain* Oxford: Blackwell.

Castle, Barbara, 1990: *The Castle Diaries 1964–1976* London: Papermac.

Cave, Alan, 1989: 'Improving the Workplace.' *New Socialist,* June/July.

Cecchini, Paolo, 1988: *The European Challenge 1992: The Benefits of a Single Market* Aldershot: Wildwood House.

Clarke, Simon, 1991a: 'The State Debate' Simon Clarke (ed.) *The State Debate.*

Clarke, Simon (ed.), 1991b: *The State Debate* London: MacMillan.

Clough, Robert, 1992: *Labour: A Party Fit for Imperialism* London: Larkin.

Coates, David, 1989: *The Crisis of Labour: Industrial Relations and the State in Contemporary Britain* Oxford: Philip Allan.

Coates, David, 1994: *The Question of UK Decline: The Economy, State and Society* Hemel Hempstead: Harvester Wheatsheaf.

Coates, David and John Hillard (eds), 1986: *The Economic Decline of Modern Britain: The Debate Between Left and Right* Brighton: Wheatsheaf.

Coates, Ken, 1995a: *Common Ownership* Nottingham: Spokesman.

Coates, Ken, 1995b: *New Labour's Aims and Values: A Study in Ambiguity* Nottingham: Spokesman/European Labour Forum Pamphlet no. 3.

Cole, Harry B., 1977: *The British Labour Party: A Functioning Participatory Democracy* Oxford: Pergamon Press.

Cohen, G A, 1994: 'Back to Socialist Basics' *New Left Review* 207 September/October.

Cohen, G A, 1995: *Is Socialism Inseperable from Common Ownership?* Nottingham: Spokesman/European Labour Forum Pamphlet no. 1.

Commission on Social Justice, The, 1993a: *Social Justice in a Changing World* London: IPPR.

Commission on Social Justice, the, 1993b: *The Justice Gap* London: IPPR.

Commission on Social Justice, The, 1994: *Social Justice: Strategies for National Renewal* London: Vintage.

Cook, Chris and Ian Taylor (ed.), 1980: *The Labour Party: An Introduction to its History, Structure and Politics* London: Longman.

Cooper, Penny, 1993: 'Blaming Messengers' *Fabian Review* vol. 105 no.6, Nov/Dec.

Cornford, James, 1990: *A Stake in the Company: Shareholding Ownership and ESOPs.* Economic study no. 3 London: IPPR.

Corrigan, Paul, Trevor Jones, John Lloyd and Jock Young, 1988: *Socialism, Merit and Efficiency.* Fabian pamphlet 530 London: Fabian Society.

Coutts, Ken, Wynne Godley, Bob Rowthorn and Gennaro Zezza, 1990: *Britain's Economic Problems and Policies in the 1990s* London: IPPR.

Cowling, Keith, 1990: 'The Strategic Approach to Economic and Industrial Policy' Keith Cowling and Roger Sugden (eds): *A New Economic Policy for Britain: Essays on the Development of Industry.*

Cowling, Keith and Roger Sugden (eds), 1990: *A New Economic Policy for Britain: Essays on the Development of Industry* Manchester: Manchester University Press.

Crine, Simon, 1991: *Labour's First Year: A Sense of Socialism.* Fabian pamphlet no. 550 London: Fabian Society.

Crewe, Ivor, 1991: 'Labour Force Changes, Working Class Decline, and the Labour Vote: Social and Electoral Trends in Postwar Britain' Frances Fox Piven (ed.): *Labour Parties in Postindustrial Societies.*

Crewe, Ivor, 1992: 'On the Death and Resurrection of Class Voting: Some Comments on *How Britain Votes*' David Denver and Gordon Hands (ed.): *Issues and Controversies in British Electoral Behaviour.*

Crewe, Ivor, Pippa Norris, David Denver and David Broughton (ed.), 1992: *British Elections and Parties Yearbook 1992* Hemel Hempstead: Harvester Wheatsheaf.

Crosland, Anthony, 1964: *The Future of Socialism* London: Jonathan Cape.

Crossman, Richard, 1991: *The Crossman Diaries* Edited by Anthony Howard. London: Mandarin.

Curran, James (ed.), 1984: *The Future of the Left* Oxford: Basil Blackwell.

Curtice, John, 1992: 'Labour's Slide to Defeat' *The Guardian* 13th April.

Curtice, John and Michael Steed, 1992: 'The Results Analysed' David Butler and Dennis Kavanagh: *The British General Election of 1992.*

Deakins, Eric, 1988: *What Future for Labour?* London: Hilary Shipman.

Dearlove, John and Peter Saunders, 1989: *Introduction to British Politics: Analysing a Capitalist Democracy* (2nd edn) Oxford: Basil Blackwell.

Defend Clause 4, 1995a: *Defend Clause 4, Defend Socialism* Issue no. 1.

Defend Clause 4, 1995b: *Defend Clause 4, Defend Socialism* Issue no. 2.

Denver, David, 1989; *Elections and Voting Behaviour in Britain* Hemel Hempstead: Philip Allan.

Denver, David and Gordon Hands (ed.), 1992: *Issues and Controversies in British Electoral Behaviour* Hemel Hempstead: Harvester Wheatsheaf.

Dorril, Stephen and Robin Ramsay, 1992: *Smear! Wilson and the Secret State* London: Grafton.

Douthwaite, Richard, 1992: *The Growth Illusion* Bideford: Resurgence.

Draper, Hal, 1977: *Karl Marx's Theory of Revolution: Volume 1 State and Bureaucracy* London: Monthly Review Press.

Drucker, H. M., 1979: *Doctrine and Ethos in the Labour Party* London: George Allen & Unwin.

Dunleavy, Patrick, 1991: *Democracy, Bureaucracy and Public Choice: Economic Explanations in Political Science* Hemel Hempstead: Harvester Wheatsheaf.

Dutton, David, 1991: *British Politics Since 1945: The Rise and Fall of Consensus* Oxford: Basil Blackwell.

Economist, The, 1995a: 'A Forward March for Labour' *The Economist* 18 March.

Economist, The, 1995b: 'Verbal Inflation' *The Economist* 18 March.

Economist, The, 1995c: 'Blair's Moment' *The Economist* 29 April.

Economist, The, 1995d: 'A Promising Party' *The Economist* 20 May.

Elliott, Gregory, 1993: *Labourism and the English Genius: The Strange Death of Labour England?* London: Verso.

Ellis, Caroline, 1993: 'Preface' Anthony Barnett, Caroline Ellis and Paul Hirst (ed.): *Debating the Constitution: New Perspectives on Constitutional Reform.*

Estrin, Saul and Julian Le Grand, 1989: 'Market Socialism' in Julian Le Grand and Saul Estrin (ed.): *Market Socialism.*

Fabian Society Taxation Review Committee, 1990: *The Reform of Direct Taxation: Report of the Fabian Society Taxation Review Committee* London: Fabian Society.

Fine, Ben and Laurence Harris, 1985: *The Peculiarities of the British Economy* London; Lawrence and Wishart.

Foot, Michael, 1975a: *Aneurin Bevan, 1897–1945* St Albans: Granada.

Foot, Michael, 1975b: *Aneurin Bevan, 1945–1960* St Albans: Granada.

Foote, Geoffrey, 1985: *The Labour Party's Political Thought: A History* Beckenham: Croom Helm.

Gamble, A. M. and S. A. Walkland, 1984: *The British Party System and Economic Policy 1945–1983: Studies in Adversary Politics* Oxford: Oxford University Press.

Gamble, Andrew, 1988: *The Free Economy and the Strong State: The Politics of Thatcherism* London: Macmillan.

Gamble, Andrew, 1992: 'The Labour Party and Economic Management' Martin J. Smith and Joanna Spear (eds): *The Changing Labour Party.*

Gamble, Andrew, 1995: *Britain in Decline* 5th edn London: Macmillan.

Garner, Robert, 1990: 'Labour and the Policy Review: A Party Fit to Govern?' *Talking Politics,* Autumn.

Geroski, P. A., 1990: 'Encouraging Investment in Science and Technology' Keith Cowling and Roger Sugden (eds): *A New Economic Policy for Britain: Essays on the Development of Industry.*

Geroski, P.A. and K.G. Knight, 1991: *Targeting Competitive Industries.* Fabian pamphlet 544 London: Fabian Society.

Giddens, Anthony, 1995: 'What Is He Up To?' *New Statesman* 24 February.

Glyn, Andrew, 1985: *A Million Jobs a Year: The Case for Planning Full Employment* London: Verso.

Gorz, Andre, 1982: *Farewell to the Working Class: An Essay on Post-Industrial Socialism* London: Pluto.

Gould, Bryan, 1989: *A Future for Socialism* London: Jonathan Cape.

Gould, Bryan, 1990: 'Introduction' Keith Cowling and Roger Sugden (eds): *A New Economic Policy for Britain: Essays on the Development of Industry.*

Green, Frances (ed.), 1989: *The Restructuring of the UK Economy* Hemel Hempstead: Harvester Wheatsheaf.

Hall, John A and G John Ikenberry, 1989: *The State* Milton Keynes: Open University Press.

Hall, Stuart and Martin Jacques (ed.), 1983: *The Politics of Thatcherism* London: Lawrence and Wishart.

Hall, Stuart, 1988: *The Hard Road to Renewal: Thatcherism and the Crisis of the Left* London: Verso.

Harris, Christopher C., 1989: 'The State and the Market' Philip Brown and Richard Sparks (eds): *Beyond Thatcherism.*

Harris, Robert, 1984: *The Making of Neil Kinnock* London: Faber and Faber.

Hattersley, Roy, 1987: *Choose Freedom: The Future of Democratic Socialism* London: Penguin.

Hawkins, Christopher, 1983: *Britain's Economic Future: An Immediate Programme for Revival* Brighton: Wheatsheaf.

Hay, Colin, 1994: 'Labour's Thatcherite Revisionism: Playing the "Politics of Catch-Up"' *Political Studies* Volume 42, Number 4 December.

Hayek, F. A., 1986: *The Road to Serfdom* London: Ark.

Healey, Denis, 1989: *The Time of My Life* Harmondsworth: Penguin.

Heath, Anthony, John Curtice, Roger Jowell, Geoff Evans, Julia Field and Sharon Witherspoon, 1991: *Understanding Political Change: The British Voter, 1964–1987* Oxford: Pergamon Press.

Heath, Anthony, Roger Jowell and John Curtice, 1985: *How Britain Votes* Oxford: Pergamon.

Heath, Anthony, Roger Jowell and John Curtice, 1992: 'The Decline of Class Voting' David Denver and Gordon Hands (eds): *Issues and Controversies in British Electoral Behaviour.*

Heath, Anthony, Roger Jowell and John Curtice (eds), 1994: *Labour's Last Chance? The 1992 Election and Beyond* Aldershot: Dartmouth.

Heath, Anthony and Roger Jowell, 1994: 'Labour's Policy Review' Heath, Jowell and Curtice (eds): *Labour's Last Chance* Aldershot: Dartmouth.

Heath, Anthony and Sarah-K McDonald, 1987: 'Social Change and the Future of the Left' *Political Quarterly*, Oct/Dec.

Heffer, Eric, 1986: *Labour's Future: Socialist or SDP Mark 2?* London: Verso.

Heffernan, Richard and Mike Marqusee, 1992: *Defeat from the Jaws of Victory: Inside Kinnock's Labour Party* London: Verso.

Hewitt, Patricia, 1989: 'Thinking Ahead.' *New Socialist*, June/July.

Hewitt, Patricia and Deborah Mattinson, 1989: *Women's Votes: The Key to Winning.* Fabian research series 353 London: Fabian Society.

Hindness, Barry, 1971: *The Decline of Working-Class Politics* London: MacGibbon and Kee.

Hodge, Margaret, 1991: *Quality, Equality, Democracy: Improving Public Services.* Fabian pamphlet 549 London: Fabian Society.

Hoggart, Simon and David Leigh, 1981: *Michael Foot: A Portrait* London: Hodder and Stoughton.

Holland, Stuart, 1975: *The Socialist Challenge* London: Quartet.

Holloway, John and Sol Picciotto, 1991: 'Capital, Crisis and the State' Simon Clarke (ed.): *The State Debate.*

Holmes, Martin, 1985: *The Labour Government, 1974–79: Political Aims and Economic Reality* Basingstoke: MacMillan.

Howell, David, n.d.: *The Rise and Fall of Bevanism.* Labour Party discussion series no. 5 Leeds: Independent Labour Publications.

Hughes, Colin and Patrick Wintour, 1990: *Labour Rebuilt: The New Model Party* London: Fourth Estate.

Hughes, John, 1995: 'Socialism in Our Time' Ken Coates *Common Ownership.*

Hutton, Will, 1991: *Good Housekeeping: How to Manage Credit and Debt.* Economic study no. 9 London: IPPR.

Hutton, Will, 1993a: 'Evicting the Rentier State' Anthony Barnett, Caroline Ellis and Paul Hirst (eds): *Debating the Constitution: New Perspectives on Constitutional Reform.*

Hutton, Will, 1993b: 'Seizing the Moment: Constitutional Change and the Modernizing of Labour' *Renewal* Volume 1, Number 3 July.

Ingle, Stephen, 1989: *The British Party System* (2nd Edn) Oxford: Basil Blackwell.

Institute of Economic Affairs, The, 1991: *The State of the Economy 1991* London: IEA.

Jenkins, Hugh, 1980: *Rank and File* London: Croom Helm.

Jenkins, Roy, 1959: *The Labour Case* Harmondsworth: Penguin.

Johnson, Christopher, 1991: *The Economy Under Mrs Thatcher 1979–1990* Harmondsworth: Penguin.

Jones, Barry and Michael Keating, 1985: *Labour and the British State* Oxford: Clarendon Press.

Jones, Bryn, 1993: 'Common Ownership: Relic or Asset?' *Renewal* vol. 1, no. 3 July.

Jordan, Bill, 1993: 'What Price Social Justice?' *Renewal* vol. 1, no. 3 July.

Kavanagh, Dennis, 1987: *Thatcherism and British Politics: The End of Consensus?* Oxford: Oxford University Press.

Keane, John and John Owens, 1986: *After Full Employment* London: Hutchinson.

Keegan, William, 1984: *Mrs Thatcher's Economic Experiment* Harmondsworth: Penguin.

Keegan, William, 1992: *The Spectre of Capitalism* London: Vintage.

Kelly, John, 1987: *Labour and the Unions* London: Verso.

King, Anthony, 1992a: 'Why Did They Get it Wrong?' *Daily Telegraph* 11 April.

King, Anthony, 1992b: 'Tory "Super-party" Born out of Last Minute Vote Switching' *Daily Telegraph* 13 April.

King, Anthony, 1992c: 'The Implications of One-Party Government' Anthony King *et al*: *Britain at the Polls 1992.*

King, Anthony, Ivor Crewe, David Denver, Kenneth Newton, Philip Norton, David Sanders, and Patrick Seyd, 1992: *Britain at the Polls 1992* New Jersey: Chatham House.

King, Desmond S., 1987: *The New Right: Politics, Markets and Citizenship* Basingstoke: Macmillan.

King, Preston (ed.), 1996: *Socialism and the Common Good: New Fabian Essays* London: Frank Cass.

Kinnock, Neil, 1978: 'Foreword'. In Aneurin Bevan: *In Place of Fear*.

Kinnock, Neil, 1989: 'Meeting the Green Challenge.' *New Socialist*, Oct/Nov.

Kogan, David and Maurice Kogan, 1982: *The Battle for the Labour Party* London: Fount.

Kreiger, Joel, 1991: 'Class, Consumption and Collectivism: Perspectives on the Labour Party and Electoral Competition in Britain' Frances Fox Piven (ed.): *Labour Parties in Postindustrial Societies*.

Labour Party News, 1995a: *Clause IV Special* no. 9 January.

Labour Party News, 1995b: no. 10 March/April.

Labour Party News, 1995c: no. 11 July/August.

Labour Party, The, 1982: *Labour's Programme 1982* London: The Labour Party.

Labour Party, The, 1983: *Labour's Plan: The New Hope for Britain* London: The Labour Party.

Labour Party, The, 1987: *Britain Will Win: Labour Manifesto* London: The Labour Party.

Labour Party, The, 1988: *Democratic Socialist Aims and Values* London: The Labour Party.

Labour Party, The, n.d.a: *Social Justice and Economic Efficiency* London: The Labour Party.

Labour Party, The, n.d.b: *Meet the Challenge, Make the Change: A New Agenda for Britain. Final Report of Labour's Policy Review for the 1990s* London: The Labour Party.

Labour Party, The, n.d.c: *Looking to The Future: A Dynamic Economy, a Decent Society, Strong in Europe* London: The Labour Party.

Labour Party, The, 1991: *Opportunity Britain: Labour's Better Way for the 1990s* London: The Labour Party.

Labour Party, The, n.d.d: *An Earthly Chance: Labour's Programme for a Cleaner, Greener Britain, a Safer, Sustainable Planet* London: The Labour Party.

Labour Party, The, n.d.e: *Future of Labour Party Conference: Possible Changes in Rules, Procedures and Voting* London: The Labour Party.

Labour Party, The, 1992a: *Labour's Election Manifesto: It's Time to Get Britain Working* London: The Labour Party.

Labour Party, The, 1992b: *NEC Report 1992* London: The Labour Party.

Labour Party, The, 1994: *Labour's Objects: Socialist Values in the Modern World* London: The Labour Party.

Labour Party, The, 1995: *Labour's Aims and Values: The Consultation Report* London: The Labour Party.

Labour Party, The, 1996: *Labour Party Rule Book* London: The Labour Party.

Lane, David, 1985: *Soviet Economy and Society* Oxford: Basil Blackwell.

Layburn, Keith, 1991: *British Trade Unionism c1770–1990: A Reader in History* Stroud: Alan Sutton.

Leach, Robert, 1991: *British Political Ideologies* London: Philip Allan.

Leadbetter, Charles, 1987: *The Politics of Prosperity*. Fabian pamphlet 523 London: Fabian Society.

Le Grand, Julian and Saul Estrin (eds), 1989: *Market Socialism* Oxford: Clarendon.

Le Grand, Julian, 1989: 'Managing the Economy.' *New Socialist*, June/July.

Lewis-Beck, Michael S., 1990: *Economics and Elections: The Major Western Democracies* Michigan: University of Michigan Press.

Linton, Martin, 1985: *The Swedish Road to Socialism.* Fabian pamphlet 503 London: Fabian Society.

Linton, Martin, 1988: *Labour Can Still Win.* Fabian pamphlet 532 London: Fabian Society.

Lipsey, David, Andrew Shaw and John Willman, 1989: *Labour's Electoral Challenge.* Fabian research series 352 London: Fabian Society.

Lloyd, John, 1989: *A Rational Advance for the Labour Party: What Labour Should do to Win* London: Chatto & Windus.

Lister, Ruth, 1989: 'Working for Equality.' *New Socialist,* June/July.

Livingstone, Ken and Peter Hain, 1989: 'Will the Impossible Materialise?' *World Marxist Review,* 9th September.

Loach, Ken, 1995: 'Questions of Ownership' *Red Pepper* no. 11 April.

MacDonald, J. Ramsay, 1920: *A Policy for the Labour Party.* London: Leonard Parsons.

Mackintosh, John P., 1981: *The British Cabinet* (3rd Edn) London, Methuen.

Mandelson, Peter and Roger Liddle, 1996: *The Blair Revolution: Can New Labour Deliver?* London: Faber and Faber.

Mann, John and Phil Woolas, 1986: *Labour and Youth.* Fabian pamphlet 515 London: Fabian Society.

Marquand, David, 1987: 'Beyond Social Democracy' *Political Quarterly,* July/Sep.

Marquand, David, 1988: *The Unprincipled Society: New Demands and Old Politics* London: Fontana.

Marquand, David, 1991: *The Progressive Dilemma: From Lloyd George to Kinnock* London: William Heinemann.

Marquand, David, 1992: 'Half-Way to Citizenship? The Labour Party and Constitutional Reform' Martin J Smith and Joanna Spear (eds): *The Changing Labour Party.*

Marquand, David, 1993: 'Collaborative Capitalism and Constitutional Change' Anthony Barnett, Caroline Ellis and Paul Hirst (eds): *Debating the Constitution: New Perspectives on Constitutional Reform.*

Martin, David, 1988: *Bringing Common Sense to the Common Market: A Left Agenda for Europe.* Fabian pamphlet 525 London: Fabian Society.

McCarthy, William, 1988: *The Future of Industrial Democracy.* Fabian pamphlet 526 London: Fabian Society.

McLean, Iain, 1980: 'Party Organisation' in Cook and Taylor (eds): *The Labour Party: An Introduction to its History, Structure and Politics.*

Meadowcroft, Michael, 1987: 'The Future of the Left: A Liberal View' *Political Quarterly,* Oct/Dec.

Meadows, Donella H, Dennis L Meadows and Jørgen Randers, 1992: *Beyond the Limits: Global Collapse or Sustainable Future* London: Earthscan.

Michie, Jonathan (ed.), 1992: *The Economic Legacy 1979–1992* London: Academic Press.

Miliband, David, 1990a: *Learning by Right: An Entitlement to Paid Education and Training.* Education and training paper no. 2 London: IPPR.

Miliband, David, 1990b: *Technology Transfer. Policies for Innovation.* Industrial policy paper no. 2 London: IPPR.

Miliband, David (ed.), 1994: *Reinventing the Left* Cambridge: Polity Press.

Miliband, Ralph, 1982: *Capitalist Democracy in Britain* Oxford: Oxford University Press.

Mill, John Stuart, 1985: *On Liberty* Harmondsworth: Penguin.

Miller, W.L., S. Tagg and K. Britto, 1992: 'Partisanship and Party Preference in Government and Opposition: The Mid-Term Perspective' David Denver and Gordon Hands (eds): *Issues and Controversies in British Electoral Behaviour.*

Milner, Henry, 1989: *Sweden: Social Democracy in Practice* Oxford: Oxford University Press.

Minkin, Lewis, 1978: *The Labour Party Conference: A Study in the Politics of Intra-Party Democracy* London: Allen Lane.

Minkin, Lewis, 1991: *The Contentious Alliance: Trade Unions and the Labour Party* Edinburgh: Edinburgh University Press.

Mishan, E. J., 1993: *The Costs of Economic Growth* 2nd edn London: Weidenfeld and Nicolson.

Mitchell, Austin, 1987: 'Beyond Socialism' *Political Quarterly,* Oct/Dec.

Mitchell, Austin, 1989: *Competitive Socialism* London: Unwin Hyman.

Morgan, Kenneth O., 1984: *Labour in Power 1945–1951* Oxford: Oxford University Press.

Morgan, Kenneth O., 1987: *Labour People: Leaders and Lieutenants, Hardie to Kinnock* Oxford: Oxford University Press.

Muellbauer, John, 1990: *The Great British Housing Disaster and Economic Policy.* Economic study no. 5 London: IPPR.

New Socialist, 1989: 'Editorial' *New Socialist,* June/July.

Nichols, Theo, 1986: *The British Worker Question: A New Look at Workers and Productivity in Manufacturing* London: Routledge & Kegan Paul.

Nove, Alec, 1983: *The Economics of Feasible Socialism* London: Unwin Hyman.

Nozick, Robert, 1974: *Anarchy, State and Utopia* Oxford: Basil Blackwell.

Owen, David, 1984: *A Future that Will Work: Competitiveness and Compassion* Harmondsworth: Penguin.

Padgett, Stephen and William E. Paterson, 1991: *A History of Social Democracy in Postwar Europe* London: Longman.

Panitch, Leo, 1986: *Working Class Politics in Crisis: Essays on Labour and the State* London: Verso.

Peden, G. C., 1991: *British Economic and Social Policy: Lloyd George to Margaret Thatcher* (2nd edn) Hemel Hempstead: Philip Allan.

Pelling, Henry, 1976: *A History of British Trade Unionism* (3rd Edn) Harmondsworth: Penguin.

Pitt-Watson, David, 1991: *Economic Short Termism: A Cure for the British Disease.* Fabian pamphlet 547 London: Fabian Society.

Piven, Frances Fox (ed.), 1991: *Labour Parties in Postindustrial Societies* London: Polity Press.

Plant Commission, The (Working Party on Electoral Systems), n.d.: *The Plant Report* London: Guardian.

Plant, Raymond, 1988: *Citizenship, Rights and Socialism.* Fabian pamphlet 531 London: Fabian Society.

Political Quarterly, 1987a: 'Commentary: The Nightmare of the Left' *Political Quarterly,* July/Sep.

Political Quarterly, 1987b: 'Commentary: Towards a Realignment of the Centre Left?' *Political Quarterly,* Oct/Dec.

Pollard, Sidney, 1984: *The Wasting of the British Economy: British Economic Policy 1945 to the Present* (2nd edn) Beckenham: Croom Helm.

Preston, Eric, 1987: *The Hitch-hiker's Guide to the Labour Party* Leeds: Independent Labour Publications.

Progress 90 Working Group, 1989: 'Making the Polluter Pay.' *New Socialist,* Oct/Nov.

Przeworski, Adam, 1985: *Capitalism and Social Democracy* Cambridge: Cambridge University Press.

Radice, Giles, 1988: 'The Case for Revisionism' *Political Quarterly,* Oct/Dec.

Radice, Giles, 1989: *Path to Power: The New Revisionism* Basingstoke: Macmillan.

Radice, Lisanne (ed.), 1985: *Winning Women's Votes.* Fabian pamphlet 507 London: Fabian Society.

Rajan, Amin, 1991: 'Britain's Labour Market Prospects in an Integrated Europe' Institute of Economic Affairs: *The State of the Economy 1991.*

Rawls, John, 1972: *A Theory of Justice* Oxford: Clarendon Press.

Rentoul, John, 1989: *Me and Mine: The Triumph of New Individualism?* London: Unwin Hyman.

Rodgers, William, 1987: 'Realignment Postponed?' *Political Quarterly,* October/December.

Roemer, John, 1988: *Free to Lose* London: Radius.

Sanders, David, 1992: 'Why the Conservative Party Won – Again' Anthony King *et al.: Britain at the Polls 1992.*

Sanders, David, Hugh Ward and David Marsh, 1992: 'Government Popularity and the Falklands War: a Reassessment' David Denver and Gordon Hands (eds): *Issues and Controversies in British Electoral Behaviour.*

Sawyer, Tom, 1989: 'Dear Member.' *New Socialist,* June/July.

Seyd, Patrick, 1987: *The Rise and Fall of the Labour Left* Basingstoke: MacMillan.

Seyd, Patrick, 1992: 'Labour: The Great Transformation' Anthony King *et al.: Britain at the Polls 1992.*

Seyd, Patrick and Paul Whiteley, 1992a: 'Labour's Renewal Strategy' Martin J Smith and Joanna Spear (eds): *The Changing Labour Party.*

Seyd, Patrick and Paul Whiteley, 1992b: *Labour's Grass Roots: The Politics of Party Membership* Oxford: Clarendon Press.

Shaw, Eric, 1988: *Discipline and Discord in the Labour Party: The Politics of Managerial Control, 1951–87* Manchester: Manchester University Press.

Shaw, Eric, 1989: *The Policy Review and Labour's Policy-Making System* Paper presented to the Annual Conference of the Political Studies Association, Warwick University 4–6 April.

Shaw, Eric, 1993: 'Towards Renewal? The British Labour Party's Policy Review' *West European Politics* vol. 16, no. 1 January.

Shaw, Eric, 1994: *The Labour Party Since 1979: Crisis and Transformation* London: Routledge.

Smith, John Grieve, 1990: *Pay Strategy for the 1990s* Economic study no. 8 London: IPPR.

Smith, Martin, 1986: *The Consumer Case for Socialism.* Fabian pamphlet 513 London: Fabian Society.

Smith, Martin J., 1992: 'A Return to Revisionism? The Labour Party's Policy Review' Martin J Smith and Joanna Spear (eds): *The Changing Labour Party.*

Smith, Martin J, 1994: 'Understanding the "Politics of Catch-Up": The Modernization of the Labour Party' *Political Studies* Volume 42, Number 4 December.

Smith, Martin J. and Joanna Spear (eds), 1992: *The Changing Labour Party* London: Routledge.

Smyth, Gareth, 1991: *Can the Tories Lose? The Battle for the Marginals* London: Lawrence and Wishart.

Socialist Society, The, 1989: *Negotiating the Rapids: Socialist Politics for the 1990s* London: The Socialist Society.

Sopel, Jon, 1995: *Tony Blair: The Moderniser* London: Bantam.

Steel, David, 1980: 'Labour in Office: The Post-War Experience' Chris Cook and Ian Taylor (eds): *The Labour Party: An Introduction to Its History, Structure and Politics.*

Stephens, John D., 1979: *The Transition from Capitalism to Socialism* London: MacMillan.

Street, John, 1990: *Politics and Technology* London: MacMillan.

Tatchell, Peter, 1983: *The Battle for Bermondsey* London: Heretic.

Taylor, Andrew J., 1987: *The Trade Unions and the Labour Party* Beckenham: Croom Helm.

Taylor, Ian, 1980: 'Ideology and Policy' Chris Cook and Ian Taylor (eds): *The Labour Party: An Introduction to Its History, Structure and Politics.*

Taylor, Gerald, 1993: 'Changing Conference: Embracing an Illusion of Democracy' in *Renewal* vol.1 no.4 Oct..

Taylor, Robert, 1989: 'Market Socialism' *New Socialist*, June/July.

Thompson, Paul, 1993a: 'Modernizing Labour' *Renewal* vol. 1, no. 3 July.

Thompson, Paul, 1993b: 'Organisation Versus Politics' *Renewal* vol. 1, no. 4 October.

Thompson, Paul, 1995a: 'Clauses and Causes' *Renewal* vol. 3, no. 1 January.

Thompson, Paul, 1995b: 'What's New in New Labour?' *Renewal* vol. 3, no. 4 October.

Tilton, Tim, 1991: *The Political Theory of Swedish Social Democracy: Through the Welfare State to Socialism* Oxford: Clarendon.

Tivey, Leonard and Anthony Wright (ed.), 1989: *Party Ideology in Britain* London: Routledge.

Townsend, Peter, 1995: 'Persuasion and Conformity: An Assessment of the Borrie Report on Social Justice' *New Left Review* no. 213 Sept/Oct 1995.

Upham, Martin and Tom Wikson, 1989: *Natural Allies: Labour and the Unions.* Fabian pamphlet 534 London: Fabian Society.

Wainwright, Hilary, 1987: *Labour: A Tale of Two Parties* London: Hogarth Press.

Webb, Sidney, 1995: 'Clause IV' Ken Coates *Common Ownership.*

Whiteley, Paul, 1983: *The Labour Party in Crisis* London: Methuen & Co Ltd.

Wickham-Jones, Mark, 1995: 'Recasting Social Democracy: a Comment on Hay and Smith' *Political Studies* vol. 43, no. 4 December.

Williams, Shirley, 1981: *Politics Is for People* Harmondsworth: Penguin.

Woolgar, Steve, 1988: *Science: The Very Idea* Chichester: Ellis Horwood.

Wright, Anthony, 1983: *British Socialism: Socialist Thought from the 1880s to the 1960s* Harlow: Longman.

Young, James D., 1988: *Socialism Since 1889: A Biographical History* London: Pinter Publishers.

Index